**booksonline**

Read SAP PRESS online also

With booksonline we offer you online access to leading SAP experts' knowledge. Whether you use it as a beneficial supplement or as an alternative to the printed book – with booksonline you can:

- Access any book at any time
- Quickly look up and find what you need
- Compile your own SAP library

Your advantage as the reader of this book

Register your book on our website and obtain an exclusive and free test access to its online version. You're convinced you like the online book? Then you can purchase it at a preferential price!

And here's how to make use of your advantage

1. Visit www.sap-press.com
2. Click on the link for SAP PRESS booksonline
3. Enter your free trial license key
4. Test-drive your online book with full access for a limited time!

Your personal **license key** for your test access including the preferential offer

    azcy-9bxu-t7id-v2ns

Demand Management with SAP®

 **PRESS**

SAP PRESS is a joint initiative of SAP and Galileo Press. The know-how offered by SAP specialists combined with the expertise of the Galileo Press publishing house offers the reader expert books in the field. SAP PRESS features first-hand information and expert advice, and provides useful skills for professional decision-making.

SAP PRESS offers a variety of books on technical and business related topics for the SAP user. For further information, please visit our website: *www.sap-press.com*.

Jörg Dickersbach, Gerhard Keller, and Klaus Weihrauch
Production Planning and Control with SAP
2007, 336 pp.
978-1-59229-106-9

Ferenc Gulyássy, Marc Hoppe, Martin Isermann, and Oliver Köhler
Materials Planning with SAP
2010, 564 pp.
978-1-59229-259-2

Marc Hoppe
Sales and Inventory Planning with SAP APO
2007, 440 pp.
978-1-59229-123-6

Balaji Gaddam
Capable to Match (CTM) with SAP APO
2009, 273 pp.
978-1-59229-244-8

Christopher Foti and Jessie Chimni

Demand Management with SAP®

Galileo Press

Bonn • Boston

Galileo Press is named after the Italian physicist, mathematician and philosopher Galileo Galilei (1564–1642). He is known as one of the founders of modern science and an advocate of our contemporary, heliocentric worldview. His words *Eppur se muove* (And yet it moves) have become legendary. The Galileo Press logo depicts Jupiter orbited by the four Galilean moons, which were discovered by Galileo in 1610.

Editor Meg Dunkerley
Developmental Editor Kelly Grace Harris
Copyeditor Ruth Saavedra
Cover Design Jill Winitzer
Photo Credit Image Copyright Michael Klenetsky, 2008.
Used under license from Shutterstock.com.
Layout Design Vera Brauner
Production Editor Kelly O'Callaghan
Assistant Production Editor Graham Geary
Typesetting Publishers' Design and Production Services, Inc.
Printed and bound in Canada

ISBN 978-1-59229-267-7

© 2010 by Galileo Press Inc., Boston (MA)

1st Edition 2010

Library of Congress Cataloging-in-Publication Data
Demand management with SAP / Christopher Foti, Jessie Chimni. -- 1st ed.
     p. cm.
  ISBN-13: 978-1-59229-267-7 (alk. paper)
  ISBN-10: 1-59229-267-4 (alk. paper)
  1. APO. 2. SAP ERP. 3. Business logistics--Computer programs. 4. Supply and demand--Computer programs. 5. Production management. 6. Sales management. I. Foti, Christopher. II. Chimni, Jessie.
  HD38.5.D46 2010
  658.8'02--dc22

2009034911

Contents at a Glance

Contents

4   Statistical Forecasting   79

5   Interactive Planning and Advanced Statistical Forecasting   101

14 Conclusion 365

Appendices 379

Acknowledgments

In the development of this book we received support from many people. This support ranged from advice and remarks, to individual chapters, to providing content of entire sections. We would like to sincerely thank the people listed below and all those not mentioned here for their support. Without your help we couldn't have completed this book.

Our special thanks go to the team at Galileo Press for all the effort that has gone into this book. Meg Dunkerley in particular was instrumental before the book was even an idea. Graham Geary and Kelly O'Callaghan also stood out with all of their hard work on the figures for this book. Their generous support along the long and sometimes difficult way helped us to get through hard times.

Christopher Foti: At SAP, Tod Stenger, Richard Howells, Chris Wiesen, Newsha Eftekhari, Claus Bosch, Cheik Daddah, and Dave Williams brought a great deal of insight into multiple topic areas. My manager, Mike Maguire was patient and understanding with this project that he inherited when he took me on. Also, Sean Dolley was a wealth of information on down stream demand.

Finally, I don't know how anyone can write anything without the emotional and sometimes tactical support of their immediate family which mine delivered superlatively.

Jessie Chimni: At Bristlecone, Anil Gupta has provided a lot of input on the flow of the content for the book. Anil coordinated all the activities on the Bristlecone side. For this type of undertaking, we knew that we would need all the help we could get. We leveraged input for a number of Bristlecone consultants, and Anil had the unenviable task of coordinating it, aligning the writing styles and ensuring my personal sanity. He made this task easier than it otherwise would have been.

Also, Ankur Raj, Vijay Venkatesh, Selwyn D'souza and V Gopinath are Bristlecone senior consultants who have provided significant contribution to this book. They provided their experience, content, and insight about SAP's various Demand

Planning solutions. Their input and contributions have enriched this book tremendously.

A number of other individuals from Bristlecone also provided input for this book, including Saroj Tripathi, Abhishek Verma, and Vasoon Sinha.

I would like to thank my wife, Sabina, and kids, Kabir and Anika, for putting up with the time that went into writing this book. This year has been a very difficult one, marred by my fathers's death in February of this year and resurgence of my mother's cancer.

Preface

In writing this book, we set out to bring together knowledge of demand management software solutions and their configuration with a business context. Our idea was that there should be a single reference that focuses as much on why to do something as how to do it. We also noted that demand management spans multiple business disciplines within each organization and is frequently supported by more than one software solution for different aspects.

So we designed the book to speak to the perspective of senior executives as well as managers and analysts in sales, marketing, and operations, with chapters focused on each. We touch on the different SAP solutions that these individuals use, but focus detailed technical discussions on the Demand Planning component within SAP Advanced Planning and Optimization (APO). Otherwise, the book would have needed to be five times as long.

Because business and technology are equally represented, the information contained in this book should be as useful to managers and vice-presidents interested in better understanding the process of managing demand as it is to analysts whose day-to-day jobs have them interacting with the individual solutions. Similarly, the discussions will be as relevant to those whose responsibilities lie in information technology as to those who deal with sales orders and production schedules.

Anyone in an organization who has an interest in projecting, impacting, or realizing demand at a future date will likely find value in multiple chapters. We hope the book encourages people to think about how managing demand better in their company could offer tangible benefits. For those it spurs into action, we have provided information not only on what those changes might be, but also on how to best bring them about.

The book begins with an introduction to the concept of demand planning and its relevance to a business organization in Chapter 1. Throughout the text we have worked to emphasize relevance by explaining how aspects of demand management impact a company's balance sheet and income statement. Chapter 2 illustrates the myriads of inputs into a demand management process from all over the organization and its ecosystem of customers and vendors. Chapter 3 offers insight into what a demand management process can look like, which SAP software solutions will support it, and how to create a business case for adopting both process and solutions

Chapters 4 through 10 explore the detailed interplay of demand management processes, techniques, and solutions from the perspective of different disciplines. Chapter 4 drills down into the detail of leveraging statistical algorithms to extrapolate future demand from information about the past. While moving from corporate goals in the executive suite using SAP BusinessObjects Planning and Consolidation to the cubicles of analysts dealing with individual forecasts in SAP APO is quite a juxtaposition, it serves as an early example of how demand management permeates the entire organization. Chapters 5 and 6 are similarly focused on forecast analysts and the information technology colleagues who support them in developing statistics-based forecasts.

Chapters 7, 8, and 9 relate more to the sales and marketing aspect of organizations. In addressing visibility of customer demand downstream of the enterprise, Chapter 7 completes the set of chapters that stress projecting demand. Chapters 8 and 9 focus on impacting demand with activities and tactics, whereas Chapter 10 shows how companies can bring all of these disparate information-generating activities together to gain consensus around a single cohesive demand plan.

Chapter 11 is an on-ramp to other great books by SAP PRESS that focus on the role of realizing demand with production planning and inventory management. It explains how the demand management process impacts these activities and in turn how the time lines and constraints of the activities impact demand management. Chapter 12 completes the portion of the book focused on demand management processes by exploring performance management, reporting, and continuous improvement.

The penultimate chapter, Chapter 13 goes into detail about how corporations can implement these new processes and their supporting technologies from governance and partner selection to tracking the value after the change is complete. This is followed by Chapter 14, which revisits many of the concepts from each of the preceding chapters to offer a perspective on how companies can perform demand management better.

While not a chapter in its own right, Appendix A contains insight into the business planning which, in a very real way, drives the demand management process. For any who have wondered at the motivations of senior executives in setting seemingly arbitrary revenue or expense targets that contradict the statistical projections, this appendix complements Chapters 1–3 and is a must-read.

Although we have attempted to include both basic and advanced concepts, in reading and considering demand management and the changes they can make in their organization, many readers will arrive at solutions, whether technical, organizational, or process-based, that we did not cover. Perhaps some will develop innovations the likes of which we have neither seen nor considered ourselves. It is our hope that this book at least offers you insight, enabling you to bring new benefits to your own organizations and offers the inspiration to bring something new to demand management.

Throughout this book, you'll learn about projecting, impacting, and realizing demand. This introductory chapter explains what demand is and what SAP tools are available to help you manage it.

1 Introduction

This book is about managing demand. More specifically, it's about projecting, managing, and impacting the sales of a business to its customers. You'll learn about the different methods that businesses use to project demand, such as statistical analysis of past customer orders and sales. You'll also gain an appreciation for the efforts of sales and marketing professionals to better adapt customer demand to a company's goals and capacity. Similarly, the book will include the role of operations personnel in meeting demand.

Because the book considers operations personnel, the examples described and some processes will tend to revolve around decisions involved in making or buying, storing, and moving a physical product. Even if your business doesn't involve physical products, you'll still derive a solid understanding of the processes and tools to enable the projecting and impacting of demand performed by most corporations regardless of product.

This book describes how SAP solutions such as SAP® ERP and SAP Advanced Planning and Optimization (APO) along with complementary solutions available from partners of SAP can be used to facilitate and expedite analytical and collaborative processes. We'll go into detail regarding both general usage and configuration with the objective of making the book useful not only to information technology professionals, but also to corporate analysts and managers responsible for sales, marketing, and supply chain areas of the business.

This first chapter introduces you to the concept of demand management and its relevance to the broader set of business decisions and processes undertaken by a corporation. It will also introduce some of the major SAP solutions that support the process.

1.1 Defining Demand Management

Thomas Watson is, correctly or incorrectly, credited with what might be one of the most famous examples of a "short forecast" in modern times when he said that there was room in the world market for maybe 5 computers. To his credit, if IBM's former chairman did indeed make this demand projection in 1943 as Internet lore has it, it has been pointed out that he was correct for about 10 years, which is probably nine years and several months longer than any of today's high tech manufacturer could claim 100% forecast accuracy.

When current business executives think about "demand," their minds tend to immediately leap to the capital F, *forecast*. This is, at its most basic, a projection of the sales of finished goods. For manufacturers, distributors, retailers, and a host of other companies whose incomes derive more from the sales of widgets than from services, the forecast is a core truth around which capital investments, staffing decisions, marketing budgets, and materials purchases swirl like snowflakes in a breeze. Figure 1.1 shows an example of such a demand projection.

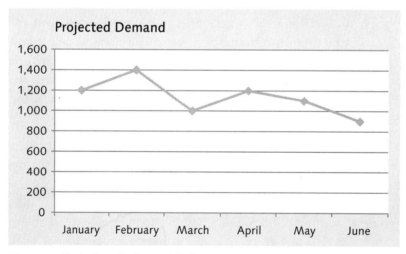

Figure 1.1 Illustration of a Demand Projection

The basic mistake that many executives make is that their concept of demand management ends with the demand projection (the forecast) and even that they interpret solely within the confines of their roles. A sales vice-president might think of the forecast as a certain number of dollars, euros, yen, yuan, and so on of finished goods to be sold to a particular customer over a certain time period, such as next month or next year. However, a plant manager might see the forecast as the number of pallets produced at a specific facility over the next two weeks. A procurement analyst may think of the forecast as the number of tons or kilograms of a certain raw material that will need to be contracted for, purchased, and in the case of some materials, hedged over the calendar year. Figure 1.2 shows a few examples of different aspects of the original forecast.

Figure 1.2 Forecasts Are Relevant to Different People in Different Forms

Marketing executives in particular have a very different view of the forecast, regardless of which units and categories it is divided into, because they know that projecting demand is just the beginning. Their role is to "move the market" or to impact demand with their four Ps (price, product, position, and promotion). Demand in the hands of an accomplished product or brand manager is the bottom row of a spreadsheet (see Figure 1.3) that begins at the top with the natural forecast and is transformed by rows of price elasticity curves, promotional uplifts, new product cannibalization, and competitive intelligence, to name a few.

	Forecasted Finished Goods Sales in Units					
	January	February	March	April	May	June
Projected Demand	1,200	1,400	1,000	1,200	1,100	900
10% Price Cut	216	252				
5% Price Increase				180	-110	
New Product Incremental			210	276	275	225
New Product Cannibalization		-70	-100	-120	-110	-90
Online Small Bus. Site (March Launch)		140	200	360	330	270
Total	1,416	1,722	1,310	1,896	1,485	1,305

Figure 1.3 Forecasts are Impacted by a Variety of Marketing Activities

After demand has been projected and impacted, it needs to be realized (see Figure 1.4). This is where the rubber meets the road or, if you prefer, where reality intrudes upon a perfectly good plan. Marketing executives engage their plans; sales executives chase after quotas; operations personnel buy, make, and move product; and (hopefully) customers begin to order. Translating the demand plan into an action plan aligning all of the stakeholders is certainly a daunting task, but most organizations find it to be much easier than getting all involved to agree on what the demand plan should be in the first place.

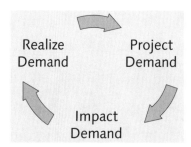

Figure 1.4 Demand Management Cycle:
Project, Impact, and Realize Demand

So managing demand can be defined as the overarching business process that entails projecting demand, impacting demand, and realizing demand along with one small addition. The process should be self-aware enough to strive for continuous improvement. Forecast accuracies should be measured, best practices researched and documented, stakeholders trained, and tools sharpened. Finally, the entire process should be examined with an eye to how it continues to contribute to the key business barometers — which brings us to a good question: What is the relevance of managing demand?

1.2   The Relevance of Managing Demand

There are two types of forecasts: wrong and wrong. If that sounds confusing, look at the bell curve describing the probability distribution of a sales forecast. The line in the middle of the bell represents the forecast, and the area under the curve is the probability that the forecast will fall within a certain range. As seen in Figure 1.5, the area of the curve to the left of the forecast line is the probability that sales will be lower than the forecast. Because it is half of the area, the probability of sales coming in below forecast is 50%. Similarly, the right half of the curve denotes a 50% probability that sales will be higher than the forecast. It doesn't take an advanced planning system to calculate 50% + 50% = 100%; stated more clearly there is a 100% chance that sales will be higher or lower than the forecasted amount.

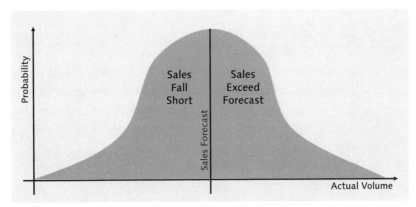

Figure 1.5 Bell Curve Describing the Probability Distribution of a Sales Forecast

But that's just the demand projection component. It doesn't take into account an organization's ability to impact or realize demand, both of which can be significant. For those who haven't tried to run a business, it might seem that the objective of impacting demand is to drive it as high as possible, and as far as realizing demand goes, it only makes sense to sell as much as the market will buy.

The questions practically ask themselves:

▶ Why forecast if you will inevitably be wrong?

▶ Why not just drive demand up as high as possible?

▶ Why not make everything that you can sell?

The answer is that it's cheaper to be wrong than reactive and more profitable to make the market want what you can make than to make what the market wants.

Imagine that you were to take a hot dog cart out to a street corner one sunny summer morning. Around lunchtime when the first customer orders a chili dog with onions you start to walk into the grocery store to buy a pack of dogs, start to steam them, heat the chili, and slice the onions. You are smiling as a line starts to form.

Five minutes later as your first dog is done, you notice people at the back of the line leaving and walking over to the falafel cart on the other side of the street. You don't even know what a falafel is, but that vendor has tinfoil packets stacked three feet in the air and he's selling them at a fast pace. Most of your line defects within five minutes.

What happened? It was cheaper for the falafel cart owner to cook in advance based on a guess of the number of customers and throw out his excess (to be wrong) than to take the time or have the number of grills to cook for each individual customer (to be late). All that time you spent talking to the construction foreman across the street to get his crew to your cart backfired when you got more demand than you could satisfy. Figure 1.6 depicts the reality for many companies, which is that it's more profitable to guess and be wrong than wait and be late.

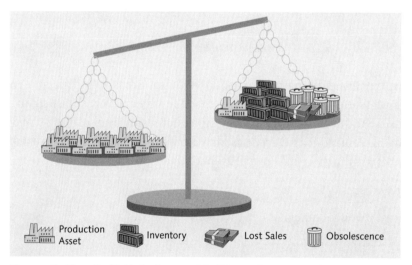

Production Asset   Inventory   Lost Sales   Obsolescence

Figure 1.6 *More Profitable to Guess and Be Wrong Than Wait and Be Late*

Demand management is relevant because it can help an organization provide a better return on time, talent, and invested capital and materials. With a decent demand projection and credible effort at impacting demand to match fulfillment capabilities, a company can keep its plants, warehouses, machines, and people busy doing what they do best to realize the impending market demand. And that is exactly what investors and stakeholders want.

1.3 The Balance Sheet and the Income Statement

Whether you work for a public or private organization, chances are that you have investors (public) or stakeholders (private), and most of them like to understand the health of their investment. The easiest way to determine this is to look at financial metrics such as revenue, expenses, profit, inventories, and assets that can be compared against other investment opportunities such as reading labels on competing products in a grocery store.

The fact that the balance sheet (Figure 1.7) and income statement (Figure 1.8) act as an investor's barometer for the health of the company is not lost on senior executives. For these people, the amount that an investor is willing to pay for a share of the company (the share price) and sometimes the numbers on the pages themselves, like revenue, dictate compensations and promotions. So these numbers are important not only to investors, but to senior executives as well.

Consolidated Balance Sheets
as of December 31

Assets

€ millions	2007	2006
Cash and cash equivalents	1,608	2,399
Restricted cash	550	0
Short-termn investments	598	931
Accounts receivable, net	2,895	2,440
Other assets	541	371
Deferred income taxes	125	108
Prepaid expenses/deferred charges	76	75
Assets held for sale	15	0
Current assets	**6,408**	**6,324**
Goodwill	1,423	987
Intangible assets, net	403	263
Property, plant, and equipment, net	1,316	1,206
Investments	89	95
Accounts receivable, net	3	3
Other assets	555	533
Deferred income taxes	146	
Prepaid expenses/deferred charges		
Noncurrent assets		
Total assets		

Figure 1.7 Example of a Balance Sheet

Consolidated Statements of Income
for the years ended December 31

€ millions, unless otherwise stated	2007	2006	2005
Software revenue	3,407	3,003	2,743
Support revenue	3,838	3,464	3,170
Subscription and other software-related service revenue	182	129	42
Software and software-related service revenue	7,427	6,546	5,955
Consulting revenue	2,221	2,249	2,071
Training revenue	410	383	342
Other service revenue	113	96	71
Professional services and other service revenue	2,744	2,726	2,484
Other revenue	71	69	70
Total revenue	10,242	9,393	8,509
Cost of software and software-related services	- 1,310	- 1,091	- 983
Cost of professional services and other services	- 2,091	- 2,073	- 1,925
Research and development	- 1,458	- 1,335	- 1,089
Sales and marketing	- 2,162	- 1,906	- 1,746
General and administration	- 506	- 464	- 435
Other operating income, net	17	56	6
Total operating expenses	- 7,510	- 6,815	- 6,172
Operating income	2,732	2,578	2,337
Other non-operating income/expense, net			
Financial income, net			
Income from continuing operations before income taxes			

Figure 1.8 Example of an Income Statement

This is important because investors and stakeholders both make their own projections about how much money a company should make and how much it needs to spend to make it. Think of the income statement and balance sheet as the scorecards for a management team and the expectations of the capital markets (investors, stakeholders, analysts) as the score of the opposing team. To win, senior executives need to meet or beat expectations.

For any organization that, unlike our ill-fated hot dog cart, chooses to commit resources to the production of a product or delivery of a service prior to entering into an agreement with a customer to pay, the demand plan drives the decision. Decisions to buy raw materials and components, to build new factories and warehouses, to launch new products, or enter new markets impact the balance sheet and income statement in multiple ways. Successful organizations align these decisions around a demand plan designed to meet investor and stakeholder expectations.

1.4 The Role of Demand Management within Sales and Operations Planning

One method to align the demand plan with all of the organization's decisions to commit resources is through a sales and operations planning process. This is a series of collaborative decisions made by executives and managers across sales, marketing, operations, and logistics disciplines. The objective of the process is to align the entire organization around a single execution plan that details how resources will be committed to build products and/or deliver services.

The demand plan is a major input into the process, but it is itself also transformed by the process. The initial demand plan is built around natural market demand in addition to any planned demand impacting sales and marketing. This acts as an initial unconstrained plan or "wish list" because it doesn't take into account the constraints on production and distribution.

The unconstrained demand plan is reviewed by executives and managers across the company to ensure that it represents their objectives and constraints. Sales executives must decide if the demand plan allows them to reach sales targets, whereas sales managers and account executives must insure that it doesn't leave any customers "short" or overload them unreasonably with more products or services than they can absorb.

Marketing executives need to confirm that the demand plan contains enough "lift" to fill the gap between natural market demand and the expectations of senior executives and analysts. Marketing managers examine the plan to be sure that their individual campaigns and activities are represented and the lift that they are planned to generate is accurately reflected.

As illustrated in Figure 1.9, when operations executives receive the demand plan, they begin to compare it to capacity in their plants. They look at their stock of finished goods, raw materials, and components to figure out if they have enough or their suppliers can deliver enough in time to satisfy the demand plan. Logistics executives perform similar constraining against the capacity of their warehouses, fleets, and services vendors.

Figure 1.9 Intertwined Planning Processes

Eventually, all of these executives and managers need to come to alignment around the demand plan and any modifications they have made to it. This might be done in a single face-to-face meeting, in multiple virtual meetings, or through mutual deadlines facilitated by software. Regardless of the actual mechanism, the final result is a single plan for demand that everyone is committed to supporting.

1.5　SAP Solutions Overview

A number of solutions are available to support the business processes of companies that want to begin a demand management process or to advance their existing process to the next level. Figure 1.10 illustrates the SAP Supply Chain Management (SCM) solutions "stack." Figure 1.11 depicts some of these solutions along a continuum of sophistication from left to right.

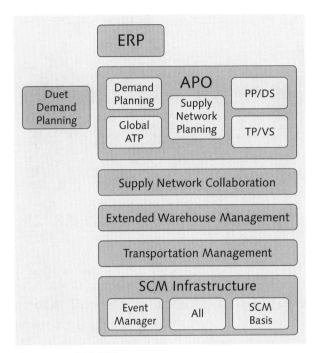

Figure 1.10 SAP SCM

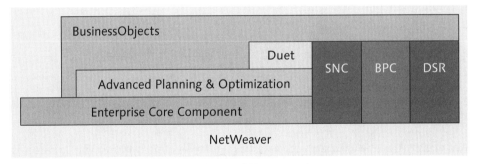

Figure 1.11 SAP Applications Supporting Demand Management

One major advantage for existing users of SAP ERP for their business transactions is that the SAP decision support tools such as SAP APO, SAP Supply Network Collaboration (SNC), and Duet™ demand planning are pre-integrated and able to interact with the SAP ERP transactional backbone in real-time as shown in Figure 1.12.

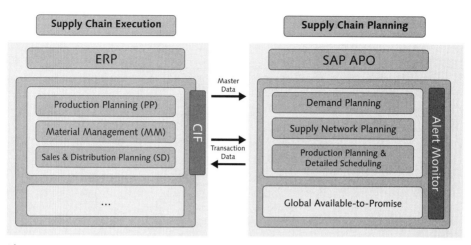

Figure 1.12 Integration with ERP

Whereas rudimentary demand management capabilities exist within SAP ERP, SAP has not improved them for nearly a decade since it released its preferred platform, SAP APO. Very few companies choose to support their planning processes with SAP ERP, and many of them are choosing to move to SAP APO. Reasons for this include:

▶ Limited flexibility in hierarchies

▶ Absence of optimization

▶ Lack of advanced algorithms, such as multiple linear regression

▶ Inability to leverage complimentary tools, such as Duet

▶ Risk of impacting the performance of critical transactional supporting tools such as order management

Adopting SAP APO alleviates these issues and offers much more. The solution is made up of multiple planning modules:

▶ Demand Planning

▶ Supply Network Planning

▶ Production Planning and Detail Scheduling

▶ Transportation Planning and Vehicle Scheduling

▶ Global Available-to-Promise

▶ Supply Chain Cockpit, which ties them all together

Because of this book's focus on demand management, the text will primarily focus on the Demand Planning component and how it develops a demand plan to be leveraged by the other modules.

Most organizations that employ SAP APO, especially those leveraging the Demand Planning component, also work frequently with SAP NetWeaver BW for reporting. Not only does SAP BW offer over 100 Level 1 reports from the Supply Chain Council's Supply Chain Operations Reference (SCOR) Model, but it is also capable of drilling into the component itself for ad hoc real-time reporting. We'll cover more of the reporting capabilities of SAP APO and SAP BW in Chapter 13.

Like the demand management capabilities in SAP ERP that were superseded by those of SAP APO, the forecasting collaboration capabilities of SAP APO have been significantly augmented by SAP SNC. SAP Supply Network Collaboration offers collaborative planning both with a company's customers and its suppliers, but the component supporting customer collaboration, called Responsive Replenishment will be more germane to the topics covered here.

Throughout the book we'll also refer to a number of other SAP solutions and complementary solutions from its partners that feed, augment, or receive information from these core demand planning solutions. These solutions include SAP Trade Promotions Management, SAP Auto-ID Infrastructure, and Vision Chain's Demand Signal Repository.

1.6 Summary

Demand management is the process of projecting demand (forecasting), impacting demand (marketing), and then realizing demand (executing). Organizations that follow this process are able to make better use of their constrained resources because they have more accurate information in time to make decisions further in advance of the actual commitment of those resources.

Decisions that are based, at least in part, on the demand plan have implications on inventories, assets, revenues, and expenses that reveal themselves to investors on the company's balance sheet and income statement. To ensure that these decisions are aligned across various business disciplines, many organizations leverage a sales and operations planning process that takes in and transforms the unconstrained demand plan into an executable sales and operations plan.

Now that you understand what demand management is, let's move on to Chapter 2, Projecting Demand, where we'll look at how to project the size and shape of the market for a company's goods.

Projecting demand is a difficult and sometimes elusive process. This chapter introduces you to the science of projecting demand, and discusses the SAP tools that enable this process.

2 Projecting Demand

In this chapter we'll begin to discuss projecting (forecasting, estimating, anticipating, guessing, etc.) demand by estimating the size and shape of the market for a company's products or services. This culminates in a sales and operations planning process.

2.1 Assembling the Parts into a Whole

Like boxes of brightly colored plastic parts strewn across a living room floor on Christmas morning, demand projections should come with a warning: Some Assembly Required. Both toys and forecasts share components that we know must fit together because there they are in the picture on the box or in the chart of last month's sales on the wall. Some pieces are obvious, like the tall piece representing a key customer's order forecast for a major product. But does this curvy piece of promotional uplift fit on top of the first one? Below it? Does it somehow bend it?

It's the nature of complex assemblies that it is difficult or impossible to envision all of the parts at once, let alone how they go together. It is also inevitable that a complex problem will attract the "help" of those who have an interest in the answer. Each new "assistant" will latch on to a component or two that becomes the center of their world as they try to figure out how everyone else's parts fit theirs. "Let me show you how your tall green customer forecast fits into my twisty blue new product launch."

Across any sizable organization there are individuals with responsibilities and perspectives that revolve around different but critical components of the business.

Their success depends on the sales through a channel, the success of a marketing campaign, the replacement of an old product with a new one, or the efficient operation of a production facility. In their respective areas they are the experts, often passionate, always focused, and rarely possessed of an unbiased perspective on the business as a whole.

Figures 2.1 and 2.2 give a perspective on different components originating from different areas making up the whole of a demand projection. Whereas shipments from a company's distribution centers continue to be strong over the previous month, it appears that based on the few key customers who share collaborative data, customers were shipping less from their distribution centers into their factories and retail outlets last week. Orders remain high, but consumption, whether measured by radio frequency identification (RFID) or through consumption (such as retail point of sale data) show that demand is slacking off downstream in the supply chain.

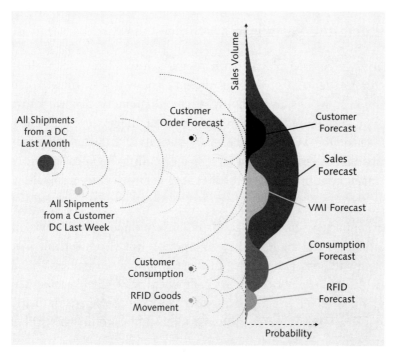

Figure 2.1 Multiple Partial Perspectives on Demand

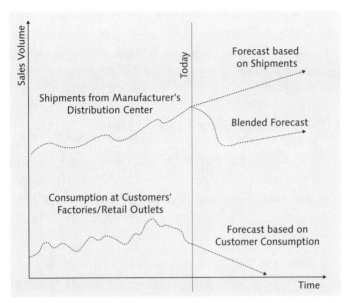

Figure 2.2 The Danger of Projecting Demand Based on a Single Demand Signal

This could be a very natural result of a customer finishing off a promotion or a large project and ordering enough to replenish their stock in anticipation of a lower, more regular demand pattern. But it would be very hard to determine without seeing both sets of data at once.

Marketing analysts at the manufacturer looking at consumption might see consumption flagging and cut their forecasts drastically, which would result in missing out on the last bit of demand to replenish their customers' shelves. Sales executives might see a strong order forecast coupled with growth over the last month or two, causing them to project higher demands for the coming months. This would result in the manufacturer being stuck with high amounts of inventory that would need to be destroyed or sold at severe discounts. Whereas both of our stakeholders have a perfectly clear view of a portion of the demand, neither would be right in their projections. In Chapter 4, we'll look at statistical forecasting and explore how information in the context of historical data can be used to forecast demand.

Spotting a divergence like this across thousands of items and hundreds or thousands of locations would be like finding a needle in a haystack without a tool like SAP APO Demand Planning. However, with Demand Planning, it is as simple as building a macro to calculate the difference between the shipment and consumption-based forecasts and setting a threshold for the value above which an analyst should be notified. Whereas Demand Planning could also recommend a mathematically blended forecast, an analyst's intuition and ability to ask questions will likely improve upon even that.

2.2   Ascertaining the Size and Shape of a Market

Although it is not a simple task, defining the market size and shape is a key component to measuring the amount of return that a company might realize if it chooses to enter the market. Given that most companies have limited capital available to invest and want to offer the best returns possible to their investors, defining the size and shape is a necessary exercise.

The market for a product is simply the amount of a product that customers will buy over a given time period. That amount determines the *size* of the market, which is simple to state in concept and deceptively complex to pin down in practice. Is the amount measured in dollars, euros, kilograms, pallets, cases, pieces, cubic feet, or any of a number of other units of measure? Does the amount include sales where the product is included in a larger kit, pack, mixed pallet, etc. together with other products? What about programs, activities, or occurrences that impact multiple products in a product group, a brand, a package size, or a business unit?

Then consider the details behind what *customers will buy*. Each sale could be described as belonging to a customer location, a geographic region, a sales channel, a country, a distribution center, an account executive, a national key account, a business unit, a price point, and so on. There are as many dimensions to the size and shape of a market as there are ways to categorize each individual sale of a product.

Unfortunately, individuals within a company tend to have partial, overlapping views of the market in varying units and across heterogeneous category groupings. So the whole needs to be understood by examining and then aggregating its disparate pieces.

Figure 2.3 shows views of portions of the market for chocolate bars in the United States. These chocolate bars can also be sold as part of a larger mixed "variety" pack or wrapped in a special promotional movie wrapper. Through market research, historical sales, and any number of methods, it's possible to estimate the size of the individual submarkets and even approximate the shape of the market against attributes such as price.

	Dimensions			
Item	**Region**	**Units**	**Channel**	**Customers**
Chocolate Bars	North America	Kilograms	Direct	All
Chocolate Bars	US	Dollars	Partner	Food Service
Mixed Chocolate Bar Pack	Pacific Northwest	Pallets	Direct	Mass Merchant
Chocolate Bars-Movie Promo	US Major Cities	Cases	Direct	All Opted In
Chocolate Bars	California	Pieces	Web	Consumer
Chocolate Bars	US	Cases	Direct	Key Customer

Figure 2.3 Market Segments Can Be Both Heterogeneous and Overlapping

Many companies have traditionally approached combining all of this information into a single useful projection of demand with the construction of a two- to four-branch hierarchy of product, location, and abstract grouping.

In the three-branch hierarchy depicted in Figure 2.4, each product rolls up to a product family that belongs to a brand or business unit. Countries are divided into regions, which are split up into production facilities, each of which services multiple distribution centers that fill local customer orders. The company goes to market through different channels (i.e., direct to customers, through resellers, over the Internet for warranty or service parts, etc.) containing key customer groupings made up of individual customer locations.

Product	**Location**	**Group**
ALL	Global	ALL
Brand/Business Unit	Country	Channel
Product Family	Region	Channel
Product Family	Production Facility	Key Customer
Product	Distribution Center	Key Customer
Product	Customer D.C.	Customer

Figure 2.4 Traditional Market Hierarchies Are Fairly Limited

Hierarchies like this work well when all of the information falls discretely into the individual buckets. However, they struggle when trying to shoehorn information across categories, such as the market for chocolate bars with movie promotion wrappers being sold in major U.S. cities only for customers who have opted in.

This is why SAP APO Demand Planning considers the market in its lowest common denominator of discrete categories or *characteristics*. The solution is then able to add up or *aggregate* amounts on the fly and then *disaggregate* any inputs or changes made to the amount upon completion.

Consider Figure 2.5, in which a number of combinations of characteristics are used to describe the market. If a marketing analyst wanted to view a demand plan for all of the items in brand alpha with a package size of one, then Demand Planning would aggregate all of the sales histories that met this criteria. The marketing analyst could then choose to increase the demand plan for this group by 10%. SAP APO would then disaggregate the new total down to each of the individual characteristics combinations. The many methods of allocating the changes made to the aggregate total down into the individual characteristics combinations will be discussed in detail in Chapter 5.

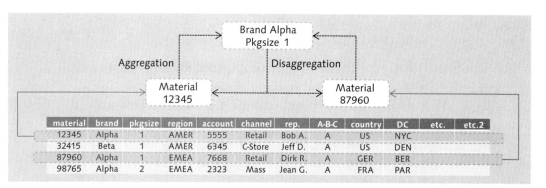

Figure 2.5 SAP APO Demand Planning Enables Aggregation and Disaggregation

By enabling an organization to store data at the lowest common denominator of market characteristics and then view and manipulate that data at any aggregation, SAP APO Demand Planning allows all of the individuals with visibility to a portion of the market to add their knowledge into the demand plan. Because Demand Planning can mathematically convert between units of measure during aggregation and disaggregation, it doesn't make a difference if the individual stakeholders think in terms of dollars, pallets, or kilograms.

Enabling individuals with different perspectives and responsibilities across an organization to enter what they know about demand in a context that is familiar to them is a key feature of Demand Planning. A brand owner can enter a dollar incremental lift for a brand resulting from a promotion. A sales vice president can add a percentage to those items sold to a key account that has just expanded within a region. A demand planning analyst can note and strengthen a growth trend in sales through the Internet channel. A marketing executive can model cannibalization of an existing product with a new one as it is rolled out from region to region. Chapter 10 will discuss a consensus forecasting process in more detail.

2.3 Sales and Operations Planning within APO Demand Planning

In Chapter 1, we discussed the importance of individual stakeholders contributing to the overall sales and operations plan and coming to a consensus. The overall demand plan is what the company intends to sell. It is heavily impacted by marketing plans and corporate revenue and profit targets, and it is a significant input into inventory planning that in turn drives the production and procurement plans.

However, like the ill-fated hot dog vendor in Chapter 1, the company can only sell what it can buy, make, or has already made and stored. So the capacity of the company to meet the demand plan becomes a constraint, and as the hot dog vendor realized in the end, there is no sense spending effort drumming up demand that you are unable to satisfy. This means that the marketing plan and the demand plan both must take the constrained demand plan back as an input, as depicted in Figure 2.6.

Figure 2.6 The Sale and Operations Planning Process Constrains the Demand Plan

SAP APO Supply Network Planning (SNP) is the main tool for developing a rough constrained plan. Further refinement of the individual components of the supply plan can be conducted in other SAP APO modules and complementary solutions. SmartOps Enterprise Inventory Optimization enhances the safety stock calculations resident in SAP APO SNP to smooth buffer inventories across the company's network of plants and warehouses. SAP APO Production Planning and Detailed Scheduling (PP/DS) refines the production plan from a daily plant- or line-level plan down to a detailed production schedule by a constrained resource at the hourly level or lower. SAP APO Transportation Planning and Vehicle Scheduling (TP/VS) breaks demand blocks into shipments that will fit within vehicles (containers, trailers, rail cars, etc.) and tenders those loads to carriers or schedules company-owned transportation resources.

In a continual process, the demand plan is constrained more granularly by capacity over time based on operational lead times. Figure 2.7 provides examples of lead times for operational decisions that impact the capacity that a company has to satisfy its demand plan.

Figure 2.7 Operations Constraints that Impact the Demand Plan over Time

Looking at the constraining factors in the example (materials purchasing, capital budgets for new facilities, truck tendering), you would come to the conclusion that these are decisions faced by most product-producing companies. Yet the multitude of individuals involved in these decisions can make it difficult to collect these capacity-impacting factors. Even more challenging is quantifying the impact of a shortage in pounds of a key raw material or of an increase in machine hours available owing to the addition of a new production line.

Demand Planning makes this collection and translation easier because of its integration to both the backbone SAP ERP system and the other SAP APO components. Bill of materials (BOM) describing how much of which raw materials, components, packaging, etc. go into a finished good are stored in the SAP ERP system as are the routings which describe the machines and activities required to convert them into a finished good. These BOMs and routings are automatically transferred over to SAP APO SNP, which then translates all of this information into capacity.

2.4 Summary

So we have seen that the challenge in projecting the size and shape of a market is compounded by the lack of a single reliable channel of complete information. Instead demand planners must compile information from multiple incomplete and sometimes overlapping sources and piece them together through a lowest common denominator. Once the demand puzzle is pieced together, it must go through a constraining process where the organization compares how much its customers are willing to buy with how much it is able to build or buy.

In the next chapter we will explore methods by which these organizations can begin to follow a demand planning process, what business cases they might leverage, and which SAP solutions they might choose to support them.

This chapter teaches you about why and where to implement demand management, including coverage about which SAP tools can help you achieve this.

3   Engaging in Demand Planning

In the two previous chapters, we discussed some of the hazards and benefits of demand planning, focusing on projecting sales volumes. This chapter will introduce you to a related topic: projecting the costs and benefits resulting from changing the way an organization does demand planning. Defining this business case for change is a critical step for any organization that wants to improve the way it manages demand.

In this chapter, we'll start out with a look at how companies typically engage in demand planning. From there, we'll move on to the supply chain challenges in today's global environment, which will lead us to an understanding of the benefits of a better demand planning process (as demonstrated in a case study). Finally, we'll end with a discussion of the various SAP solutions that can help support a demand planning initiative.

3.1   How Companies Engage in Adopting Demand Management

Executives often express their dissatisfaction over the lack of accuracy in their demand forecasts. This can often be the result of many factors, such as volatile demand, reduced customer loyalty, shorter product lifecycles, mass customization, and tougher global competition. However, it can be exacerbated by poor visibility of isolated pools of information with significant time lag. Here is an analogy: You're driving down a road that is becoming more twisty and narrow, but instead of a windshield you have 20 monitors connected together, with only 15 showing the actual road. Each of those is set to a different magnification, and each has a time lag set randomly between 5 and 20 seconds. Such a situation would make it very difficult for you to drive the car.

To maximize customer satisfaction and remain profitable and competitive, businesses need a process, organization, and information infrastructure (Figure 3.1) that can help them make decisions that are informed, accurate, and timely. The stakes are high because as we mentioned in Chapter 1, inaccurate forecasts can lead to excess inventory expense and/or failure to meet delivery dates or other commitments.

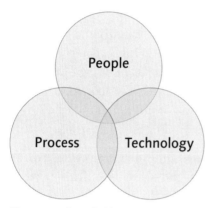

Figure 3.1 Organization

Ask three executives at three different companies who are responsible for demand management, and you'll likely get five different answers about demand. There is a maturity curve of responsibility and reporting relationships that most organizations go through in managing their demand (Figures 3.2 and 3.3).

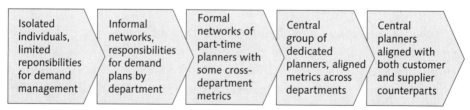

Figure 3.2 Organizational Maturity

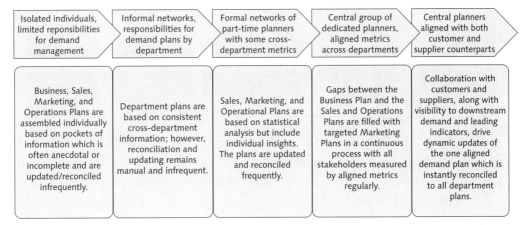

Figure 3.3 Process Maturity

Initially, the perspective and data access necessary to manage or at least project demand is spread throughout the organization, residing in the minds of isolated individuals, many of whom have no real responsibility for demand management. They may belong to sales departments, operations, marketing, manufacturing, logistics, or even finance. Each is likely to know one piece of the puzzle, but their knowledge is applied only to the decisions made by their own departments. In such a scenario, the demand planning is done informally. These individuals sometimes form an informal network either in response to requests for information that goes beyond their own knowledge or just out of their own curiosity.

Organizations that are more mature try to create a central competency for demand projection that likely resides within an existing business function such as sales, finance, or marketing. The focus of the group depends on the host department. Demand planners in a sales organization likely think in terms of accounts and collect information from sales executives. If these same planners were instead in the finance organization they would probably be more concerned with the revenue plan. Planners aligned to marketing tend to pay attention to promotions, pricing, and new product introduction.

The next evolutionary step for an organization is when demand planning is a well-defined function and the planning process is centralized. This organization is accountable for forecast accuracy. When planning is centralized, it relieves the other departments of the burden of developing their own forecasts, but obliges them to plan and execute according to the central team's demand projections.

As the planning group is measured on the accuracy of their projections, each discipline or department is measured on their attainment to the plan. This configuration evolves to where they are aligned with their customer and supplier counterparts for an integrated demand planning process.

3.1.1 Process

Chapters 1 and 2 discussed the sales and operations planning process at a high level. Chapters 4 through 10 will go into more detail in each of the areas of business planning, statistical forecasting, leading indicators, downstream demand, marketing, and sales.

In a typical demand planning process, each department creates its own plan, based on their own set of assumptions and perspectives. For example, the sales organization may look at the current pipeline and annual sales goals to create their version of the demand plan. The finance team may create their own plan based on the current year's budgets and next year's projections. Marketing's forecast may be based on their market research activities. These different plans have very different perspectives, and as a result various organizations within the company are no longer on the same page. In a consensus demand planning process (Figure 3.4), these departments work together to create a single forecast, so everyone is on the same page.

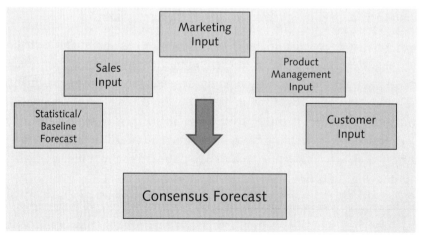

Figure 3.4 Demand Planning Best Practices

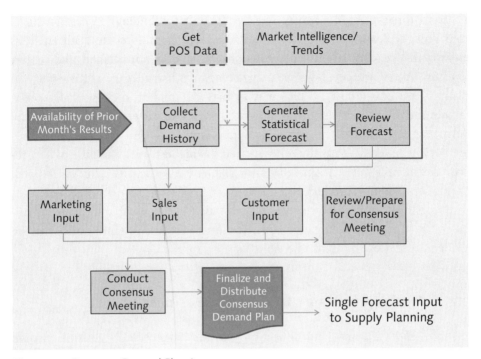

Figure 3.5 Consensus Demand Planning

The consensus demand planning process (see Figure 3.5) baseline forecast is generated using history [and may include point of sales (POS) data]. Each of the departments then reviews the forecast and provides inputs. For example, marketing provides inputs to forecast adjustments based on their promotions plan. Similarly, finance and sales provide input to that forecast. A consensus meeting helps everyone come to a common number for the demand forecast. This then becomes the basis for all related execution, that is, developing an inventory and production plan, refining the financial plan, and so on.

3.1.2 Technology

Technology is the third leg of the stool and is equally important as the organization and process. Consequently, none of the three should be designed or implemented without consideration for the others.

There are three stages of maturity levels in the use of technology. In the first stage, companies typically use spreadsheets to create a demand forecast. Their environment is very reactive, and the planning process is long, not detailed, and subject to errors. At the next level, we see many companies using legacy or basic demand planning systems. These systems may or may not support a consensus process, are not scalable, and are not well integrated with ERP systems. As a result, many departments work off their own plans, and the planning and execution processes are not integrated in these environments. At the highest level is the use of best-in-class demand planning systems that are scalable, use consensus planning, support promotions and new product introductions, and enable customer collaboration. In addition, these systems have sophisticated statistical modeling to leverage historical perspectives and leading indicators. These systems are well integrated with the ERP and reporting solutions to enable decision support.

3.2   Finding the Value to Create a Business Case

Section 1.3 in Chapter 1 introduced you to the balance sheet and the income statement and explained its importance to shareholders and managing executives. Because the money invested in bringing about change is reflected in the balance sheet and income statement, the associated benefits should be as well. A good business case for a change in demand management should highlight existing issues or opportunities currently facing the organization and the cost of the change in a manner that can be traced directly to the company's assets and liabilities as well as costs and revenues.

Figure 3.6 exposes the links to the balance sheet, and Figure 3.7 illustrates the impacts that demand management has on the income statement. Done well, demand management can positively impact not only inventories but also the manufacturing and distribution assets used to produce and distribute them. Costs associated with obsolete products, overtime, expedited raw materials, and components can also be affected.

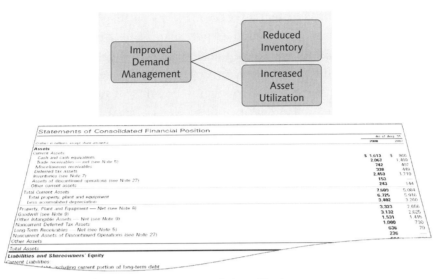

Figure 3.6 Demand Management Impacts on Balance Sheet

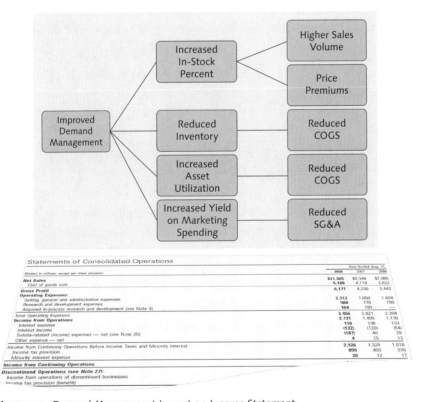

Figure 3.7 Demand Management Impact on Income Statement

On the revenue side of the equation, better demand management can free up capacity to broaden a company's product portfolio, penetrate new markets, or both. Slightly more difficult to directly attribute to revenue, but no less real, improving the chance that you are carrying in stock what a customer wants where and when they want it can improve your ability to command and maintain higher prices than your competition or demand other beneficial terms such as faster payment. It can raise the barrier to entry for the competition while simultaneously increasing the *switch over* cost.

Once you know that a demand management initiative can bring benefits to the organization, the next questions are where to start, which area to attack first, and how to calculate the resource requirements. This helps you create a plan of attack culminating in a business case to be presented to the people whose roles and responsibilities must change and the people who are responsible for the resources and budgets required to make the change happen.

A Word about Incremental versus Integral Improvements

As companies add more products, suppliers, and distribution plants into their supply chains, a slow erosion of effectiveness tends to follow. Despite incremental investments in people, processes, and technology, many companies are finding that as time passes, key metrics such as on-time delivery, order fulfillment lead time, and supply chain response begin to deteriorate.

Like a production line, speeding up or improving the quality of individual machines on a case-by-case basis can actually lead to an imbalance, where some machines produce faster than others, piling up inventory while downstream another machine is "starving" for input. Both the production line and the demand management process must be looked at as an integral whole, with subcomponents tuned together.

A successful company with motivated employees is likely to have several options in which to invest time, talent, and money. Most have more options than they have the capability to pursue at one time. This means your business case doesn't simply need to prove that improving the company's demand management capabilities will deliver a positive return on the investment. It needs to prove that the return will have a greater reward to risk ratio (Figure 3.8) than all of the other proposals that will not be authorized and funded.

Figure 3.8 Risk to Reward Ratio for Project Approval

A good business case helps get a commitment from the senior management, which is an essential step in change management, and helps show quantifiable benefits that can be tracked to realize the full potential of the initiative. Developing a business case provides an opportunity to identify the following:

▸ Quantifiable results that can be owned by line executives

▸ Creation of ownership and adoption in the organization for systems decision

▸ Showcase for value that implementation brings to the business and corporate strategy

▸ Alignment between IT and business perspectives within your organization

▸ Opportunity to review your overall IT strategy

▸ Implementation plan that is actionable and measurable

It's essential to highlight the following benefits as part of the business case:

▸ Strategic benefits

▸ Quantitative business benefits

▸ Qualitative business benefits

▸ Total cost of ownership and return on investment

53

The first step in creating a business case is conducting a supply chain opportunity assessment. Supply chain opportunity assessments can help you determine what may be happening at your company. Like an annual doctor's physical provides a snapshot of overall health, a supply chain opportunity assessment gives your company a complete look at the overall state of one of its most critical functions and provides you with a comprehensive list of opportunities for improvement.

Armed with the report from a supply chain opportunity assessment, a company can immediately begin to take a series of actions that help improve its operating efficiency, and ensure that the supply chain is structured to meet any growth trends or expected sales increases. An assessment also guarantees that processes and data can be more tightly integrated and shared with partners, helping fulfill the ultimate goal of realigning the supply chain with business and operations strategies.

An assessment is appropriate for companies that are investing time and money to understand their current supply chain challenges and are ready to identify opportunities to maximize the strategic value of their supply chains. The focus of the assessment exercise is to:

▶ Evaluate the effectiveness of the client's supply chain

▶ Identify the opportunities for improvement or optimization

▶ Estimate the value of realization of these opportunities

▶ Recommend a realistic roadmap for achieving the optimized results

Do It Yourself or Call in the Professionals?

Anyone who has ever tried to fix or upgrade their own computer or car or bicycle has faced the decision to do it yourself, pay someone to assist, or completely outsource the task. The criteria for deciding to seek help in developing an assessment is likely very similar.

Because at the end of any project you propose you'll likely be judged by how closely the expenses and benefits met the business case, it is probably not realistic to completely outsource the assessment. A good assessment requires so much knowledge of existing roles, responsibilities, processes, and technology that it would be impractical and imprudent not to be involved to some degree.

Alternatively, unless you have experience with projects involving significant organizational, process, and technological change in addition to knowledge of industry-specific best practices in the area of demand management, you would likely benefit from working with someone with such experience. Another benefit is the ability to share administrative responsibilities because it's likely that you and many other people whose input would be required also have other responsibilities in the day-to-day operation of the organization.

The assessment framework, as shown in Figure 3.9, is an example of a framework developed to quickly assess the supply chain processes and benchmark their performance to discover issues and challenges and identify improvement opportunities for clients. This results in an extremely rich and actionable assessment of the organization's supply chain process in a short amount of time.

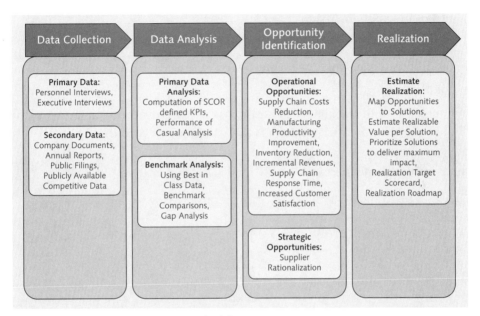

Figure 3.9 Steps in the Assessment Methodology

3.2.1   Deliverables

The deliverables from the supply chain assessment include:

► Executive presentation
  ► High-level presentation indicating the current supply chain processes, challenges and key findings, optimization opportunities, solution map, and business benefit and return on investment (ROI) analysis
► Assessment details
  ► Description of the existing supply chain processes for selected organization entities
  ► Supply chain process: Best practice comparisons and gap analysis

▶ Identification of key information flow and process integration and their impact on supply chain metrics and root cause analysis

▶ Optimization opportunities including to-be process recommendations

▶ Opportunities and solutions map

▶ Business benefits and ROI analysis details

▶ Benefit realization roadmap

▶ External benchmark comparisons and competitive ranking chart

▶ Solution implementation roadmap

▶ Solution proposal

  ▶ Proposal with recommended next steps for achieving the optimization based on the solution roadmap defined as part of the assessment

3.2.2 Engagement Plan

Figure 3.10 illustrates a typical project plan for the assessment engagements.

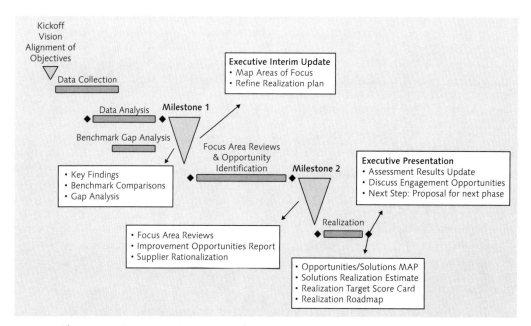

Figure 3.10 Assessment Engagement Plan

The key milestones for the engagement plan are as follows:

- Kickoff meeting
  - Participants: Executives sponsor and key stakeholders
  - Purpose: Understand the vision, existing challenges and concerns, and alignment of objectives and ensure timely participation from the key personnel
- Executive interim update
  - Participants: Executive sponsor and key stakeholders
  - Purpose:
    - Provide a brief update on key findings, benchmark comparisons, gap analysis, some key opportunities for improvement, and so on
    - Map areas of focus and a high-level realization plan
    - Ensure that the team is on the right path and get alignment on the challenges and to an extent on possible solution opportunities
- Final executive presentation
  - Participants: Executive sponsor and key stakeholders
  - Purpose:
    - Final presentation of findings
    - Presentation of solution roadmap
    - Recommendations and next steps

3.2.3   Process

Successful completion of an assessment engagement requires tight cooperation between information technology and line of business employees. A combination of primary data gathering using interviews and workshops along with secondary data gathering through publicly available information is used to arrive at the final deliverables.

The assessment engagement typically begins with a "kickoff" meeting with the executive sponsor and key stakeholders. The expectation is that the executive sponsor provides the high-level (big picture) vision for the engagement to all participants. This also helps set the scope of the engagement and ensure timely participation from the key stakeholders and their teams. In addition, the expectation is set that the executive sponsor will be available for interviews during the course of the engagement.

> **Value Lifecycle Management**
>
> SAP has constructed a dynamic and collaborative business process evaluation platform, including typical subprocess and industry issues, opportunities, and key performance indicators to help an organization diagnose business process health and quantify the impact of process improvement.
>
> This tool, the Value Lifecycle Manager (VLM), includes results from analyses performed on benchmark data volunteered by thousands of organizations across multiple industries and empirical evidence gathered from clients who have implemented transformational strategies. This information is a gold mine for not only an initial investigation of potential areas of opportunity, but also for a collaborative and in-depth validation required to build world-class business cases.

The assessment process consists of four key steps in a sequence to ensure that all of the appropriate and required data are gathered in a timely manner. In the following sections, we'll discuss each of these steps in more detail.

Step 1: Data Collection – Understand and Capture Stakeholder's Concerns

As a starting point, the team listens to key stakeholders describe their order-to-delivery process issues that emanate from efficiency and effectiveness issues within their supply chain. This helps in understanding the key supply-chain-related pain points and their impact on the business and focuses the data collection process to appropriate areas to capture key supply chain process information (Figure 3.11). Through a series of meetings and structured workshops, the team maps the current supply chain topology and processes, as well as information and material flows in these processes for each of the product lines and business units. In addition, key operating metrics are used to measure how the performance of each of these processes are captured and how these metrics are collected, reported, and utilized to identify, diagnose, and correct issues.

All of this is achieved using the predefined detailed questionnaires or templates developed as part of the framework. The templates are designed to collect quantitative, and qualitative, data.

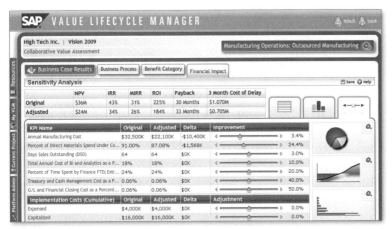

Figure 3.11 Data Collection with Focus on Supply Chain Vision

Step 2: Data Analysis – Discover Key Issues and Perform Root Cause Analysis

Once the data is collected, resources with deep demand management expertise identify key issues and root causes (Figure 3.12) for each of the issues. This analysis prepares them to identify and propose solutions that address the issue at its core.

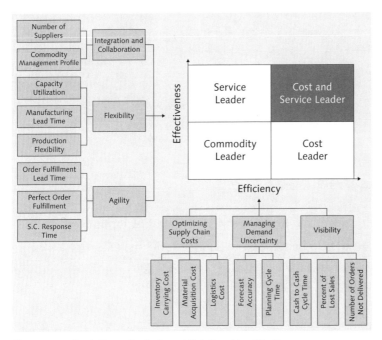

Figure 3.12 Root Cause Analysis and Solution Identification

During this time, the project team also assesses the current findings and compares them with industry best practices to determine where the client stands with respect to their peers and best in class in several categories or metrics within the supply chain spectrum (Figure 3.13). In addition, if business benefits and ROI analysis is part of the scope, then the team works on collecting relevant information from the finance and operations organization that will help ensure building the business value realization and benefits scorecard.

Issue	Root Cause	Best Practice	Process Recommendation	IT Recommendation
Forecast Accuracy	No history of demand patterns available to sales team for analysis	Data Analysis Capability	Single data source for decision-making	Forecasting using APO Demand Planning and APO BW (I a)* and BW analytics (II)*
	Large manual effort required in collation of demand forecast	Timely and correct updating of forecast	Planning calendar to be followed	Automation using APO planning books (I a)*
	Low visibility into Customer's business plan	Customer Collaboration	Integrate with customer's planning process	Facilitate the process using APO Collaborative Planning (I b)*
	No fool proofing mechanism to validate forecast number	Exception based planning		Consensus planning and Alert functionality in APO DP (I a)*
	No measurements in place	Closely monitoring and tracking metrics	Design and monitor metrics and targets for each organization level	Metrics reporting and tracking using SAP BW (II)*

* Phases of solution implementation: I a, I b, II, III

Figure 3.13 Data Analysis and Benchmarking

Step 3: Identify, Prioritize, and Recommend Opportunities for Improvement

Once the issues and their root causes are identified, the next step is to identify those issues that can quickly have the highest impact (Figure 3.14). Key opportunity areas may include, but are not limited to, the following:

- ▸ Operational opportunities
  - ▸ Supply chain cost reduction
  - ▸ Manufacturing productivity improvement
  - ▸ Inventory reduction
  - ▸ Incremental revenues
  - ▸ Supply chain response time improvement
  - ▸ Customer metrics improvement
- ▸ Strategic opportunities
  - ▸ Supplier rationalization

Demand Planning	Supply Planning	Order Promising and Allocation Planning	Data Management	Metrics
One Number	Centralized	Allocation Rules	Clean Data	Use Metrics
Consensus	Constrained/ Concurrent	Global ATP Check	Data Management Process	Standardized
Statistical	Collaborate	CTP Check		Hierarchy
Lifecycle	Exception Based	Supply Change Update		Information System
Collaborate	Simulate	Integrated		SCOR
Decoupling Point	Supplier Capacities			
Frequency	Alternate Item Logic			
Integrated	Integrated			

KEY: ☐ Some Alignment with Best Practices ☐ Strong Alignment with Best Practices ☐ No Alignment with Best Practices

Figure 3.14 Example of Conclusions from Data Analysis and Benchmarking

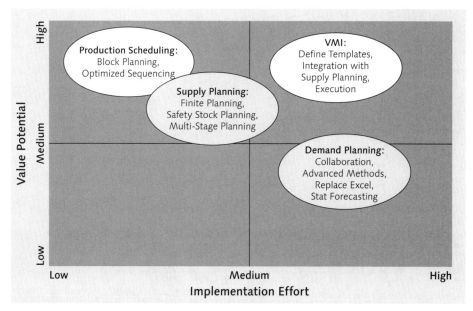

Figure 3.15 Value Potential versus Implementation Effort

Step 4: Develop Solution Roadmap

The final step in the process is to develop a clear solution roadmap for prioritized opportunities. As shown in Table 3.1, the roadmap identifies clear systems deployment steps involved in realizing the qualitative and quantitative benefits that were identified and prioritized in the opportunity identification step.

Area	Phase I	Phase II
Demand planning	▶ Replace Excel-based planning ▶ Deploy statistical and consensus forecasts ▶ Lifecycle and promotion planning	▶ Collaborative planning ▶ Facilitate safety stock planning
Supply planning		▶ PP/DS heuristics to propagate demand across the supply network (CPD, beverage, mills) ▶ Finite planning ▶ Safety stock planning

Table 3.1 Solution Roadmap with Deployment Phases

Area	Phase I	Phase II
Production scheduling		▸ Optimized sequencing ▸ Block planning
Vendor-managed inventory (VMI)		▸ Define template processes for Excel, EDI, and other VMI approaches ▸ Integration with supply planning processes ▸ Possible integration with Sales and Distribution
Master data	▸ Product and location hierarchy ▸ Refine planning characteristics	▸ Review PP master data ▸ Review MRP views and purchasing related master data ▸ Review SD master data

Table 3.1 Solution Roadmap with Deployment Phases (Cont.)

3.2.4 Case Study

In this case study, the organization in question is a market leader in materials integrity management. It provides technological expertise, a broad product line, a wide base of semiconductor supplier experience, and services to customers. Customers throughout the semiconductor, data storage, fuel cell, aerospace, medical, and emerging technologies industries use its products and services to precisely control micro-contamination and reliably handle substrates. With a global infrastructure of manufacturing, service, and research facilities, it services customers across the globe.

The organization was an existing SAP customer and was using SAP ERP to run its day-to-day business. Though having an SAP solution in place for execution purposes, the organization lacked any supply chain tool to support the process and make it measurable

The demand planning process at the organization was revenue driven, where sales and finance functions were forecasting the revenues instead of the unit quantities for various product lines. There was no customer demand visibility for the manufacturing and procurement functions, resulting in all-pervasive *expedites,* where people were more busy managing the sudden demand spurts or material shortages then improving the process efficiency. Frequent changes to the production schedules had to be made to accommodate customer demand. No scientific method was used to calculate or review the safety stock levels; everything followed the gut feelings of the individuals.

When the organization was asked about their forecast accuracy, it was reported to be 96%, but the line fill rate was 50–60%, and the entire order delivery cycle time was as long as four weeks. These fill rates were in spite of the fact that a commit date was used to calculate the fill rate against the customer requested delivery date. We know from our previous discussion that a relationship exists between demand forecast accuracy and order fulfillment. Something was wrong with these numbers.

A supply chain assessment exercise was conducted to determine the root cause of the pain areas and identify the focus areas for improvement. The result of the study showed some eye-opening results: The forecast accuracy was 96% as claimed, but it was measured by revenue on a quarterly basis. The forecast accuracy number, however, came down to a mere 20% when measured by SKU/DC on a monthly basis, which is far below the industry best in class. Inventory days in supply were 98 days, which was almost three times the industry best in class. Now the numbers started to make some sense.

Top management identified inventory reduction and reduction in order delivery cycle times as the objectives for a supply chain transformation exercise. It was determined that the organization was following make-to-stock (MTS) and build-to-order (BTO) manufacturing strategies. Almost 60% of the products were following an MTS manufacturing strategy — about 11,000 products. Inventory analysis revealed that almost 90% of the finished goods inventory and 50% of the raw materials inventory was for the MTS products. Average lead time for the MTS products was 3.5 weeks, with the variability at four weeks; that is, 85% of the time, it takes manufacturing between 1 and 7.5 weeks to meet MTS demand. Most of the finished products were single sourced with a dedicated manufacturing plant, and the majority of the raw materials was also single sourced.

Based on the above analysis, MTS products were identified as the first opportunity to bring maximum benefits instead of diluting the efforts on a wider scope, but demand planning for 11,000 products takes a lot of time and effort from the planners. A further analysis revealed that only 5% of these products were contributing to 80% of the revenue, whereas 77% of the products contributed just 5% of the revenue. Similar customer analysis revealed that only 4% of the customers were contributing 80% of the revenue while 85% of the customers were contributing just 5% of the revenue.

A demand planning process was designed based on the above analysis, where planners had to focus only on a smaller subset of products and customers contributing the majority of the revenue, and the large number of products contributing to a small amount of revenue were moved to an autopilot mode where inventories were managed using min/max levels, and planners will intervene only in exceptions. A consensus demand planning process was put in place providing upstream function demand visibility, helping them anticipate future schedules.

A conservative set of benefit estimation showed that with an estimated forecast accuracy of 50% and line fill rates of 95% after the implementation, the organization will get annual savings of over $2.0 million and one-time savings of over $11 million. After the successful implementation of the new demand management process, the organization managed to achieve benefits much greater than the earlier projected numbers. The estimated RoI for the entire initiative was just over a year, which gave management the confidence to give approvals and commitment for the initiative.

Something to keep in mind throughout the process is that the business case should focus on issues and opportunities that can be met. If the proposed process or organizational change exceeds the company's willingness to change, then it is unlikely to be successful. In these cases, proposals that feature phased approaches can express the full vision while reaching a compromise with executives concerned with the risks. Similarly, if the new process and organization depend on a solution that does not exist or is significantly more sophisticated than existing technology used by the organization, then a phased approach may be best.

3.3   What SAP Solutions Can Support This?

Without information technology, it would not be possible to plan demand for hundreds and thousands of product items and communicate this plan to the supply organization on an ongoing basis and in a consistent and accurate manner. Thirty years ago, few companies performed demand management. It was simply too time-consuming to gather information on customers' buying patterns, integrate this information with marketing and sales plans, and perform statistical forecasting. Most of this work had to be performed manually — without even the aid of spreadsheets.

Today, software applications can statistically forecast hundreds of items in just minutes. Sales orders and demand schedules can be communicated via electronic data interchange (EDI) and the Internet in real time. Retail companies can share point-of-sale information with their trading partners. Salespeople can sit in their customers' offices and look up product availability, specifications, and pricing on their companies' information systems, using hand-held devices.

> **The Spreadsheet**
>
> With all of the advanced technological capability available to them today, it's surprising how many companies, regardless of whether their revenue is measured in millions or billions of dollars, have incredibly powerful and sensitive demand information contained within PC spreadsheets.
>
> One company tells a story about a single analyst with the entire organization's demand plans built into a single spreadsheet so large that it requires a new computer each year as technological advancement races to keep pace with the organization's growth.
>
> The benefits of using enterprise software to support demand management processes include scalability and reduced risk of losing, corrupting, or inadvertently releasing sensitive data and the ability to share relevant information quickly and easily across the organization and beyond to suppliers and customers. All of these benefits are nullified if the solutions do not align with the process and organization that they are put in place to support, forcing people to reach for flexible alternatives.

Figure 1.11, first introduced in Section 1.5 of Chapter 1, illustrates a number of SAP solutions that can support an organization in performing demand management. As with best practices in both process and organization, solutions that enable demand management have evolved over time even among SAP solutions. Consequently, whereas there is some redundant functionality among the applications, there is significant synergy among them because each successive solution was built to take advantage of the capabilities of the existing applications.

3.3.1 SAP Business Suite for Demand Management

As shown in Figure 3.16, the SAP Business Suite provides integration of information and processes, collaboration, industry-specific functionalities, and scalability. The toolset supports industry best practices and is closely integrated with standard data transfer interfaces, resulting in error-free communication with enterprise-wide data visibility. SAP ERP forms the central component of the SAP Business Suite, helping run the enterprise in accordance with strategy and plans by providing access to the right information in real time, and helping identify the concern areas.

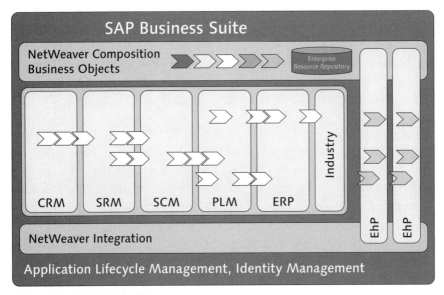

Figure 3.16 SAP Business Suite

SAP ERP supports a broad range of business processes including financial management, human capital management, procurement and logistics execution, product development and manufacturing, sales and service, and corporate services. Using the robust functionality that SAP ERP provides for these business processes, you can:

▶ More tightly link your business operations and improve visibility

▶ Enhance financial management and reporting

▶ Effectively manage your workforce — both locally and globally

▶ Achieve superior flexibility for addressing new business requirements

▶ Gain easier access to enterprise information and reports

▶ Give employees tools to perform their jobs efficiently

▶ Take advantage of software designed for adaptability that grants you the freedom to innovate

3.3.2   Core Demand Planning with SAP ERP

Embedded with the SAP ERP solutions comes a simple demand planning solution known as Flexible Planning. It is a simple table-based solution with statistical forecasting capabilities for univariate forecasting. Flexible Planning is capable of capturing the information for up to nine levels of planning hierarchy — by customers, sales division, material group, and line item — providing user flexibility to slice and dice the data, and allows planning at any level of a hierarchy. Automatic aggregation and disaggregation functionality ensures that you can propagate a demand plan at all levels of a hierarchy consistently. The disaggregation ratios can be automatically calculated using historical data and can be manipulated by the planners if needed.

Flexible Planning contains most of the textbook univariate forecasting techniques for forecasting future demand based on historical data. Statistical forecasting has various graphical checks and capability to adjust historical data and forecast results. With the help of transparent tables, Flexible Planning can store logistics information system data available in SAP ERP, which can be used as an input for the statistical forecasting. The limitation of this approach is the inability to run simulations for the forecasting models, which prevents planners from seeing the impact of various forecasting models on the data.

Flexible Planning allows you to define multiple key figures to capture the input from multiple departments in an organization with the capability to define custom views for each entity. This helps in providing data security and convenience for the planners. For periodically running simple mathematical calculations, macros are provided that are easy to configure and can be scheduled to execute these calculations in the background. You can use macros for a wide range of purposes, such as finding differences between the forecasts created by two different departments or automatically creating a final demand plan as a weighted average of statistical forecast and planner input.

Though Flexible Planning offers a range of features to help planners plan demand, it has some severe limitations in terms of the number of planning hierarchies, which can't exceed nine, and inability to run forecast simulations. Also, macros don't support any advanced logical and mathematical functions, and Flexible Planning doesn't offer any advanced functions to support promotion management or track the lifecycle of a product. To overcome these impediments you need to use advanced demand planning tools.

3.3.3 SAP Supply Chain Management (SCM)

As we mentioned briefly in Chapter 1, a step up from SAP ERP Flexible Planning is the SAP Supply Chain Management (SAP SCM) application (Figure 3.17). It is a complete supply chain management application that enables collaboration, planning, execution, and coordination of the entire supply chain, empowering organizations to adapt their supply chain processes to an ever-changing competitive environment. SAP SCM can help transform traditional supply chains from linear, sequential steps into a responsive supply network in which communities of customer-centric, demand-driven companies share knowledge, intelligently adapt to changing market conditions, and proactively respond to shorter, less predictable lifecycles.

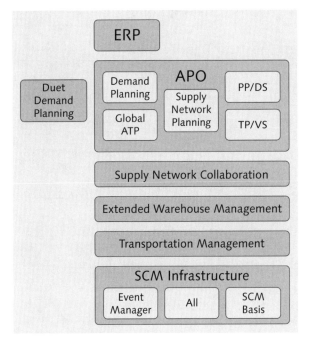

Figure 3.17 SAP SCM Suite

SAP SCM is closely integrated with the SAP ERP system, ensuring that the planner is working with the real-time information in the organization. This helps planners react to the changing demand and supply scenario and replan to fill gaps and maintain service levels without increasing the network inventory. The latest plan can be sent to the SAP ERP system in real time for execution.

As shown in Figure 3.18, planners can create a demand plan using various user-friendly functionalities in SAP SCM Demand Planning and transfer it to the SAP ERP system, where it can be used as an input for Material Resource Planning (MRP) and Rough Cut Capacity Planning (RCCP). Any changes in the demand situation (in the form of actual customer orders) the supply situation (in the form of available stock), or planned production can be communicated back to the SAP SCM system in real time, giving planners visibility into the changing business situation. Planners can react to changes by re-creating the demand plan, which can be sent back to the SAP ERP system to close the loop.

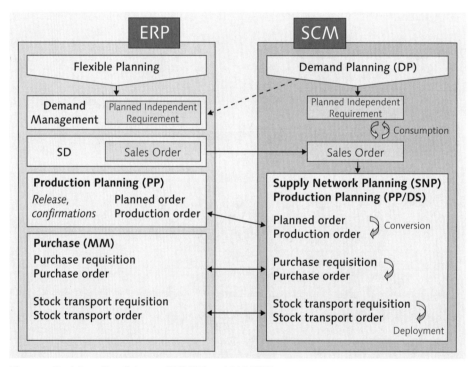

Figure 3.18 Integration Between SAP ERP and SAP SCM

3.3.4 Advanced Demand Planning with SAP APO

SAP Advanced Planning and Optimization (APO) Demand Planning is a key component of SAP APO, which is itself the centerpiece of SAP SCM. The Demand Planning functionality is focused at enabling a business to define a forecast of future demand for its products from the customers — usually drawing on knowledge of the actual demand in the past.

SAP APO Demand Planning offers a complete range of advanced functions for data analysis, multilevel planning, lifecycle management, forecasting, and promotion planning. In addition, it supports collaboration and supply chain partnerships such as vendor-managed inventory and collaborative planning, forecasting, and replenishment. As shown in Figure 3.19, SAP APO Demand Planning helps combine state-of-the-art forecasting techniques with user-friendly functionalities to capture the planner's knowledge of the ever-changing business environment, helping deliver more accurate demand plans that are in sync with the market realities.

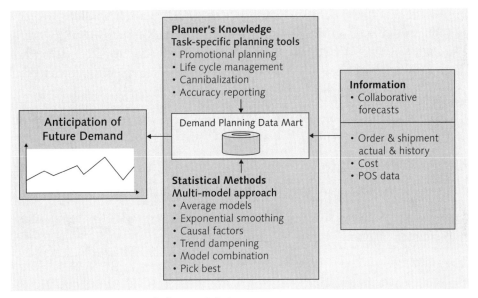

Figure 3.19 SAP SCM Demand Planning Solution

SAP APO Demand Planning utilizes an innovative database technology known as Livecache, which helps capture and process large amounts of information at a much faster rate than an RDBMS database. This tool can capture the information at multiple levels — individual customer, sales territory, sales channel, product category, family, and item — providing planners with the ability to slice and dice the data for analysis. User-specific data views with telescopic time buckets allow planners to create short-term, mid-term, and long-term demand plans, reducing the work load significantly. Another advantage of this innovative approach is the capability to run forecast simulations, which helps planners run through multiple scenarios and realize their impact on the demand plan. Planners can then easily choose the best forecasting model or scenario reflecting the market realities and use it as a final demand plan.

For organizations with a large number of products and a large customer base, Demand Planning offers automatic aggregation and disaggregation of data with completely flexible rule definition. This allows planners to plan the data at the aggregate level and automatically create the item-level forecast to be sent to the supply planners, facilitating the implementation of the one-number principle in the organization. With the help of a built-in business intelligence (BI) system, Demand Planning can receive and store historical information from the SAP ERP system, customer systems, or any third-party application that forms the basis for the state-of-the-art statistical forecasting. This also allows planners to run operational reports to analyze and compare the historical data and make course corrections.

Demand Planning has several primary planning methods. Some are alternatives and some are complementary:

▶ Interactive planning with user-friendly and fully configurable planning books

▶ Statistical forecasting using univariate or multiple regression techniques

▶ Collaborative planning with partners via the web

▶ Promotion planning

▶ Like-modeling and lifecycle management

▶ Automatic planning alerts

By providing all of the historical data, current data, and forecasts for future demand generated by either system or various departments in the organization (such as sales and marketing), SAP APO Demand Planning significantly improves the transparency and accuracy of demand planning numbers. It also significantly shortens the planning cycle time by eliminating redundant data exchange and consolidation, making the entire planning process exception based instead of planners running through each and every item. This allows planners to forecast more frequently, improving forecast accuracy.

SAP APO Demand Planning enables organizations to collaborate and negotiate with their suppliers by providing more accurate long-term demand schedules, helping in reducing overall supply chain costs without compromising on the service levels. Figure 3.20 lists some of the benefits of implementing SAP APO Demand Planning.

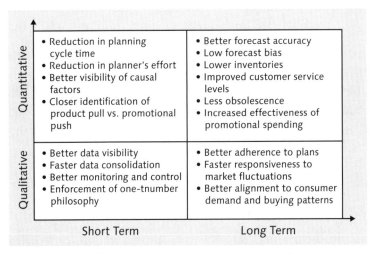

Figure 3.20 Benefits of Implementing SAP APO Demand Planning

3.3.5 Composite Demand Planning with Duet and SAP SCM

Used with a fully configured SAP demand planning application in the backend, Duet offers a comprehensive array of interactive planning functions for creating, controlling, and modifying demand plans or forecasts. Duet links the advanced demand planning features of SAP SCM with the familiar and flexible interface of Microsoft Excel. Together, Duet and SAP SCM support users' needs for comprehensive interactive functions that are flexible, intuitive, and easy to use. In addition, users have the option to work offline, allowing, for example, a sales representative to enter forecast data while on the road.

The biggest advantage Duet offers in a demand planning implementation is that it reduces the training effort because user familiarity with Microsoft Excel means instant usability and reduced cost. User acceptance is high, and training costs are close to zero, whereas it takes some effort to make users well acquainted with the newly introduced demand planning interface. Another advantage that Duet offers is that it complements SAP APO Demand Planning by providing key planning information available offline for sales representatives and product-marketing staff. Ultimately, demand planning becomes faster and more accurate thanks to input from those closest to the demand requirements. To ensure data security and accuracy, data access can be restricted for individual users.

Using Duet and SAP SCM, employees who don't specialize in the planning process but have the best possible understanding of their customers' requirements can enter information via a simple interface, thereby contributing greatly to the accuracy of the overall demand plan. Such employees gain an unprecedented view of planning data as it relates to their areas of responsibility. Specialized demand planners also benefit from the flexible Excel-based functions that complement the SAP SCM functions they already use.

3.3.6　Easy to Use Planning Sheets

A *planning sheet* is an Excel worksheet that is used as a template into which users load planning data from SAP SCM demand planning software. Users can then analyze, modify, and add to this data as required and save the changes in SAP SCM. Users with administrator or power-planner authorization can create planning sheets, which can be used multiple times.

Working with a planning sheet is like working with any other Microsoft Excel file. As shown in Figure 3.21, a planning sheet has the look and feel of a regular Excel worksheet. You can use many standard Microsoft Excel functions, such as adding rows and columns, creating graphics, and making calculations with specific formulas. You can even make calculations that reference data from another source that is included within the same Excel workbook. A highlight feature identifies the changes you make to the planning data so that you can review those changes before saving the data in SAP SCM.

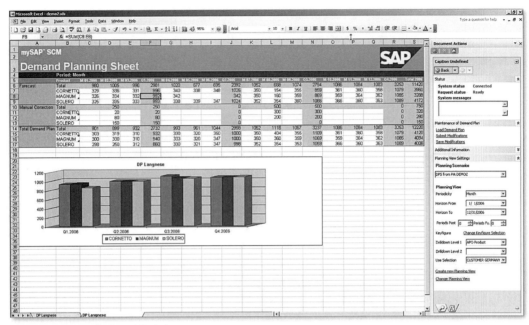

Figure 3.21 Sample Duet Worksheet

3.3.7 Flexible and Efficient Planning

When working online, the user can load up-to-date data from SAP SCM into the planning sheet with one click and then analyze and edit the data as required. A highlight feature identifies the changes you make to the planning data so that you can review them before saving the data to SAP SCM.

If you want to work offline, you can load the data into the planning sheet while you're still online and connected to SAP SCM. The date and time that a user last loaded data into the planning sheet or SAP application are shown in the status area of the Duet action pane to ensure that you always know the status of the data in planning sheet. The next time you're back online and connected to SAP SCM, you simply save any changes that were made while offline to the SAP backend application.

3.3.8 Customer Collaboration Using SAP Supply Network Collaboration

In an economic environment that challenges profit margins, one must reduce costs while increasing innovation, customer service, and responsiveness. To meet these challenges, you can outsource manufacturing to partners in low-cost regions, develop relationships with global suppliers, outsource other nonstrategic activities, and leverage real-time demand data across your supply chain. All of these actions require collaborative relationships with suppliers, contract manufacturers, and customers.

Developing collaborative relationships is not always easy. Connecting to a customer with limited technical capabilities can be costly, complicated, and time-consuming. Telephone, fax, and email remain the most common methods of communication. Even though electronic data interchange (EDI) may be more reliable, it is cost-effective only in high-volume situations. How, then, can you extend the benefits of collaboration to your entire ecosystem? How can you get all your partners to connect automatically, efficiently, and cost-effectively to your internal processes? The answer lies in the SAP Supply Network Collaboration (SNC) application, part of the SAP SCM. SAP SNC helps customers operating SAP or non-SAP systems collaborate through a range of supply, demand, and inventory replenishment processes. Figure 3.22 shows various levels of collaboration provided by SAP SNC for upstream and downstream collaboration.

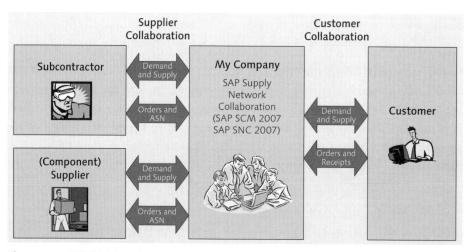

Figure 3.22 SAP SNC Overview

SAP SNC has an out-of-the-box approach for customer collaboration that supports capabilities designed for all levels of sophistication. You can deploy these capabilities on a customer-by-customer basis, allowing management of the inventory at each customer's location.

Responsive Replenishment enables organizations to leverage state-of-the-art VMI capabilities. These include true demand-driven replenishment based on forecasting, short-term forecasting through replenishment planning, and truck load building with or without promotion management. With Responsive Replenishment, you can manage inventory at customer locations based on demand and min/max stock balance limits using replenishment orders.

Responsive Replenishment also enables web-based collaboration with which organizations can share and compare forecasts with both suppliers and customers. You can calculate your forecast based on consumption data, customers transmit their forecasts, and SAP SNC calculates the difference — triggering exceptions if limits are breached. Workflow mechanisms ensure that a final, consensus-based forecast is reached. You can integrate this forecast into an overall forecasting process using the Demand Planning application that is part of SAP APO — or use the forecast within SAP SNC to ensure replenishment accuracy.

3.4   Summary

Regardless of the level of organizational, procedural, and technological sophistication currently possessed by a company in the area of demand management, there is room for improvement. Although this improvement can include many intangibles, the most relevant benefits are those that can be directly attributed to the income statement and balance sheet. The projection of these tangible benefits against the costs and less tangible risks of the proposed change makes up the business case that is used to weigh the potential of a demand management project against other investment opportunities faced by the organization.

The assessment process is a critical objective look at the organization's current and potential level of sophistication. It may benefit from external assistance and should be conducted keeping in mind the amount of organizational and procedural and technological change that the organization is prepared to undergo. For changes that exceed organizational comfort thresholds, phased plans combine the ability to build up to a vision with the reduced risk of smaller steps.

SAP offers an integrated suite of tools to address various aspects of demand management and help provide organization-wide integration of information and processes, collaboration with business partners, and scalability. This toolset addresses the needs of a wide variety of organizations with different levels of maturity in the demand management process.

Now let's move on to statistical forecasting, where you'll learn how you can use historical data to project future demand.

In this chapter, you'll learn about statistical forecasting. You'll gain perspective on using historical data to project future demand and learn how SAP APO Demand Planning supports this process.

4 Statistical Forecasting

Business planning is inherently "top-down," meaning it begins with single enterprise-wide numbers such as quarterly or annual revenue, which must then be allocated to individual accounts and products. This chapter focuses on *statistical forecasting*, which can be done not only top-down, but bottom-up or even middle-out, as we'll discuss.

The chapter begins with an overview of the use of historical data to project future demand, and then goes on in detail about how the SAP APO Demand Planning component supports this process. Statistical forecasting with Flexible Planning in SAP ERP is also briefly discussed in the final section of the chapter.

4.1 Looking Back to See Ahead

Statistical forecasting is mostly about looking at what has happened in the past to extrapolate what is likely to happen in the future. (Of course, it is also possible to use statistics to develop a demand projection based on knowledge of leading indicators, but that will be covered in Chapter 6.) In the spirit of studying the past to project the future, it might benefit us to consider what brought about the prevalence of statistical forecasting in business today.

Driven by Moore's law, the rise of computing power in the later decades of the 20th century enabled simple mathematical algorithms to be applied to unimaginable amounts of data at unparalleled speeds, provided that the raw data was available in electronic memory. Projecting future demand for products requires static master data information about products and customers, as well as dynamic transactional data, such as how many of which products were ordered by which customers on what date.

The algorithms and processing power needed to accomplish this were available long before organizations had achieved a disciplined approach to storing and updating master and transactional data. For many corporations, much of this data was available but stored and maintained in disparate systems (i.e., order management, finance, etc.) that often resided on different technological platforms. Demand planning and, later, demand management applications, owe their popularity to the Y2K issue inherent in these earlier disparate corporate systems. Because of concerns about the viability of critical enterprise systems such as order management when the two-character variable field coded into many of these applications shifted from (19)99 to (20)00, organizations invested en masse in the new generation of ERP solutions that, for the first time, brought together financial, customer, and product data within the same database.

Because the urgency of resolving the Y2K issue resulted in explosive growth in the market for ERP systems and because of the risk of trusting data that was vital to companies' day to day operations, there was an extremely accelerated pace of growth concentrated in a few top vendors. Unlike the previous decades' slow growth of multiple solutions offered by multiple companies who may not have even specialized in software, the new generation of ERP software vendors was reduced to a handful of successful software companies.

So, in the mid-to-late 1990s, with sufficient computing power, thanks to information technology, talented analysts experienced and business employees trained in enterprise-level projects, and a freshly developed sense of process integration, companies were in a position to apply statistical algorithms to their newly available master and transactional data for the purposes of demand management. Meanwhile, with a limited number of types of ERP databases spread across an enormous market of customers, software companies offering demand planning solutions sprang up in an echo "boom" to the Y2K ERP rush.

It is interesting to consider that sufficient computing power was available a decade or two before statistical forecasting was widely adopted. It took consolidation of data on a foundational platform and the willingness of companies to accept new business processes and organizational roles and responsibilities for statistical forecasting to be widely adopted. This seems to lend credibility to the assertion that it is the confluence of people, process, and technology that makes demand management successful. A corollary to this is that each investment in people, process, and technology serves as a foundation for the next step. This emphasizes the importance of a long-term vision from the organizations making the change and the importance of vision and viability in the vendors whose tools they choose to support the change.

SAP is one of the handful of companies that came out on top of the Y2K ERP rush and subsequently recognized the market for demand management software. Statistical analysis of orders from a company's customers and shipments to those customers was built into Flexible Planning, a tool that continues to exist today in the SAP ERP solution and that will be discussed in the final section of this chapter. The bulk of the chapter, however, will be dedicated to SAP APO, specifically the Demand Planning component, which was built with lessons learned from Flexible Planning and insights gleaned from SAP customers.

4.2 Basic Statistical Forecasting Algorithms

Statistical algorithms in demand management work to identify repeating patterns within historical demand data (i.e., customer orders, shipments to customers, etc.). These patterns can be constant, trending up or down, or even cyclical, each of which we'll explore in this section. SAP APO Demand Planning uses univariate models that focus on a single data set. A single algorithm cannot look at both customer orders and shipments to the customer at the same time to create a forecast. However, in Chapter 11 we'll discuss how to bring multiple forecasts, such as a statistical forecast based on orders and a statistical forecast based on shipments, together.

A Word about Order History and Demand History

In using statistical algorithms to project future demand based on information about historical demand, companies often run up against the seemingly trivial question of what past demand really is. For audits, returns, recalls, and other purposes, organizations must keep track of what was shipped to customers. Therefore, this is probably the easiest form of demand history to access.

However, when projecting what the customers will want in the future, it might make more sense to base the calculations on what they asked for, not necessarily what you delivered. The difference between the customers' orders and the shipments to them would be zero for any company that has never delivered a short or late shipment, expedited production, shipped a substitute product, or shipped from an alternate manufacturing or distribution source. That rules out most companies.

By choosing to use shipment information as the basis for a statistical forecast, a company sets itself up to miss the same orders in the following years as they did in the past in a sort of self-fulfilling prophesy. The initial requested delivery date, amount, and product are harder for organizations to capture, but most ERP solutions are able to do so. Because there may not be a reason to store original order information, it may take time for companies to accumulate a large enough pool of historical data to support a forecast.

Until the pool has reached sufficient depth, it makes sense to base forecasts on shipment history because most companies that are still in business are meeting at least the majority of their customers' orders. However, leveraging demand data either in a parallel process or in replacement of shipment data will likely lead to better forecast accuracy and the benefits (Chapter 3) that it entails.

4.2.1 Constant Demand

At its most rudimentary, the univariate (single variable) model that SAP and most other software vendors use for history-based statistical forecasting operates by applying different mathematical formulas and tweaking their individual constants to match the pattern of demand history. The simplest example of this is a constant demand pattern as shown in Figure 4.1.

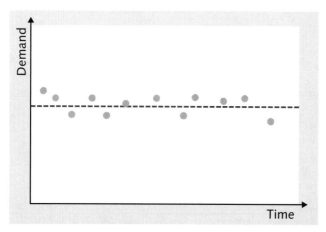

Figure 4.1 Constant Demand

In a constant demand pattern, demand is expected to vary little from its historical norm. This might be something like the number of light bulbs that a city requires for its street lights. Because they are not erecting any more light posts and because the lights are all on for the same amount of time, the demand is fairly flat. This type of model can be described with the equation $y = b$, where y is the demand (which in our example is the number of bulbs that need to be replaced at any time period x), and b is simply a constant number.

4.2.2 Trend Demand

Whereas constant demand is wonderfully predictable and can result in very low inventory safety stock requirements, it is not necessarily a growing business for a manufacturer, distributor, or retailer. Most of them would prefer to be in a business where the market is expanding. So instead of street lights, let's look at the casket business.

If the only two certainties in life are death and taxes, then this would appear to be a fairly constant business. However, because most countries in the world are experiencing population growth, it is not a flat business. It is logical to assume that the number of sales is increasing each year or, to put it in more mathematical parlance, "trending up." Staying as simple as possible, the easiest model to understand for trend demand is the equation of a straight line: $y = mx + b$, where y is again the demand and b is a constant value. The m, therefore, must represent our trend as captured in the line's slope (i.e., how much higher sales get for every incremental time period). This is pictured in Figure 4.2.

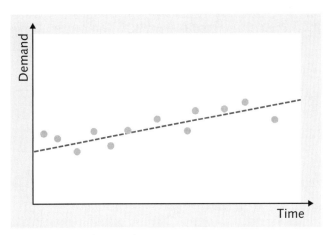

Figure 4.2 Trend Demand

Notice that in both Figure 4.1 and Figure 4.2, the data points do not all fall on the line. This is the *variance*, or the amount of sales that the model is unable to predict even after the constants (*m* and *b* in the examples) have been tuned as well as possible. Whereas some variance (sometimes called error) is nearly inescapable, we know that when organizations make operational decisions based on these demand projections, error results in excess inventory or lost sales, both of which cost money. So it makes sense to explore more sophisticated models as long as it does not lead to diminishing returns, where the amount of time and resources invested is larger than the cost of being wrong.

4.2.3 Seasonal Demand

Sometimes data that appears constant or trending may have a second pattern that plays around the initial line. If we revisit our street light example, we'll note that for cities a good distance north or south of the equator, the periods of darkness when the lights are lit tend to be longer during winter days and shorter during the summer days. So where the annual demand for streetlights may be constant, the demand varies in a cycle from summer, when it is lower, to winter, when it is higher. This is an aptly named seasonal demand. However, seasonality could apply to any repeating cycle, such as consumers buying more every two weeks when they get paid by their employers or demand for Olympic merchandise every two years. Figure 4.3 shows a seasonal demand model.

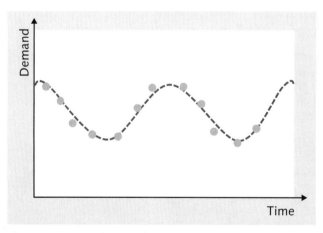

Figure 4.3 Seasonal Demand

4.2.4   Seasonal Trend Demand

Similarly, seasonality can be applied to trended models as well. If we return to our certainties and choose taxes, we can safely state that the market for tax software for individual citizens in the United States is constantly growing with the population. However, the demand for tax software tends to grow just before the April 15 filing deadline and then wane for the remainder of the year until April 15 rolls around again. Figure 4.4 shows such a seasonal trend model.

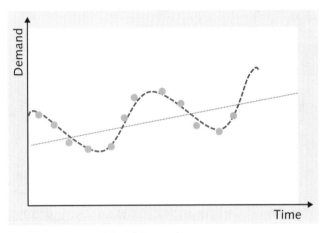

Figure 4.4   Seasonal Trend Demand

4.2.5   Lumpy Demand

The last and possibly most difficult demand pattern we'll discuss is the intermittent demand pattern. Some demand occurs less frequently and/or across a broader area. The need for equipment to set up a new oil refinery or the demand for service parts for a construction vehicle are two examples. Even demand that appears constant, seasonal, or trended can become intermittent if the time and place on which you focus is discrete enough. The annual need for caskets in Europe is probably very regular, but the number needed from day to day for one small town in Australia can probably vary significantly. Figure 4.5 approximates an intermittent demand pattern.

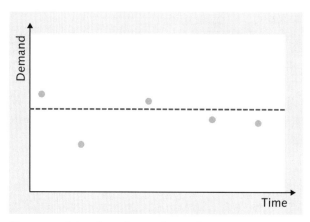

Figure 4.5 Intermittent/Lumpy Demand

4.2.6 First-Order Exponential Smoothing

Before we can discuss mathematical models for seasonal and intermittent demand, we need to understand one more thing about these demand patterns: Even the way that they change over time changes over time. Cities may choose to conserve energy by reducing the number of lights on at certain hours. Governments may choose to enable electronic filing and payment of taxes over the Internet. Both of these choices will result in changes to the demand pattern that make the orders and shipments after the change more relevant to projecting future demand than the orders and shipments before the change. Figure 4.6 shows the change in demand pattern over time as a hot new product settles into steady state.

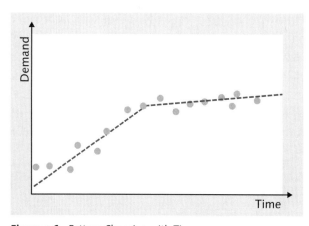

Figure 4.6 Pattern Changing with Time

Demand planners compensate for these changes with *smoothing*, which weighs the more recent data points more heavily than their older counterparts in calculating the forecast. This increases the complexity of the algorithms, but it still uses the same underlying algebra and trigonometry. Figure 4.7 shows our forecast before and after smoothing.

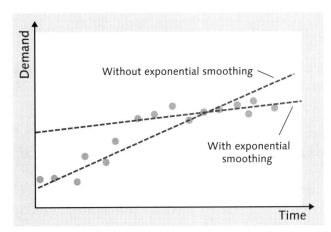

Figure 4.7 Forecast Before and After Exponential Smoothing

To return to our simplest constant model, where $y = b$, a demand planning application might look for a moving average based on the previous n time periods, where n could be the past ten days or the past five years. If M were the moving average and $V(t)$ were the sales in time period t, then the equation would look something like this:

$$M = \frac{\sum_{t=1}^{n} V(t)}{n}$$

However, this gives equal weight to every data point in that series (i.e., sales for the past ten days or past four years). We could instead increase the importance of more recent data and reduce the importance of older data by *weighting* it. If Wt is the relative weight (importance) of the data point (sales volume) at time period t, then the equation becomes:

$$M = \frac{\sum_{t=1}^{n} W_t \ne V_t}{\sum_{t=1}^{n} W_t}$$

M = Average value
V = Actual value
W = Weighting factor
n = Number of periods in the weighting group

Again, this is just for a constant model because, as you can see, without an x in the equation the result stays the same regardless of whether it is next week or next year.

A preferred method for setting the relative importance of time periods is an exponential smoothing that reduces the weight of data points exponentially as they age. This rapidly invalidates all but the most recent data points individually but retains the influence of longstanding trends. Those with children will recognize this as the naturally occurring process by which they arrive at the clothes and music that are cool to wear and listen to. The formula would be as follows:

$$G(t) = \alpha V(t) + (1-\alpha)G(t-1)$$

$G(t)$ = The current basic value for the current period (t)
$WG(t-1)$ = The previous basic value from the previous period
$V(t)$ = Actual demand for the current period (t)
α = Smoothing factor for the basic value

So if a planner were to choose a smoothing factor of 0.5, then the weight on historical data points would be:

▸ Most recent data point: 50%

▸ Second most recent data point: 25%

▸ Third most recent data point: 12.5%

▸ Fourth most recent data point: 6.25%

SAP APO Demand Planning has an algorithm that can be employed to automatically set this first-order exponential smoothing factor based on the historical data.

Beyond the constant model, first-order exponential smoothing can be applied to the trend, seasonal, and even seasonal trend models. Three smoothing factors are employed in this algorithm: one each for the basic value, trend, and seasonality. When brought together, the equations look like this:

Forecast Value for the Period (t+i)

$$P(t+i) = (G(t)+i * T(t)) * S(t-L+i)$$

Where:

Basic Value: $\quad G(t) \quad = G(t-1)+T(t-1)+\alpha \left[\dfrac{V(t)}{S(t-L)} - G(t-1) - T(t-1) \right]$

Trend Value: $\quad T(t) \quad = T(t-1)+\beta \left[G(t) - (G(t-1)+T(t-1)) \right]$

Seasonal Index: $S(t) \quad = S(t-L)+\gamma \left[\dfrac{V(t)}{G(t)} - S(t-L) \right]$

For Constant Model $\quad T(t) \quad = 0, \beta=0, S(t)=1.0, \gamma=$ Gamma $=0$

For Trend Model $\quad\quad S(t) \quad = 1.0, \gamma =$ Gamma $=0$

For Seasonal Model $\quad T_{(t)} \quad = 0, \beta=0$

$P(t+i) =$ Forecast calculated in the current period (t)for the period (t+i)
$i \qquad\quad =$ Forecast horizon
$G(t) \quad =$ Current basic value for the current period (t)
$G(t-1)=$ The old basic value from the previous period
$L \qquad\quad =$ Period length (often 12)
$V(t) \quad =$ Actual requirement (past) for current period (t)
$T(t) \quad =$ Current basic value calculated for the current period
$T(t-1) =$ Old trend value from previous period
$S(t) \quad =$ Seasonal index for the period (t)
$S(t-L) =$ Old seasonal index for the period (t)
$\alpha \qquad\quad =$ Smoothing factor for the basic value 'G', $0 < \alpha < 1$
$\beta \qquad\quad =$ Smoothing factor for the trend value 'T', $0 < \beta < 1$
$\gamma \qquad\quad =$ Smoothing factor for the seasonal indices 'S', $0 < \gamma < 1$

For many people, the mathematical formulas are intimidating to try to interpret, which is why we've broken them down into their components. What can be understood almost immediately is that these are the same equations used without exponential smoothing, but with a different smoothing factor applied to each.

4.2.7 Second-Order Exponential Smoothing

Second-order exponential smoothing can be used to make the demand plan even more responsive to changes in historical demand data. To accomplish this, the result of the first exponential smoothing (which we called $G(t)$ in the previous figures) is then run through the equation a second time, replacing $V(t)$. The equations for this would be:

$$G^{(1)}(t) = \alpha V^{(1)}(t) + (1-\alpha)G^{(1)}(t-1)$$

$$G^{(2)}(t) = \alpha G^{(1)}(t) + (1-\alpha)G^{(2)}(t-1)$$

$G^{(1)}$	=	Simply smoothed basic value
$G^{(2)}$	=	Doubly smoothed basic value
V	=	Historical value
α	=	Smoothing factor

The success of all of these equations is predicated on a demand stream that's fairly regular. If historical demand data is sparse or lumpy, as we saw in Figure 4.5, then a different model is called for. SAP APO Demand Planning uses the Croston method, which initially calculates the average demand with an exponential smoothing model and then identifies the average interval from demand point to demand point. The equation looks like this:

```
If V(t)=0
  q=q+1
Else
  Z(t)=Z(t-1)+α [V(t)-Z(t-1)]
  X(t)=X(t-1)+α [q-X(t-1)]
Endif
```

$V(t)$	=	Historical value
$P(t)$	=	Forecasted value
q	=	Interval between last two periods with demand
Z	=	Smoothing factor for the estimates
X	=	Estimate of demand volume
α	=	Estimate of intervals between demand

If the first, oldest value in the time series, $V(0)$, is zero, then the algorithm sets it to one and sets the initial time between demand, $X(0)$, to two.

For the more recent SAP APO Demand Planning versions (v4.0 or greater), the forecast quantity can either be spread across each bucket in the forecast horizon as it was in older versions of the software, or it can be distributed according to the mean interval that was calculated above.

In reviewing the equations, it becomes apparent why organizations would prefer to employ software to execute them for any problems of significant scale or frequency. Whereas all of the computation is merely algebra, the number of steps in the algorithm and the number of times the algorithm must be run to identify the approach and smoothing factors that result in a good forecast is significant. This is especially true when we consider that most of these organizations look at two to three years of historical orders and shipments for each of potentially thousands of products sold to potentially tens of thousands of customers.

4.2.8 Model Fit: Ex-Post Forecast and Outliers

One thing we haven't established yet is how to judge when a statistical model is "good." Obviously a forecast's quality can be judged on how well it predicts future results, but that requires waiting for future results — which can be not only time consuming, but expensive (in terms of the excess inventory and lost sales that may result as you tune your algorithms and smoothing constants).

A more expeditious method is to apply the algorithm and constants to an older portion of your historical data, perhaps the oldest two years of a three-year data set, to see how well it predicts the most recent year's results. This simulated historical forecast is called an ex-post forecast (Figure 4.8), and the difference between the values it predicts and the actual values can be aggregated into a forecast error measurement for each set of algorithms and constants used.

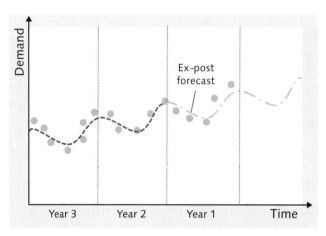

Figure 4.8 Checking Model Fit with Ex-Post Forecast

There are many ways to aggregate the differences between the predicted and actual values of each time period into a single number expressing the relative accuracy of the forecast. Chapter 11 will cover error measurement in more detail, but for now it is important to know that the methods by which ex-post forecast accuracy and thus the fit of the model, or *model fit,* can be judged using SAP APO Demand Planning are:

▸ Mean absolute deviation (MAD)

▸ Error total (ET)

▸ Mean absolute percentage error (MAPE)

▸ Mean squared error (MSE)

▸ Root mean squared error (RMSE)

▸ Mean percentage error (MPE)

One use for these error measures is to develop *tolerance lanes*, which serve as boundaries for statistical outliers. Outliers are data points that are so far removed from the forecast model that they might be suspected of not accurately representing history. Figure 4.9 shows an outlier outside of the tolerance lane. Customer orders for that period might be abnormally low because of a competitor's marketing promotion or a problem that shut down the main production line of a key customer. These outliers are easily identified within SAP APO Demand Planning, and can be automatically or manually brought back into conformance with the rest of the data. The solution uses a sigma factor to dictate how tightly the tolerance lane should be positioned around the forecast. The resulting forecast is simply known as the *corrected forecast*.

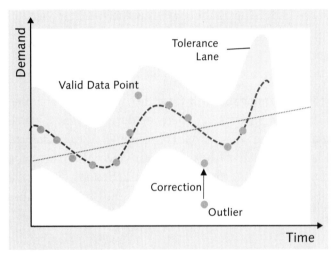

Figure 4.9 Identifying and Correcting Outliers with Tolerance Lanes

Chapter 12 will go into more detail and expand error and accuracy measurements with concepts like time lagging and weighting. What should be apparent at this point is that whereas these equations are not extremely complex, the size and number of data sets make them fairly unusable at any useful level of detail without software tools to support the numerous calculations. Some organizations could be forecasting based on two to three years of historical data in weekly buckets across thousands of items and tens of thousands of customers or more.

In the next chapter, we'll discuss in detail how information technology and demand planning analysts can configure and use SAP APO Demand Planning to generate statistical forecasts based on historical demand data. First, however, we'll take a look at the planning books that are your window into all of the data and analyses that Demand Planning offers.

4.3   Planning Books

Planners working in Demand Planning can see and manipulate their demand data in interactive planning screens called *planning books,* the main mechanism for planners to enter and change data. These planning books are usually designed to support the planning process. Consequently, there can be as many planning books as there are departments engaged in developing the consensus demand plan — sometimes even more. Planning books can be configured based on the preferences of the individuals using them. They contain key information about the plan, including figures, characteristics, planning horizons, macros for calculations, and so on.

To access the planning book, a planner selects it from the list of other planning books and data views, as shown in Figure 4.10. There are different views, which can be used based on the data you're working on. For example, to run a statistical forecast, a planner would select the statistical forecast view. Alternatively, a marketing manager could view and make changes to a marketing plan using the marketing view. The number of planning books created depends on the number of roles and participants in the planning process.

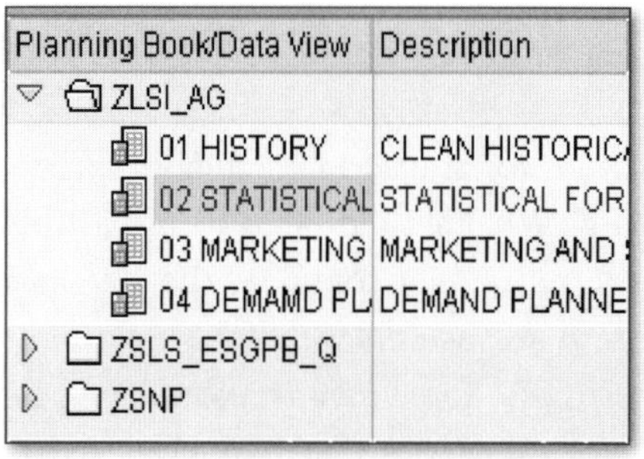

Planning Book/Data View	Description
▽ 🗁 ZLSI_AG	
🗐 01 HISTORY	CLEAN HISTORIC
🗐 02 STATISTICAL	STATISTICAL FOR
🗐 03 MARKETING	MARKETING AND
🗐 04 DEMAMD PL	DEMAND PLANNE
▷ 🗀 ZSLS_ESGPB_Q	
▷ 🗀 ZSNP	

Figure 4.10   Selecting a Planning Book

The data views are based on the planning book and contain a subset of the key figures in the planning book. These *key figures* are the categories of data which make up the rows in the spreadsheet-like table on the right-hand side. Examples of key figures might be historical shipments, statistical forecasts, marketing plans, and so on.

The data view screen is divided into two main sections: the data view itself and the shuffler, which allows you to choose different characteristics combinations.

4.3.1 Data View

Figure 4.11 shows the spreadsheet-like data view in tabular form. A graph form is also available either in addition to or replacing the tabular form. With key figures as the row headings, the aggregated data for the characteristics combinations that have been selected are shown across a number of periods. Months are used in the example below, but they could just as easily be in weeks, quarters, financial periods, or even seasons. Telescoping time buckets are also available, permitting planners to see a combination of time periods, such as the next three weeks, then the following two months, and the rest of the year in quarterly buckets.

	Un	P 06/2007	P 07/2007	P 08/2007	P 09/2007	P 10/2007	P 11/2007
System Generated Forecast	EA	10,214	7,520	8,289	7,416	7,591	7,980
Sales Forecast Quantity	EA	8,542	9,974	8,680	7,892	7,982	8,433
Market Final Forecast	EA	8,542	9,974	8,680	8,416	9,000	8,433
Demand Planner Forecast	EA	5,125	5,984	5,208	4,735	4,789	5,060
Consensus Forecast Quantity	EA	7,175	8,378	7,291	6,786	7,010	7,084
Customer Forecast Input	EA	3,000	5,904	5,177	5,032	4,839	5,120
Consensus Forecast 2	EA	3,000	5,904	5,177	8,416	9,000	8,433

Figure 4.11 Data View (Tabular)

4.3.2 Selection Profile

As alluded to in the previous paragraph, until you choose the characteristics combinations that you want to work with, the data view will simply be an empty table or graph. To choose the products, customers, brands, or combinations of these, a planner chooses the stored data selection in the selection profile by clicking on it. Alternatively, the user can create an ad-hoc selection (see text box below for details).

The following steps illustrate the ad hoc selection of data loading and display.

1. Go to the planning book with Transaction code /SAPAPO/SDP94.

2. Select the specific planning book and data view, as shown in Figure 4.12.

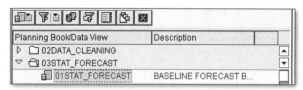

Figure 4.12 Planning Book/Data View

3. Click on the selection window icon, as shown in Figure 4.13.

Figure 4.13 Selection Window

4. The previous step opens the window for object selection (Figure 4.14).

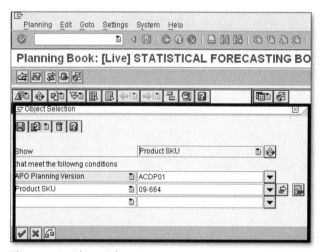

Figure 4.14 Object Selection

5. Select the objects as shown in Figure 4.14. The selection is for Product 09-664 and planning version ACDP01.

6. Based on the configuration of the planning book, other characteristics can be selected as shown below, and respective objects can be selected.

The selection profile, shown in Figure 4.15, is a grouping of previously stored combinations of characteristics that represent a data set. The selections can be created by planners, such as TOP 5 Products or Brand ABC. This ensures that the they don't have to remember the item number or go searching for it every time they want to review the information in the system. The selection profile can be created in the planning book.

Selection profile
▽ ⌷ SDSOUZA
❖ BRAND ABC
❖ TOP 5 PRODUCTS

Figure 4.15   Selection Profile

Once the data set corresponding to the stored combination of characteristics selected in the selection profile is retrieved, the planner can look at the aggregate results for the entire set or choose subsets as shown in Figure 4.16.

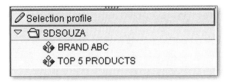

Material/Product	Material/Product
700083713.0	M-L-STRIDER-BI-MP

Figure 4.16   Choosing a Subset of the Characteristics Combination

Once the data is loaded, the views look like a spreadsheet. With grids made of rows (usually key figures) and columns (usually dates), data can be manipulated in highlighted cells, as shown in Figure 4.17.

	Un	P 06/2007	P 07/2007	P 08/2007	P 09/2007	P 10/2007	P 11/2007
System Generated Forecast	EA	10,214	7,520	8,289	7,416	7,591	7,980
Sales Forecast Quantity	EA	8,542	9,974	8,680	7,892	7,982	8,433
Market Final Forecast	EA	8,542	9,974	8,680	8,416	9,000	8,433
Demand Planner Forecast	EA	5,125	5,984	5,208	4,735	4,789	5,060
Consensus Forecast Quantity	EA	7,175	8,378	7,291	6,786	7,010	7,084
Customer Forecast Input	EA	3,000	5,904	5,177	5,032	4,839	5,120
Consensus Forecast 2	EA	3,000	5,904	5,177	8,416	9,000	8,433

Figure 4.17   Highlighted Cell in Data View

In addition to the tabular view of the data, planners can select a sometimes more intuitive graphical view, illustrated by Figure 4.18. The graphing capability is very flexible, and adjustments will be familiar to most people who have used graphs in common spreadsheet software packages.

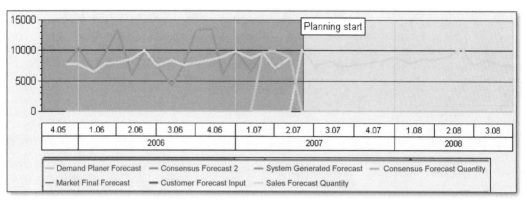

Figure 4.18 Graphical View

Along with the data selection and data view areas, there are many other features such as download to Excel, look at disaggregated or aggregated view, and hide key figures. Exceptions or alerts can be shown, notes or comments can be entered and viewed in individual cells.

Besides this standard SAP graphical user interface (GUI), *Collaborative Planning* allows planners and other stakeholders in demand management to view and change data via a web browser. Once the planning books are created in the SAP GUI, they can be viewed over the Internet; the Transaction code for this is /SAPAPO/CLPISDP. Using web access, sales and customers can collaboratively review and manipulate forecast figures. Alerts and exceptions can be shown on the web interface in real time as well. Figure 4.19 shows the planning book in a browser.

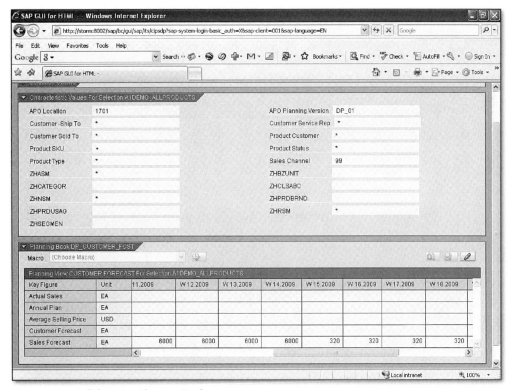

Figure 4.19 Collaborative Planning Book

4.4 Summary

With the basics of both statistics and planning books behind you, we can now move to Chapter 5, which will go into detail about configuring Demand Planning to generate statistical forecasts based on your historical data, and will focus on univariate forecasting based on historical demand data. Chapter 6 will go into more detail about augmenting univariate forecasts with causal forecasts derived from multiple linear regression models applied to leading indicators.

This chapter introduces you to SAP APO Demand Planning and SAP ERP Flexible Planning according to the statistical techniques covered in the previous chapter. These tools help provide clear, accurate data for you to use in your day-to-day processes.

5   Interactive Planning and Advanced Statistical Forecasting

Running more than two years of weekly historical demand data through iterative statistical algorithms to analyze model fit against an ex-post forecast to correct outliers for hundreds of thousands of product-customer combinations is no small task. However, given a solid footing based in clean master data and a dependable technical architecture, the SAP APO Demand Planning component can do the job.

In this chapter we'll look at how an organization's demand data can be represented in SAP APO Demand Planning. This will give us the basis to move into the hows and whys of configuring the tool and beginning to produce statistical forecasts. From there, we'll move on to applying statistical forecasts to new products without any demand history on which to draw, and finish with a brief discussion of the use of custom forecasting algorithms and the basic yet functional statistical forecasting capabilities embedded in the SAP ERP solution.

5.1   Characteristic Combinations and Data Selections

In Chapters 1 and 2, we discussed the importance of each stakeholder in the demand management processes having access to information in a familiar context. Marketing may think in terms of dollars and brands or product groups, sales in terms of regions and accounts and euros, operations in pallets or kilograms and individual products. If you were to think about any one order that the organization has filled or will fill, you would see that it can be described in terms of an amazingly large number of characteristics, such as:

▶ Product

▶ Product group

▶ Brand

▶ Business unit

▶ Customer account

▶ Sales region

▶ Sales channel

▶ Originating distribution center

▶ Price point

Each person's familiar context for demand information is likely made up of a combination of these characteristics, which SAP calls a *characteristics value combination* (CVC). This section explores how SAP APO Demand Planning leverages CVCs and stored selections of data (data selections) to enable individuals to quickly and efficiently get the demand information they want to see.

5.1.1 Introduction to Characteristic Combinations

CVCs are part of the master data for demand planning in SAP APO. They determine the levels at which demand plans are created, changed, aggregated, and disaggregated. A combination of a specific sold-to-party (1000) serviced from a specific distribution center location (2400) for a specific product (P-102), represented by P-102, 2400, and 1000 is an example of a CVC. Each planning level is represented by a characteristic, and planning is done for a combination of characteristics represented by a CVC. Figure 5.1 illustrates individual characteristics being grouped into CVCs.

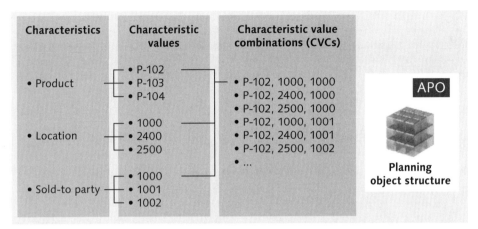

Figure 5.1 Characteristics Value Combination

Data is stored at the level of these characteristic combinations, and can only be planned if a CVC exists. If there is no valid combination, no plans can be defined for it. A Demand Planning system typically has anywhere from a few thousand to several hundred thousand combinations. This is dependent on both the nature of the business and the design of the system.

5.1.2 Creating Characteristic Combinations

CVCs are usually generated automatically from past sales history stored in Info-Providers. *InfoProviders* are data repositories that store historical data and archive planning data. However, sometimes they are created manually — typically for new products for which no sales have yet been made.

From the SAP APO Easy Access menu, go to ADVANCED PLANNING AND OPTIMIZA-TION • MASTER DATA • APPLICATION-SPECIFIC MASTER DATA • DEMAND PLANNING • MAINTAIN CHARACTERISTICS VALUES, as shown in Figure 5.2.

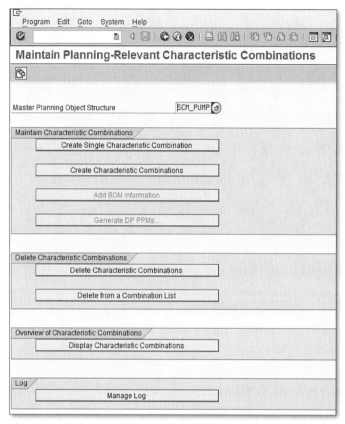

Figure 5.2 Maintaining Planning-Relevant Characteristic Combinations

Here you can perform a variety of activities, detailed in the following sections.

Creating Single Characteristic Combinations

You use this option to create characteristics combination manually, when the combination of values is new and no suitable past sales history exists in the InfoProvider. Typically, you use this option for creating characteristic combinations for a new product.

Creating Characteristic Combinations

Figure 5.3 displays the screen that appears when you click on the Create Characteristic Combinations button. You use this option to create characteristic combinations for the following scenarios:

- ► Manually
- ► Using an InfoProvider
- ► Using combinations maintained in a flat file

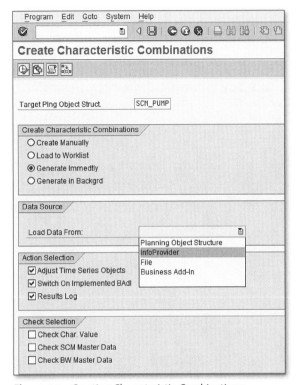

Figure 5.3 Creating Characteristic Combinations

Creating Manually

You use this option to create multiple characteristic combinations manually. The use is similar to the Create Single Characteristic Combination option, to create characteristic combinations for new products. However, it differs in that it allows you to create multiple combinations at a time manually as shown in Figure 5.4.

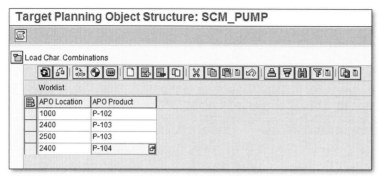

Figure 5.4 Creating Multiple Combinations Manually

Creating from an InfoProvider

Using the Create from an InfoProvider option as shown in Figure 5.5, you can create characteristic combinations based on the content of an InfoProvider. Typically, the past sales history InfoProvider is used to create characteristic combinations automatically.

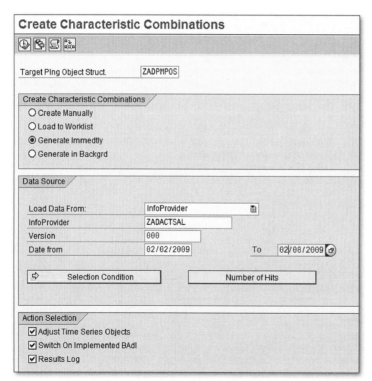

Figure 5.5 Generating Characteristic Combinations from an InfoProvider

In this case, the system generates all CVCs that it detects for a particular time period. You need to enter the InfoProvider that contains the data and the period for which the data needs to be evaluated in the InfoProvider. It is also possible to restrict the data by entering certain filter criteria in the selection condition. To maintain the CVCs so that they are up to date, you can save the parameters as a variant and schedule the program that generates the characteristic combinations to run periodically as a background job that generates the new CVCs. When you update data into the past history InfoProvider, such as a sales order for a new customer, the background job generates new combinations for it.

Creating from a File

Another method for maintaining several characteristic combinations is to edit the combinations in a flat file and then use this file to create the CVCs (Figure 5.6).

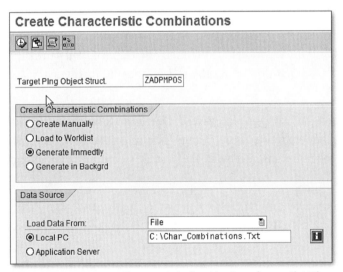

Figure 5.6 Generating Characteristic Combinations from a Flat File

5.1.3 Displaying Characteristic Combinations

You can view the created characteristic combinations using the Display Characteristic Combinations button in Figure 5.2. In the screen that appears, you can choose to display all of the characteristic combinations or display the combinations only for a subset such as for a certain product or customer. Based on the selection criteria, the system displays the characteristic combinations as shown in Figure 5.7.

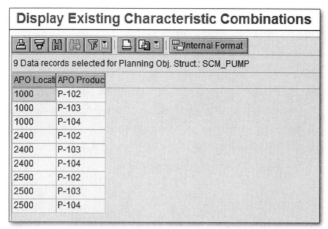

Figure 5.7 Displaying Existing Characteristic Combinations

5.1.4 Data Selections in Interactive Demand Planning

As mentioned previously, data can only be planned for CVCs that exist. The CVCs shows all characteristics for which data can be planned and queried. You can select the data for particular characteristic values in the selector area of interactive planning table.

As a review from the previous chapter, Interactive Demand Planning is the primary tool that enables planners to view and change planning data. Using Interactive Demand Planning, planners interact with the system to create, change, and analyze the demand plan.

To access Interactive Demand Planning, follow the menu path ADVANCED PLANNING AND OPTIMIZATION • DEMAND PLANNING • PLANNING • INTERACTIVE DEMAND PLANNING.

As shown in Figure 5.8, the interactive planning table is divided into two sections: the selector area and the work area.

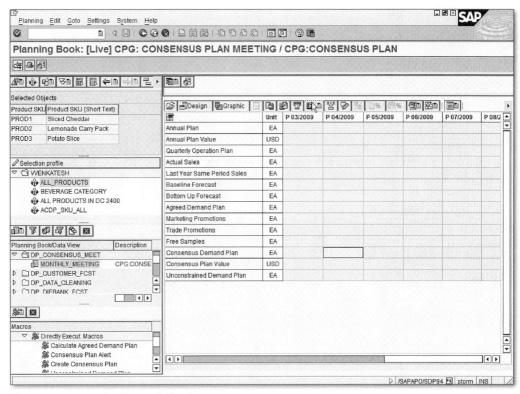

Figure 5.8 Interactive Demand Planning

The selector is divided into four areas:

▶ **Selection window**

The selection window shows all of the characteristic values for which data can be planned and viewed. Characteristics in Demand Planning can be a specific product, location, customer, and so on. You can select the objects that meet certain selection criteria from the dropdown box in the shuffler as illustrated in Figure 5.9 or by choosing an existing selection from the selection profile. The Selection Window, also referred to as the *shuffler,* is the window in which you select the characteristics you want to plan. For example, you might want to show all products that belong to a particular category (e.g., Beverage). The first row labeled show indicates what you would like to see. The remaining rows acts as filters to only show those objects that meet the selection criteria.

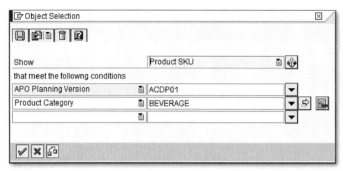

Figure 5.9   Selector Window

▶ **Selection profile**

Frequently accessed objects can be stored in a selection ID. The Selection profile, as shown in Figure 5.10, enables the user to quickly access frequently accessed selections.

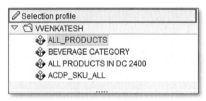

Figure 5.10   Selection Profile

The Selection IDs, shown in Figure 5.11, enable the user to slice and dice data in the interactive planning table. They allow the user to view and change at a particular planning level. Selection IDs are also used in background jobs to enable certain actions to be processed on the objects contained in the selection IDs.

▶ **Planning Book/Data View**

The planning book section is where the planner can select the planning book and data view. Planners have the opportunity to filter which views are accessible.

▶ **Macro area**

The macro area shows the macros that are active in the currently selected planning book and data view. Macros can be executed directly from this window.

▶ **Work area**

The work area consists of the planning grid for display and planning purposes. This is the area where numerical quantities such as forecast, shipments, and so on are displayed in the grid. Data can be displayed both in a tabular format and in a graphical format.

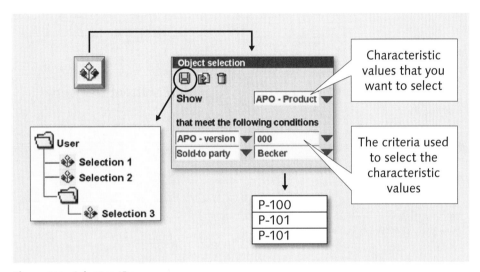

Figure 5.11   Selection IDs

5.2   Statistical Forecast: Core Functionality Setup

SAP APO provides a set of standard statistical tools that can be used in the forecasting process. These include:

▶ Univariate, or one-dimensional, methods

▶ Multidimensional, or causal, methods

▶ Composite methods

Univariate methods were described in Chapter 4, Section 4.2, but Figure 5.12 serves as a brief reminder. The use of causal and composite forecast methods will be addressed in more detail here and in Chapter 6. For consistency, however, we will cover their configuration here after briefly introducing the concepts.

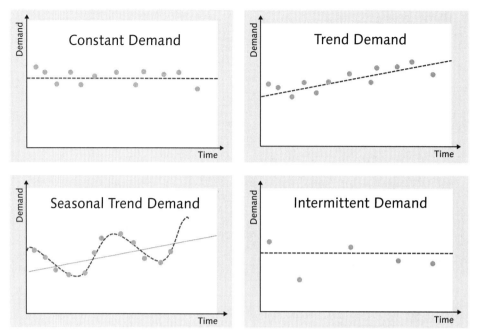

Figure 5.12 Time Series Patterns

Causal methods are based on the assumption that demand is influenced by several known factors. Causal methods in SAP APO use multiple linear regression (MLR), which is a statistical technique that analyzes the relationship between a single dependent variable and several independent variables. For example, the demand for winter clothing is influenced by temperature. Other influencing factors can be price and promotions. MLR is used to determine how the dependant variable such as sales is connected with the influencing factors of temperature, prices, and promotions. Once the relationship is established, the independent variables can be used, the values of which are known, to predict the single dependant value.

Causal methods can provide more accurate forecasts than time series models and support "what-if" analysis. However, they require more data than times series models. It is also difficult to identify all of the independent variables.

A *composite forecast* is the combination of different forecasting methods such as univariate and causal methods. The objective is to take the benefit of the strength of each method and combine them to create a single forecast. Several univariate and MLR forecasts can be combined to generate the composite forecast. While combining, you can either average the forecast, giving equal weights to each forecast, or you can weigh each one differently. For example, you can combine 30% of time series model and 70% of causal model to generate a single forecast.

5.2.1 Forecast Profile

A forecast profile needs to be created before statistical forecasting can be executed either interactively or scheduled as a background job. A forecast profile contains the parameters for executing a statistical forecast.

Master Forecast Profile

The *master forecast profile* is the mechanism for controlling which particular method — univariate, causal, or composite — will be used for forecasting and the parameters for controlling them. To create or change a forecast profile, follow the menu path ADVANCED PLANNING AND OPTIMIZATION • DEMAND PLANNING • ENVIRONMENT • MAINTAIN FORECAST PROFILES. The system displays the screen shown in Figure 5.13.

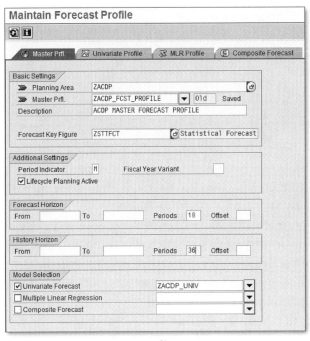

Figure 5.13 Master Forecast Profile

In the Basic Settings area, you enter the planning area for which you want to create the master forecast profile and a name and description for the master forecast profile. The forecasted key figure indicates the key figure in which the results of the statistical forecast will be stored. The Period Indicator, in the Additional Settings area, defines the time bucket in which the statistical forecast will be carried out, whether in weeks, months, or some other time period. The Lifecycle Planning Active checkbox is used for lifecycle planning. In the Forecast Horizon section, you define the horizons or the number of periods for which you want to run the forecast into the future. In the History Horizon section, you define the horizon or the number of periods you want to use as historical data. If the horizon is defined in terms of periods, it rolls forward with time, whereas the horizon does not roll forward if entered as specific date ranges.

Depending on the forecast method to be used, you must create a subprofile for each of the methods in the Model Selection section. If you plan to use univariate forecast method, select the Univariate Forecast checkbox and enter the name of the univariate profile. Next, you need to enter the parameters for the univariate forecast in the Univariate Profile tab. Similarly, if you plan to use MLR methods, select the Multiple Linear Regression checkbox and enter a name for the MLR profile and the parameters for the MLR forecast in the MLR Profile tab.

Univariate Forecast Profile

The Univariate Forecast Profile contains all of the parameters required for controlling the univariate forecast, shown in Figure 5.14. In the Read Historical Data area, you define the key figure and the version to be used for historical input.

In the Model Parameters area, you select which particular univariate forecasting model is to be applied for generating the forecast. SAP APO offers more than 30 models for running the univariate forecast. The parameters available for entry depend on the selected model. You define the values of alpha, beta, and gamma. The system uses the alpha factor to smooth the basic value in every time series forecast model in which exponential smoothing is carried out. The beta factor is used to smooth the trend value in a trend or seasonal trend model. The gamma factor is used to smooth the seasonal index in a seasonal or seasonal trend model. Enter the number of periods that make up a season in the Periods field. The system uses this parameter to execute a seasonal test. The system uses the sigma factor to correct outliers in the historical data if outlier correction is enabled. The smaller the sigma factor, the more values are identified as being outliers and are corrected.

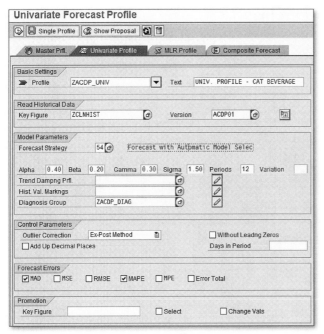

Figure 5.14 Univariate Forecast Profile

In the Control Parameters area, if you want outliers in the historical data on which the forecast is based to be corrected, choose either Ex-Post method or the Median method in the drop down menu in the Outlier Correction field. In case you do not wish the system to perform any outlier correction, choose none. If you want to apply work days correction, you set the average number of workdays in the Days in Period field. The system corrects the historical values using this average number of workdays. The new values are contained in the Corrected history row of the demand planning table. The system then runs the forecast based on this average number of workdays in the forecast period and recalculates the figures to account for the actual number of workdays in the forecast period. The corrected forecast row shows the results of this calculation. In this way, you account for differences in the number of days per month. Select the Without Leading Zeroes checkbox to exclude leading zeros from the historical data on which the forecast calculation is based. In the Forecast Errors area, you select which error should be calculated and reported while executing the forecast.

Multiple Linear Regression Forecast Profile

The MLR Profile, shown in Figure 5.15, contains all of the parameters required for controlling the causal forecast.

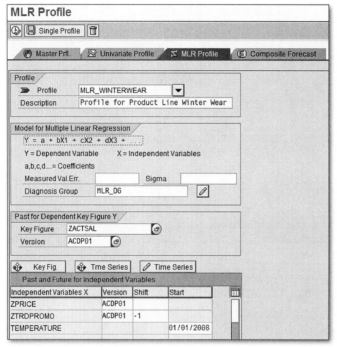

Figure 5.15 MLR Profile

In the Profile area, enter the name of the MLR profile and a description of the profile. In the MLR profile, you can maintain a diagnosis group that specifies the upper and lower limits for MLR errors. If the errors exceed the threshold values, alerts are generated. Planners can review the alerts and make changes to the forecast if required.

In the Past for Dependent Key Figure Y area, you specify the key figure in which the historical data of the dependent variable is saved and the version of the historical data. Normally this would be the key figure that stores the historical past sales data. The system uses this data to calculate the coefficients in the MLR model. In the MLR equation, this key figure represents the historical values of Y, such as past sales.

In the Past and Future for Independent Variables area, you specify the causal factors that influence the dependent variable. In the Shift field beside the variable, you can define a lag for that variable. For example, -1 for the Trade Promotions variable means that it takes 1 month for trade promotions to impact demand. The variable's values are shifted one period into the future.

Composite Profile

The Composite Forecast Profile, shown in Figure 5.16, contains parameters for combining several univariate and/or MLR forecasts to create a single forecast.

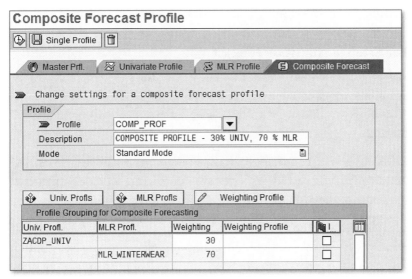

Figure 5.16 Composite Forecast Profile

Here you include the name of the univariate profile and the MLR profile for creating the composite forecast. You can specify a percentage to signify the weighting of a particular forecast in the composite forecast. For example, the composite forecast can be created considering 30% of the univariate forecast and 70% of the MLR forecast. This weighting is not time based. The composite forecast combines forecasts from alternative forecasting methods (such as times series and casual) for a particular brand, product family, or product. Each forecast is based on the same historical data but uses a different technique. The underlying objective is to take advantage of the strengths of each method to create a single "one-number" forecast. Either you can average the forecasts, giving each one equal weight, or you can weight each one differently. Alternatively, you can vary the weightings of each forecast over time by entering a weighing profile that assigns different weightings to different periods.

5.2.2　Executing the Forecast

The statistical forecast can be executed in the Interactive Demand Planning or as a scheduled background job. Normally, the statistical forecast is run as a scheduled job, and alerts are generated when errors exceed threshold values. The planners can view these alerts and then review the forecast of these characteristic combinations in Interactive Demand Planning and tweak the models if required.

Planning Book Setup for Statistical Forecast

Planning books are user-defined views that allow the users to view and change planning data, as illustrated in Figure 5.17. In Interactive Demand Planning, users access planning books to interact with the system to create, change, and analyze the demand plan.

A planning book has both user-specific views and SAP-defined standard views. SAP provides three standard forecast views, one for each forecast method, univariate, causal, and composite, and a standard view for promotion planning.

Based on the forecasting method you choose to execute, the appropriate standard forecast view needs to be selected while creating the planning books. A button for executing each of the forecast methods becomes visible in the planning book depending on the forecast view selected, as illustrated in Figure 5.18.

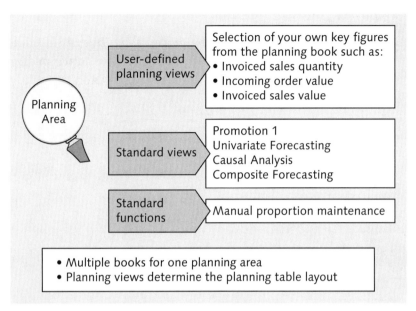

Figure 5.17 Planning Books within a Planning Area

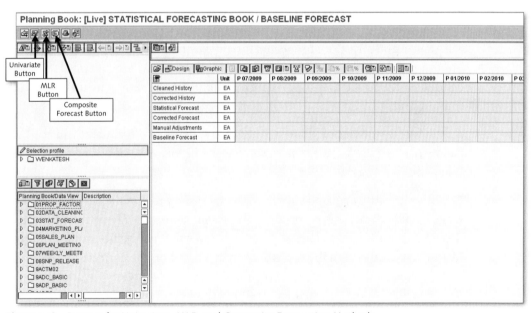

Figure 5.18 Buttons for Univariate, MLR, and Composite Forecasting Methods

Forecasting Process Flow

Figure 5.19 illustrates the univariate forecasting process flow. During statistical forecasting, the system reads the historical data and calculates the corresponding forecast based on the models and parameters maintained in the forecast profile.

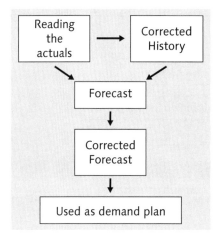

Figure 5.19 Forecasting Process Flow

The statistical forecast can be created for any key figure depending on the key figure maintained in the master forecast profile. The forecast can be calculated using actual data or corrected historical data depending on the setting maintained in the forecast profile.

If the average number of workdays per forecast period is maintained in the Univariate Forecast Profile, the system corrects the historical values using this average number of workdays.

The new values are contained in the Corrected History row of the demand planning table. If outlier correction is enabled, the system automatically corrects the actual data that is outside the tolerance zone and stores the new values in the corrected history row. The system then runs the forecast based on the corrected history. The system recalculates the figures to account for the actual number of workdays in the forecast period. The Corrected Forecast row shows the results of this calculation.

You can also choose to correct the history manually in your own key figure in the interactive table. Normally, you make manual corrections to the statistical forecast in your own key figure.

5.3 Running the Forecast in Interactive Planning

A forecast can be executed in interactive planning by using the appropriate buttons for the univariate, causal, or composite forecast. Load the historical data for the products for which the forecast needs to be run by either using a selection profile or using the shuffler to select the objects such as products. Once the desired object is visible in the selection window area, you can load the data for all of the objects together or individually by clicking on the Load data button.

Figure 5.20 shows the interactive planning table with the historical data loaded for the product PROD1. The statistical forecast row is empty because the forecast has not yet been executed.

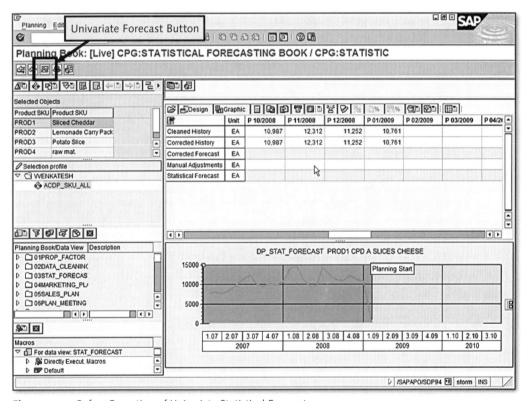

Figure 5.20 Before Execution of Univariate Statistical Forecast

To execute the forecast, click on the appropriate button based on the forecast method that you have chosen to use. To execute the forecast, click on the appropriate button based on the forecast method you have chosen to use. To execute a univariate forecast, click on the Univariate Forcast, shown in Figure 5.20.

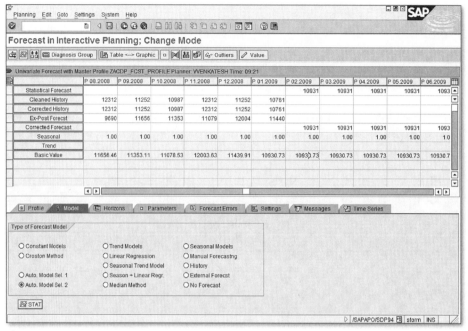

Figure 5.21 Univariate Forecast View

When you click on the button, the univariate forecast is executed immediately, and you'll see the screen shown in Figure 5.21. The Univariate forecast is executed with the forecasting model set up in the forecast profile. The results of the forecast are displayed in a tabular format in the upper portion of the screen. The forecast models and their parameters can be changed interactively by navigating to the various tabs in the lower portion of the screen.

The upper portion of the screen displays the following rows:

▶ **Statistical Forecast**
   This row displays the results of the statistical forecast.

▶ **Cleaned History**
   This is the key figure that is maintained in the Read Historical Data section in the forecast profile. It is the historical input key figure containing the actual data.

▶ **Corrected History**

This row shows the values of the corrected history calculated by the system.

▶ **Ex-Post Forecast**

Ex-post forecast is run in past periods for which actual historical data is available. The system performs forecast accuracy measurements by comparing the ex-post forecast and the actual data.

▶ **Corrected Forecast**

This row displays the results of the corrected forecast calculated by the system. If the average number of workdays per forecast period is maintained in the Univariate Forecast Profile, the system recalculates the figures to account for the actual number of workdays in the forecast period. If the average number of workdays is not maintained, the corrected forecast equals the statistical forecast.

▶ **Seasonal, Trend, and Basic Values**

The seasonal, trend, and basic values calculated by the system are shown in their respective rows.

It is possible to display the forecast results in a graphical format as well, as shown in Figure 5.22. You can select the row to be displayed in the graph.

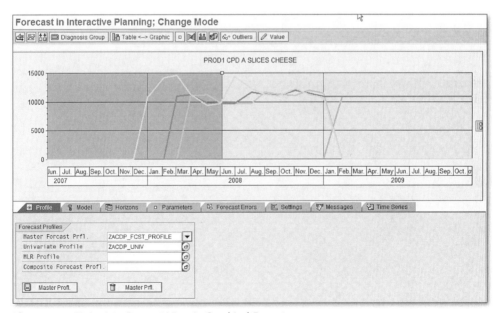

Figure 5.22 Univariate Forecast View in Graphical Format

5.3.1 Forecast View Tabs

The tabs available in the lower portion of the forecast view display additional information regarding the forecast. We'll discuss each of these in the following sections.

Profile Tab

As shown in Figure 5.23, the Profile tab is where you can save the various forecasting settings for the current selection in a new forecast profile or assign an existing profile to the current selection. If the Parameter /SAPAPO/FCST_GUID is set in the user master record, the changes to the forecast profile are saved for the selection as a GUID. In the subsequent interactive forecasting for the selection, the system uses the parameters stored in the GUID profile. It's also possible to set up the background job to use the GUID profile in the next background run. In the event of a forecast alert generated for a forecast error exceeding threshold values, the planner can tweak the forecast parameters to adjust the forecast.

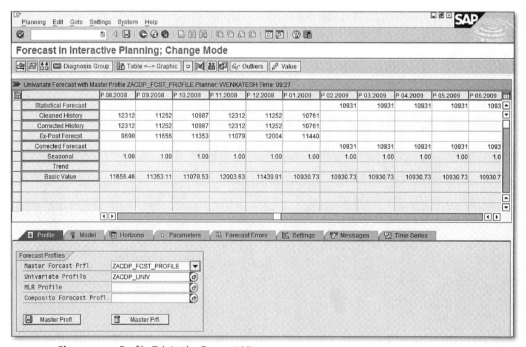

Figure 5.23 Profile Tab in the Forecast View

Saving the changed parameters in the GUID profile specific to the product for which the alerts are generated allows the background job run to use the forecast parameters for that product using the revised parameters set by the planners.

Model Tab

The Model tab, shown in Figure 5.24, displays the currently used forecasting model. It also allows the user to choose a different forecasting model and rerun the forecast.

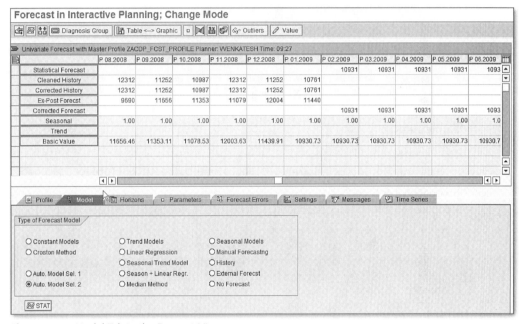

Figure 5.24 Model Tab in the Forecast View

Horizons Tab

The Horizon tab (Figure 5.25) displays the history and the future horizon. It's possible to change these horizons here and rerun the forecast.

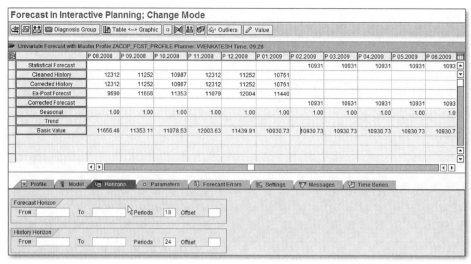

Figure 5.25 Horizons Tab in the Forecast View

Parameters Tab

In the Parameters tab, as shown in Figure 5.26, you can change the setting for the currently applied forecasting model. The parameters available for change depend on the selected model.

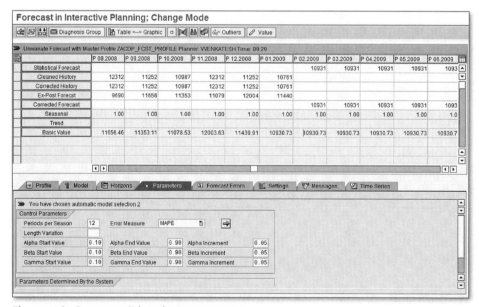

Figure 5.26 Parameters Tab in the Forecast View

Forecast Errors Tab

The Forecast Errors tab (Figure 5.27) displays the values of the forecast error. Only errors that have been selected for display in the forecast profile are displayed. If the error exceeds the threshold values set in the diagnosis group, a visual alert is indicated next to the value of the forecast error. The ex-post forecast value is used for calculating the forecast error by comparing the ex-post forecast value to the actual data. Not all forecasting models calculate ex-post value and consequently do not report any forecast error.

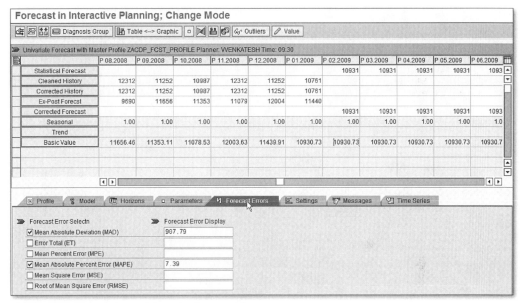

Figure 5.27 Forecast Errors Tab in the Forecast View

Settings Tab

In the Settings tab (Figure 5.28), you can select various settings, such as Outlier Correction, ignoring leading zeroes in the historical data, and the LIKE profile that will be applied for lifecycle modeling.

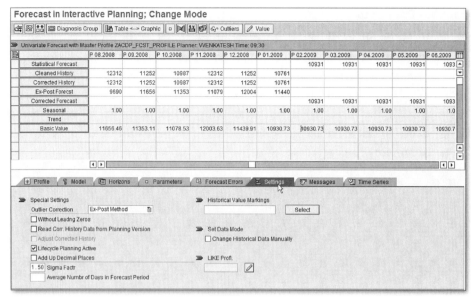

Figure 5.28 Settings Tab in the Forecast View

Messages Tab

The Messages tab (Figure 5.29) shows the various forecast messages generated during the course of forecast execution.

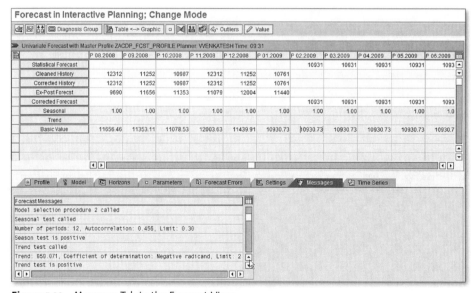

Figure 5.29 Messages Tab in the Forecast View

Time Series Tab

The Time Series tab (Figure 5.30) displays the various phase in and phase out profiles (as discussed in Section 5.4), the trend damping profile, and the weighting profile. The values maintained in these time series can be displayed and used for forecasting.

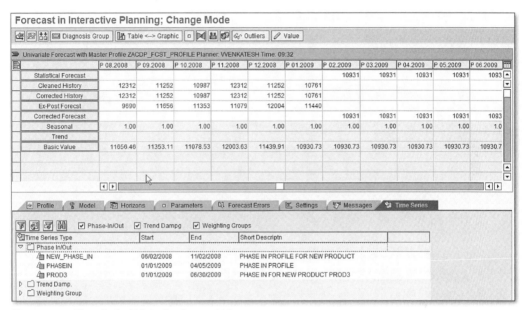

Figure 5.30 Time Series Tab in the Forecast View

5.3.2 Forecast Comparison

The system remembers the results of the previous ten forecasts executed by the user by default. In a forecast comparison, you can compare the forecast errors and parameters for the various forecasts executed. It is possible to change the numbers of forecast versions saved for comparison.

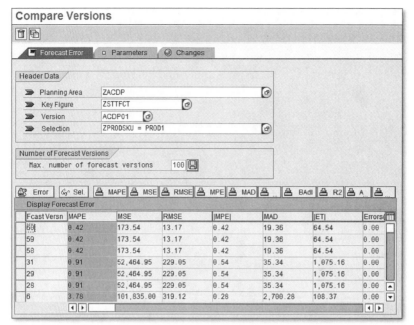

Figure 5.31 Forecast Comparison

To start the forecast comparison, in the interactive statistical forecasting screen, shown in Figure 5.31, follow the menu path GoTo • FORECAST COMPARISON.

The forecast comparison screen consists of three tabs:

▶ **Forecast Error**
Here you can see the forecast error for each of the forecasts executed by the user. To see the error for each of the forecast runs, click on the Error button as illustrated in Figure 5.31. The system then displays a number of forecast runs with error measures for each run. It is possible to sort the different versions according to any measure of error by clicking on the Error measure button. You can select any of the versions and generate a forecast profile using the settings in the version.

▶ **Parameters**
The Parameters tab displays the forecasting model and the parameter values for each of the forecast versions. The usual practice is to sort the forecast run in ascending order of errors based on the chosen error measure in the Forecast Error tab and then click on the Parameter tab to find what parameter resulted in the least errors.

▶ **Changes**

The Changes tab lets you see general information such as the planner who executed the forecast version, the date and time when it was executed, the profile used, and the type of the forecast method.

After executing the forecast, click on the Back button to copy the forecast values and return to interactive planning.

Figure 5.32 shows the forecast values in interactive planning. The periods from P 02/2009 onward now contain the values of the statistical forecast.

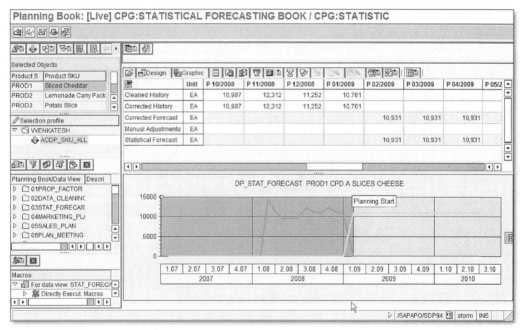

Figure 5.32 After Execution of Univariate Statistical Forecast

5.4   Using Like-Modeling and Phase-In/Phase-Out to Support Product Planning Across Its Lifecycle

A product goes through various phases in its lifecycle: launch, growth, maturity, decline, and discontinuation (shown in Figure 5.33).

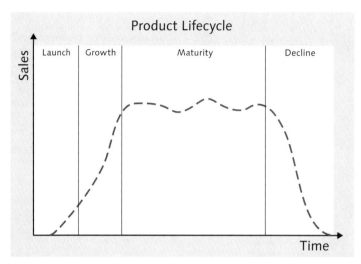

Figure 5.33 Product Lifecycle

During the growth phase, there is a rapid increase in demand after launch, as shown by the upward sales curve. As the product enters into the maturity stage, the demand reaches a plateau. The forecasting methods used during the growth phase will no longer apply in the maturity phase. Demand planning should account for this change or else the forecast will be too high and result in excess inventory. Products in the maturity stage have a stable history and therefore have no major changes to their forecast pattern. Quantitative methods are best suited for this stage. Toward the end of the product's life, demand declines steadily, and finally the product is discontinued.

You can model the various phases by using the lifecycle planning functionality with SAP APO. Lifecycle planning consists of two features: *like-modeling* and *phase-in/phase-out modeling*. Lifecycle planning can be used for univariate forecasting, multiple linear regression, and composite forecasting.

5.4.1 Like-Modeling

A new product being launched is unlikely to have historical data that can be used as a basis for forecasting. The statistical forecasting for such products would yield poor results because of insufficient data. Using like-modeling, you can create a forecast for the new product using the historical data of a similar product or products with similar sales behavior. Using the historical data from the similar product or products, the system can create a forecast for the new product. To create or display a like profile, follow menu path ADVANCED PLANNING AND OPTIMIZATION • DEMAND PLANNING • ENVIRONMENT • LIFECYCLE PLANNING. In the screen that appears, enter the planning area and click on the Like profiles button.

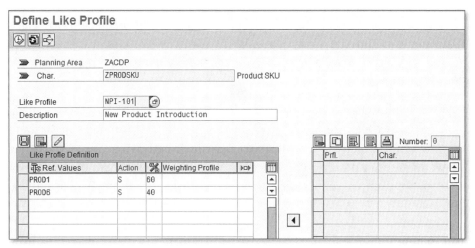

Figure 5.34 Like Profile

Figure 5.34 shows the like profile in which two existing products, Prod1 and Prod6, have been included as reference products. When this like profile is assigned to a new product, the system uses the weighted historical data of the products included in the like profile to generate a forecast for the new product. The forecast for the new product will be created using 60% of the historical data of Prod1 and 40% of the historical data of Prod6. It's not necessary for the weighing factors to total 100%. If you expect your new product to have much better sales than other similar products, you can maintain a weighing factor exceeding 100%, and conversely the factor can be less than 100% for lower-volume new products.

5.4.2 Phase-In/Phase-Out Modeling

The demand for a product in the launch phase and the discontinuation phase is quite different from that of a product in the mature phase. In the introductory phase of the launch period, demand usually increases with every period, whereas it declines toward the end of the lifecycle. Statistical forecast modeling behavior suited for the mature phase will result in an inaccurate forecast for the launch and discontinuation phases, and would not predict the behavior accurately. In phase-in/phase-out modeling, a time-dependent factor is stored in a phase-in/phase-out profile. The result of the statistical forecast is multiplied by this factor to produce the actual forecast. For phase-in profiles the factor generally increases with time, whereas for phase-out profiles it decreases.

To create or display a phase-in/phase-out profile, follow the menu path ADVANCED PLANNING AND OPTIMIZATION • DEMAND PLANNING • ENVIRONMENT • LIFECYCLE PLANNING. In the screen that appears, enter the planning area and click on the Phase-In/Out button.

Figure 5.35 illustrates a phase-on profile for six periods in which factors are maintained in increasing order to forecast the new product. This mimics the upward sales trend that you'd expect during the launch and growth phases. Figure 5.36 shows a phase-out profile with decreasing percentages, which mimics the downward sales curve that you'd expect the product to display during its discontinuation phase.

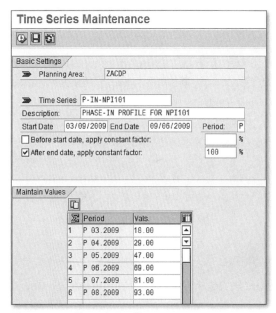

Figure 5.35 Phase-In Profile

Time Series Maintenance

Basic Settings

Planning Area: ZACDP

Time Series: P-OUT-EOL087

Description: PHASE-OUT PROFILE

Start Date: 05/11/2009 End Date: 11/08/2009 Period: P

☐ Before start date, apply constant factor: _____ %

☑ After end date, apply constant factor: _____ %

Maintain Values

	Period	Vals.	
1	P 05.2009	100.00	▲
2	P 06.2009	76.00	▼
3	P 07.2009	64.00	
4	P 08.2009	49.00	
5	P 09.2009	23.00	
6	P 10.2009	9.00	

Figure 5.36 Phase-Out Profile

The like profile and the phase-in/phase-out profile needs to be assigned to the material, as shown in Figure 5.36. To perform the assignment, follow the menu path ADVANCED PLANNING AND OPTIMIZATION • DEMAND PLANNING • ENVIRONMENT • LIFECYCLE PLANNING. In the screen that appears, enter the planning area, select the Assignments radio button, and click on the execute button. In the Assign Life Cycle screen, shown in Figure 5.37, enter the new product in the Product SKU column and the like profile and phase-in/phase-out profile in their respective columns. Click on the execute button to save the assignment.

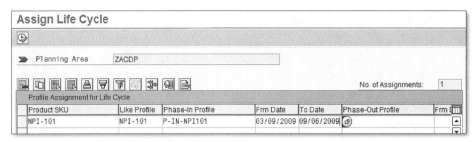

Assign Life Cycle

Planning Area ZACDP

No. of Assignments: 1

Profile Assignment for Life Cycle

Product SKU	Like Profile	Phase-In Profile	Frm Date	To Date	Phase-Out Profile	Frm
NPI-101	NPI-101	P-IN-NPI101	03/09/2009	09/06/2009		

Figure 5.37 Assigning the Lifecycle Profiles

When a statistical forecasting run is executed for the new products with the life-cycle assignments, the system uses the historical data of the reference products in the like profile to generate the forecast for the new product. The statistical forecast is then multiplied by the percentages maintained in the phase-in profile.

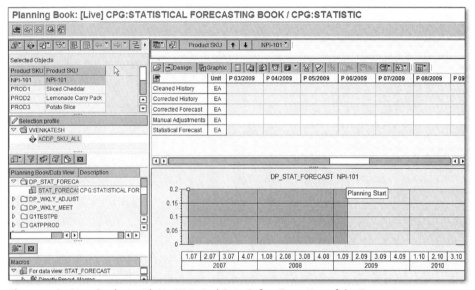

Figure 5.38 New Product with No Historical Data Before Execution of the Forecast

Figure 5.38 shows the interactive planning table with the data loaded for the new product NPI-101. To load the data for the new product, select the product from the shuffler window or by using a selection profile and either double-click on the product in the shuffler window or click on the Load Data button. The empty row for the history indicates that no historical data is available for the new product.

Figure 5.39 shows the statistical forecast values in interactive planning. The forecast has been generated using the historical data of the reference products maintained in like profile NPI-101. The statistical forecast results have been multiplied by the factors maintained in the phase-in profile P-IN-NPI101 to generate the upward curve shown in the figure.

The Messages tab in the forecast view of the interactive statistical forecast (Figure 5.40) shows the lifecycle profiles used, if any, while generating the forecast.

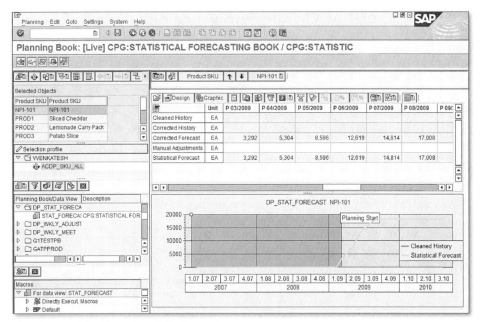

Figure 5.39   After Execution of the Forecast

Figure 5.40   Messages Tab Showing Usage of Lifecycle Profile

A Note about New Product Introductions

When organizations launch new products, they often accompany the launch with marketing activities (advertising, price promotions, etc.), which will be covered in more detail in Chapter 8. Demand planners generating phase-in profiles for new products that are being so accompanied should work closely with their marketing counterparts to ensure that they do not build redundant growth into their plans.

5.5 Incorporating Custom Forecasting Algorithms

SAP offers the business add-in (BAdI) /SAPAPO/SCM_FCSTPARA to allow customers to incorporate their own custom forecasting algorithms in addition to the standard models available in Demand Planning. Customers can write their own algorithms in the method EXTERN_FCST available in the BAdI. To display the BAdI available for statistical parameters enhancement, execute Transaction SPRO, click on the SAP Reference IMG button, follow the menu path ADVANCED PLANNING AND OPTIMIZATION • SUPPLY CHAIN PLANNING • DEMAND PLANNING • BUSINESS ADD-INS (BADIs) • FORECASTING, and click on Additional statistical parameters enhancement.

Figure 5.41 shows the methods available in the BAdI /SAPAPO/SCM_FCSTPARA. This BAdI lets you create and change the statistical processing in univariate forecasting.

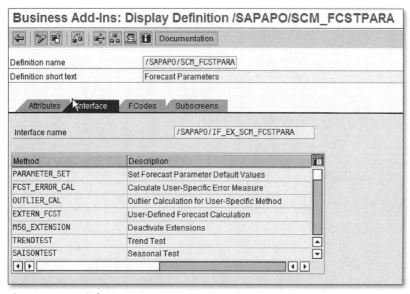

Figure 5.41 BAdI for Custom Forecasting Algorithms

BAdI /SAPAPO/SCM_FCSTPARA consists of the following methods, among others:

▶ PARAMETER_SET

Here you can change the limits that are used for the statistical tests in automatic model selection. These are:

- ▶ Seasonal limit (default value 0.33)

- ▶ Trend limit (default value 0.33)

- ▶ Croston limit — test for sporadic data (default value 0.33)

▶ FCST_ERROR_CAL

Here you can define a further measure of error.

▶ OUTLIER_CAL

Here you can define your own outlier control.

▶ EXTERN_FCST

Here you can define your forecast method. You can also use this method to connect to an external forecasting tool.

5.6   Statistical Forecasting in SAP ERP and SAP APO

Embedded within the SAP ERP solution is a table-based statistical forecasting capability known as Flexible Planning. Although it has remained basically untouched for nearly a decade, it is still functional. In Flexible Planning, data is stored in LIS-based table structures using a simple hierarchical forecasting structure limited to nine characteristics.

The forecast can be executed from within the product master as shown in Figure 5.42 by executing Transaction MM02 and selecting the Forecasting Tab.

The forecasting parameters are maintained in the Forecasting tab of the product master. Clicking on the Execute forecast button runs the forecast.

A forecast can also be executed within Flexible Planning. To execute a forecast in flexible planning, execute Transaction MC94. Select the Infostructure configured for the flexible planning and enter the product and other hierarchy details for which you want to execute the forecast. Then select the version and press Enter (Figure 5.43).

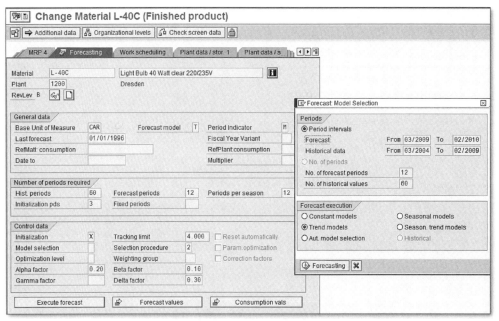

Figure 5.42 Executing Statistical Forecasting from Product Master

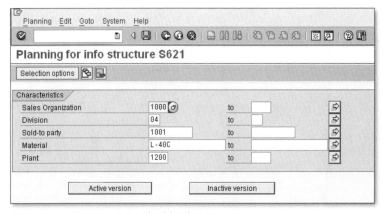

Figure 5.43 Forecast Using Flexible Planning

In the screen that opens up, follow menu path EDIT • FORECAST. The screen in Figure 5.44 is displayed. Enter the forecast and the history horizon in the Periods sections, select the model for forecasting in the Forecast Execution section, and click on the Forecasting button to execute the forecast.

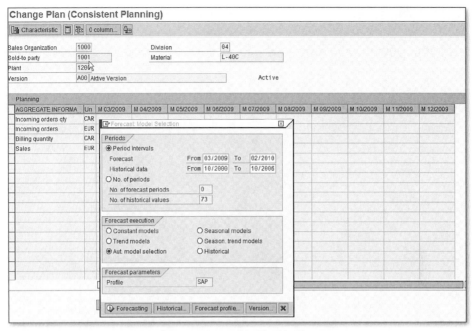

Figure 5.44 Executing Statistical Forecasting within Flexible Planning

Clicking on the Historical button displays the historical data values, as shown in Figure 5.45.

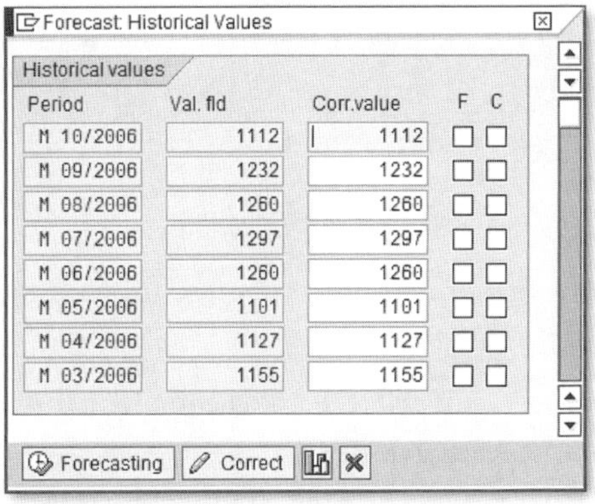

Figure 5.45 Displaying Historical Values

It is possible to automatically correct the outliers by maintaining the tolerance zone in the forecasting profile. It is also possible to manually correct the outliers. Clicking on the Forecasting button generates the forecast, as shown in Figure 5.46.

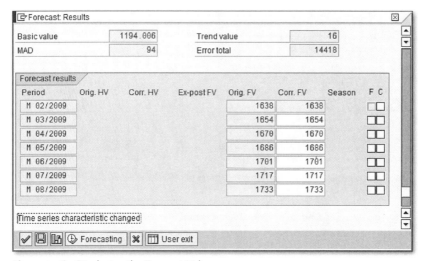

Figure 5.46 Displaying the Forecast Values

The system also displays the error measures for the forecast run.

Statistical Forecasting Differences in SAP ERP and SAP APO

Flexible Planning contains many of the forecast algorithms found in SAP APO. Figure 5.47 shows the univariate forecasting algorithms found in SAP ERP.

The major differences between SAP ERP and SAP APO are as follows:

▶ Flexible planning in SAP ERP offers only the univariate statistical forecasting technique. No causal or composite forecasting is possible.

▶ Whereas flexible planning offers most of the univariate forecasting algorithms found in SAP APO, more models are available in SAP APO.

▶ Lifecycle and phase-in/phase-out modeling is not available in Flexible Planning in SAP ERP.

▶ Flexible Planning's table-based structure and lack of simulation capabilities limit its effectiveness to more simplistic scenarios.

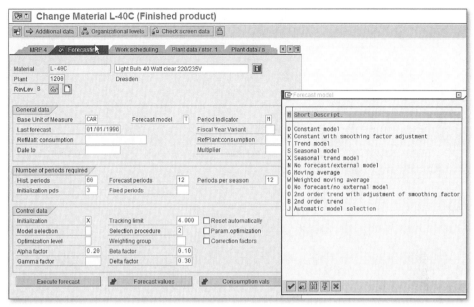

Figure 5.47 Forecast Algorithms in SAP ERP

▶ Flexible Planning is limited to a simple hierarchical forecasting structure consisting of a maximum of nine characteristics.

▶ Flexible Planning offers a limited macro capability for simple arithmetic operations, whereas SAP APO offers much more powerful macro capabilities.

5.7   Summary

In this chapter, we've reviewed SAP APO Demand Planning and SAP ERP Flexible Planning according to the statistical techniques discussed in Chapter 4. Whereas the number of parameters and amount of configuration needed to set this up is certainly not trivial, once everything is up and running, you, as the planner, will spend the majority of your time focused on the data and its analysis, as opposed to gathering information, crunching numbers, and formatting spreadsheets.

The univariate forecast becomes even more important in the following chapters, which offer different methods of augmenting the base statistical forecast. In Chapter 6, we'll look at the use of leading indicators to generate a forward-looking demand projection that can be compared to the backward-looking statistical forecast to improve the accuracy of the overall demand plan.

This chapter discusses leading indicators when projecting demand. You'll learn how it can enable a planner to quantitatively state the likely impact on the sales item.

6 Leading Indicators

The previous two chapters were about looking at the past to project the future. Whereas historical information can offer insight into the future, there's something to be said for looking ahead. Knowing that the weather was sunny for the previous week is important, but it's likely less relevant than hearing thunder and seeing clouds on the horizon in deciding whether or not it's going to rain soon. In this chapter, we'll look at leading indicators and how to leverage them in projecting demand.

6.1 Examples of Business Indicators

From Chapter 4 we learned that in calculating a statistical forecast, an organization can lend greater weight to more recent sales figures by increasing the exponential smoothing factors or even applying second-order exponential smoothing. Whereas this can make the model more responsive, it can also cause it to respond to variations that are more "noise" than significant new trends. To be more responsive, it is a good idea to augment backward-looking univariate models with forward-looking causal models.

For example, a company contemplating a price increase usually considers the impact on sales volumes based on at least a loose understanding of a price elasticity curve. A planned but unannounced price increase could create a decline in sales volume, if not sales revenue. Similarly, a competitor's price increase or decrease can be used to inform the demand projection if they are known in advance. Although we'll dig deeper into manipulating price as a method of impacting demand in Chapter 8, it's safe to say here that price, when known in advance, can be a leading indicator of demand, and can therefore be used as a leading indicator.

However, price is by no means the only such indicator. Most organizations do not lack for anecdotal indicators that executives use to "gut check" (approximate) their sales projections for the near future. The weather for the coming weekend might be relevant to a soft drink distributor, whereas the predictions for the coming hurricane season might be important to home supply stores and the mill product manufacturers who supply them.

An indicator can be just about any data set that's at least partially known in advance and has a decent correlation to a product's sales. Some companies that service customers with unusually strong growth have used the schedule for the opening of new facilities or retail outlets as an indicator of future demand.

Most organizations don't have a formal approach for quantifying the impact of sales of some products on sales of other products. Instead, these companies rely on rough estimates based on anecdotal information. The demand plan for a line of toys might be incremented by 10% after unexpectedly strong ticket sales to the related movie. Meanwhile, a decrease in new home sales could be taken as a justification to reduce the sales forecast for kiln-dried timber by 15%.

A more disciplined approach is to identify the correlation between ticket sales and toys or home sales and lumber by looking at past data. This leads to a more generalized form of price-elasticity curve that tells you how demand for your product responds to changes in your indicator. That sounds like a lot of number crunching, especially for regional or account-based correlations, but SAP APO Demand Planning can help. Although it cannot immediately identify all of the indicators that might have a correlation to your product's sales, it can tell you what the relationship is if it is given historical data of both for comparison.

> **Retail Point of Sale Data**
>
> A fairly advanced usage of leading indicators is the tracking of the consumption of an organization's product either by the sale at a store to an end consumer in the case of a bottle of detergent or into another product, such as a semiconductor being built into a laptop computer. We'll discuss using *downstream* demand data like this to project customer replenishment orders in Chapter 7.

Using sales data as a leading indicator can be useful in projecting demand for some types of items. The sale of specific models of cars might correlate with later sales of a specific tire or brake pad. Similar examples are air filters for furnaces, pads for duster mops, and replacement batteries for laptop computers. What all of these examples have in common is that they are consumable components of larger finished goods. That is, they are meant to be used up, and replacements will likely be purchased by customers to extend the life of the original purchase.

Slightly different from consumables is the demand for certain replacement components of original devices. For instance, instead of (or perhaps in addition to) a battery, a laptop's hard drive might fail. Perhaps the anti-lock sensor is what breaks on the car. Whereas sales of the master product can be good indicators of future demand for consumable replacements, planning for service parts needs to take into account probabilities of failure.

In another closely related scenario, some products that are neither consumable nor service parts have a natural correlation. Imagine the impact that the sales of digital cameras had on photo-quality inkjet printers and flash memory cards, or the relationship between the sales of high-definition DVD players and high-definition DVDs. In these cases, the sale of a product can be foretold by the sales of other products that are complementary.

6.2 Complementary Products

Looking backward, it's fairly obvious that the rise of the Apple iPod should have been a good indicator to many manufacturers of audio speakers, headphones, and other similar items of ensuing sales growth for their products that complemented the music player. Still, many companies were caught out-of-stock during the critical Christmas buying season for the first year or two on those products.

One issue is that, unlike consumables, the relationship between the two products isn't always obvious. Organizations need to engage in market research to better understand what is in their customers' "market baskets" and even directly work with end users and consumers to understand how their products are being used or consumed.

Even after a relationship is suspected, the complementary product might belong to another company, which makes getting the sales data problematic. This is especially true if that other company is a competitor. In the latter case the company in question would likely need to rely on a combination of customer, market and financial analyst, and syndicated data to develop visibility of the sales for the complementary product.

Regardless of the source of the information, as long as the sales figures can be provided in a fairly consistent stream of data, SAP APO Demand Planning can use them to provide a causal counterpoint to the existing univariate forecasting. We'll look at the method for doing exactly that in the next section.

6.3 Causal Forecasting in SAP APO Leveraging Multiple Linear Regression

As mentioned in Chapter 5, in causal forecasting the future sales of a particular product or service are closely associated with changes in some other variable. Sales of lumber are impacted by the number of severe storms in an area, summer temperatures may affect the sales of air conditioners, swimming pools, and so on. Multiple Linear Regression (MLR) is the statistical method for establishing the relationship between the sale of the product in question and the proposed leading indicators. Figure 6.1 contains the general notation for MLR where:

Y_i = Dependent variable

β_0 = Y-intercept or constant

β_i = Coefficient or weights

X_i = Independent variables

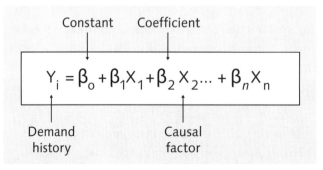

$$Y_i = \beta_0 + \beta_1 X_1 + \beta_2 X_2 \cdots + \beta_n X_n$$

Constant   Coefficient

Demand history   Causal factor

Figure 6.1 MLR Model

The MLR procedure uses the method of least squares to estimate the model parameters. This procedure adopts a linear approach to multiple regressions and minimizes the total of the square of the differences between the actual and the forecasted values that are determined by the model.

MLR enables you to analyze the relationship between a single dependent variable and several independent variables. You use the independent variables, the values of which are known to you, to predict the single dependent value, which is the value you want to forecast. Each predictor variable (Xi) is weighted. The coefficients or weights denote their relative contribution to the overall weighting. They describe the relative importance of the variables. MLR uses historical data as a basis for calculating the coefficients for causal analysis. The coefficients in a causal model indicate how value changes in each of the independent variables (Xs) influence the values of the dependant variable Y. For example, you can determine the effect on the sales quantity when the temperature drops by 10 degrees Fahrenheit, if all the other variables remain constant.

MLR forecasting enables you to answer some of the frequently asked questions of causal analysis:

▸ How can you achieve a sale of X units? What is the most cost-effective way?

▸ Is it more cost-effective to reduce the price or increase the promotional spend?

▸ How will the markets behave if you or your competitor reduce or increase the price?

▸ How effective were past marketing programs?

▸ How strongly is the demand influenced by the weather?

▸ How will sales be affected by changes in overall economic factors?

▸ What factors determine the long-term sales effectiveness?

6.3.1 Data Requirements

Causal forecasting does not identify individual variables that are relevant to the future sales. The demand planner has the task of identifying and quantifying the most important independent variables and modeling the causal relationship. The causal analysis has the following data requirements:

▶ Actual data is required for all of the variables. In contrast to a univariate forecast, which requires just the historical sales data for analyzing the patterns, causal analysis requires actual data for both the dependant and independent variables to establish the relationship between them.

▶ Often competitor's activities are one of the significant influencing factors. So a causal model involving competitor activities requires competitor's data. However, it is very difficult to obtain the actual data from the competitors.

▶ Forecast for the independent variables. Apart from the historical data of the independent variables, causal forecasting also requires the forecast values of the independent variables to predict the future values of the dependant variable. For instance, if temperature is one of the influencing factors in the sales of winter wear, the forecast values of temperature for future periods is required to predict the future sales of winter wear. The quality of the forecast of the dependant variable will be dependent on the quality of the forecast for the independent variable.

It can be challenging to determine which variables affect sales. The quality of the causal forecast will suffer if any of the significant influencing factors is not included in the analysis. It can also be difficult to estimate how the independent variables influence sales.

The advantages of causal analysis are as follows:

▶ Support for "what if" analysis. Using different forecast values of the independent variables, we can do the what if analysis to determine the values of the dependant variables. For example, you can determine how sales will behave for different promotional spends.

▶ Causal methods can provide more accurate forecasts than time series models.

▶ It is possible to model complex relationships using causal forecasting.

Causal forecasting has the following disadvantages:

▶ Causal forecasting requires a higher quantity of data than time series models because past data is required for both dependant and independent variables, and the forecast value of the independent variable is required to forecast the dependant variable.

▶ It is difficult to identify all significant independent variables that influence the dependant variable. The historical data of all of the independent variables may not be readily available, and it may require a lot of effort to acquire the historical data for the variables.

▶ Causal forecasting is more complex than the Univariate methods and is somewhat difficult to understand.

▶ Causal forecasting needs more processing time because the data quantity involved is larger.

SAP APO Demand Planning uses the following methods to test how well the MLR model fits the data:

▶ R square, adjusted R square

▶ Durbin-h, Durbin-Watson

▶ T-test

▶ Mean elasticity

The R square measure is one of the most important ways to evaluate the quality of the forecast. R square indicates how well a particular combination of X variables (the model drivers or independent variables) explains the variation in Y (the dependent variable). It is automatically calculated during the forecasting process, and its value is always between 0 and 1. A value of 0 implies that am MLR model cannot explain the variation in Y. A value of 1 means the model is a perfect fit. A value of 0.9 or more indicates an acceptable model.

6.3.2 Executing the MLR Forecast

To execute an MLR forecast, you need to create an MLR forecast profile. Section 5.2.1 in Chapter 5 discusses the MLR profile. If the planning book is configured for the causal view, the Execute MLR Forecast button becomes visible on the upper left of the planning book. Figure 6.2 shows a planning book with historical data stored in the actual sales row. The data for the influencing factors of price and promotions are displayed in their respective rows. Both the historical and forecast data are displayed for the influencing factors.

To execute the MLR forecast, click on the MLR Forecast button. The system generates an MLR forecast, as shown in Figure 6.3, and stores the forecast in the key figure that you specified in the forecast profile. Clicking on the Parameter On button displays the coefficients and the MLR measures of fit.

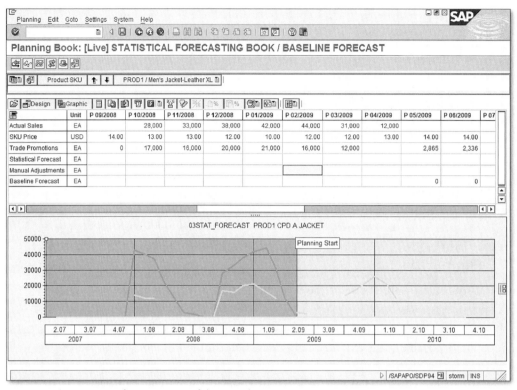

Figure 6.2 Before Execution of the Causal Forecast

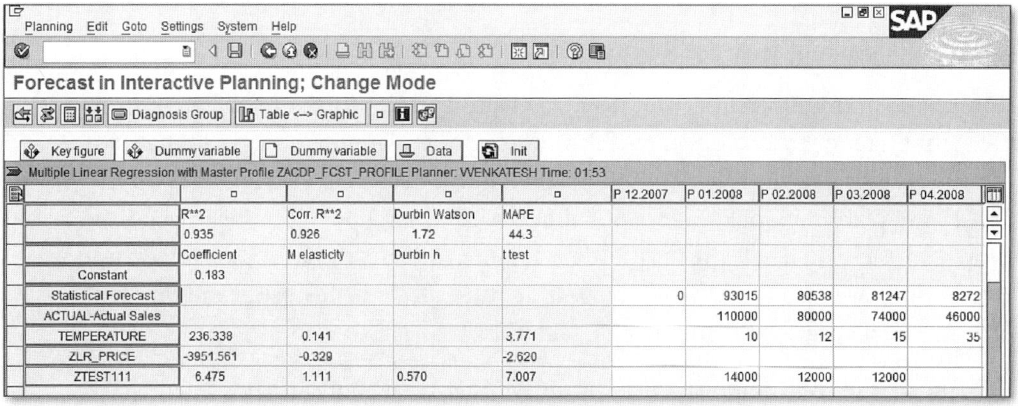

Figure 6.3 Executing the MLR Forecast

The R square value of 0.935 indicates that it is an acceptable model. Using the value of the constants and the coefficients and the forecast value of the independent variables (temperature, price, and promotional spending), the system calculates the value of the dependent variable.

After executing the forecast, click on the Back button to copy the forecast values and return to interactive planning. As you can see in Figure 6.4, the forecast values are now populated in the statistical forecast row.

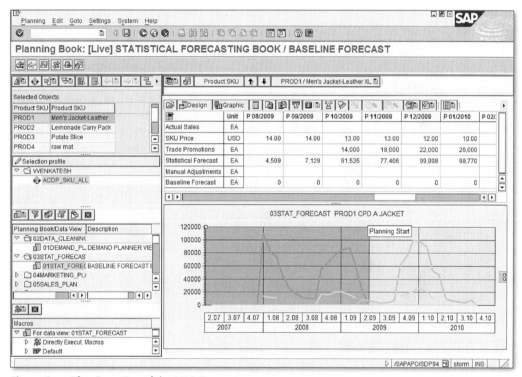

Figure 6.4 After Execution of the MLR Forecast

6.4 Summary

Leveraging leading indicators in projecting demand in a more formal method is a great way to get beyond the anecdotal references of how the weather or the price is likely to impact sales volume in the future. It is not only a way to separate the wheat from the chaff, but it enables a planner to quantitatively state the likely impact on the sales volume.

Causal forecasting is an excellent way to augment a univariate forecast (discussed in Chapters 4 and 5). In Chapter 10, we'll discuss how all of these forecasts can be brought together, but in the next chapter we'll first look at how downstream demand information can be brought to bear.

In this chapter, you'll learn about the different methods of collaborating with customers so you can increase visibility to downstream demand for your products.

7   Downstream Demand

With an understanding from the previous chapters of how you might leverage both historical and forward-looking information, the logical next step is to look beyond the bounds of your organization for more sources of demand data with which to enrich your demand plan. One source of this information is data from organizations that are *downstream* in your supply chain. Downstream in this case refers the companies and organizations to and through which your products flow to get to their ultimate consumers. These might be your immediate customers or even their customers. Information that you might receive from these downstream sources could be how much of your product has been sold by them or integrated into their own products, how much of your products they have in inventory, and so on.

This chapter will focus on different methods of collaborating with customers to increase visibility of downstream demand for your products. Because not all vendor-customer relationships lend themselves to collaboration, we'll explore other means of securing and leveraging downstream data as well.

7.1   Vendor-Managed Inventory and Collaborative Planning, Forecasting, and Replenishment Leveraging SAP APO

As we discussed in the earlier chapters, past supply chain structures for many organizations were linear. Manufacturing was done based on a forecast without much input from any external stakeholders. The manufactured products were then pushed to the respective distribution centers and from there were pushed to the retailers or the dealers. It was a push strategy from the beginning to the end of the supply chain, which resulted in high inventory levels, volatility in the demand plan, and difficulty perceiving and responding to changes in the market.

Today, manufacturers are striving hard to become more responsive to customer demand across a wide range of products without needing to maintain large buffers of inventory. Many companies are working to develop demand-driven supply networks where they have the ability to quickly sense and respond to actual demand. New methods such as collaborative planning, forecasting, and replenishment (CPFR), efficient consumer response (ECR), and lean customer relation management and supplier relation management have emerged to minimize or, preferably, eliminate inventory that acts as a buffer for demand uncertainty, while maintaining, if not increasing, service levels.

One such technique based on the pull strategy is *vendor-managed inventory* (VMI). This is a collaborative process between the supplier and the customer, where the supplier generates orders for the end-customer based on demand and supply information that they have provided. During this process, the supplier is guided by mutually agreed-to objectives for service levels, such as inventory levels, order fill rates, and transaction costs. The supplier is responsible for optimizing the availability of products by following a continuous replenishment approach to the stock within the supply chain.

By transferring responsibility for demand planning and inventory management, the customer frees up analytical talent and reduces the risk of stock-outs. Though the overall responsibility is with the vendor organization that manages the stocks, the customer remains involved in setting the framework within which the replenishment system operates and in continually monitoring and adjusting the characteristics of this framework. The vendor also benefits by gaining visibility into downstream demand, which offers greater lead time to respond to changes in the market.

Vendor-Managed Inventory

VMI starts with the a product activity report containing demand information such as sales and transfers, along with inventory position information such as on-hand, on-order, and in-transit figures for any items experiencing movement since the last report. This information forms the backbone of VMI and is sent by the customer on a prearranged schedule, typically daily.

The supplier reviews this information to determine if an order is needed. This review process may vary from organization to organization and so may the kind of software that is being used to automate the process. Normally, though, the process includes the following steps:

1. Verify that the data is accurate and meaningful.

2. On a scheduled basis, a reorder point for each item is calculated based on the inventory movement data and any market intelligence possessed by the manufacturer, such as promotions, seasonality, new items, and so on.

3. Determine if a replenishment order is necessary by comparing the quantity available at the customer with the reorder point for each item at each location. If the quantities at the manufacturer's location are less than the reorder level, then replenishment orders are created.

4. Calculate the order quantities. Typically, the calculation of order quantities takes into account important factors such as future demand and transaction costs.

5. Enter the order quantities into the vendor's order management process and system. From here on, the order is identical to an order placed directly by any other customer, with one exception. Customers can reserve the right to confirm or decline the order following their receipt of either the purchase order acknowledgment or the advanced shipment notification (ASN). Both documents contain information about the items and quantities being ordered, but the ASN includes additional information such as carrier and waybill information.

7.2   CPFR Process Overview

Collaborative planning, forecasting, and replenishment (CPFR) helps organizations be more demand driven by incorporating collaboration into the process of planning and forecasting. The goal of CPFR is to increase each supply chain partner's revenue by integrating both the planning and execution aspect of supply chain.

Trading partners engaging in CPFR agree to a set of business objectives and measures, develop joint sales and operations plans, and electronically collaborate to generate and update sales forecasts and replenishment plans. This increase in the frequency and depth of the communications between the trading partners results in better visibility of the changes in both supply and demand. Such clear visibility enables the partners to proactively make adjustments and reduce costs associated with excess inventory, stock-outs, and order expediting.

The Voluntary Interindustry Commerce Solutions (VICS) Association published the first guidelines for CPFR, which are based on the efficient consumer response (ECR) principles that grew out of the grocery industry in the mid 1990s. As illustrated in Figure 7.1, the CPFR generic model consists of three areas: planning, forecasting, and replenishment.

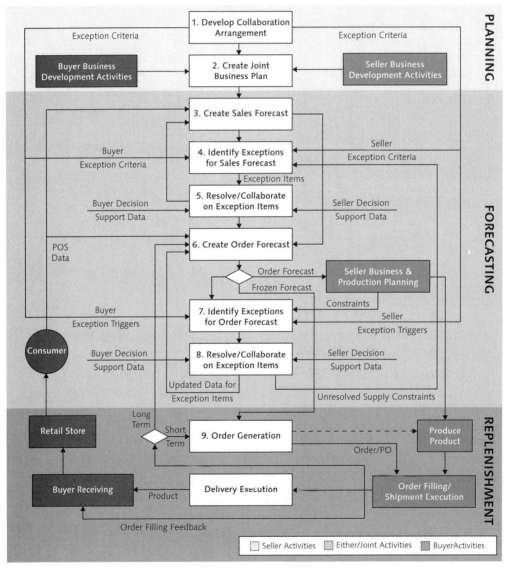

Figure 7.1 Nine-Step CPFR Process

7.2.1 Stage 1: Initial Agreements

The first stage of the CPFR process deals with initial decisions that define the type of collaboration the vendor and customer want to pursue. This tends to be a one-time process in which the organizations define service levels and lay out expectations for the frequency and mechanism of the exchange of information and what information is being exchanged. The two steps in this first stage are:

1. Develop the frontend agreement.
2. Develop a joint business plan.

Step 1: Develop Frontend Agreement

The first step of CPFR involves the establishment of rules for collaboration between the trading partners. It also details the roles and responsibilities of resources and business partners involved in the successful implementation of CPFR. The metrics for measuring the performance of trading partners involved in CPFR are also defined during this step.

The development of a frontend agreement typically involves:

1. **Mission statement for CPFR**
   The mission statement forms the basis for cooperation between the business partners, continuous availability of resources pledged for the CPFR initiative, and trust between the trading partners involved.

2. **Goals and objectives of CPFR**
   Determination of concrete goals and objectives of CPFR for a CPFR implementation includes agreement on the metrics developed for performance measurement.

3. **Resources and system**
   CPFR requires the continuous involvement of identified resources and their ability to contribute to the process in the long term and short term as a key success factor. The systems that will enable the CPFR processes and automate the proceedings are also identified.

4. **Collaboration points definition**
   The touch points for collaboration between the trading partners are identified and clearly mapped, along with the details of functional departments that will be involved in these collaborations.

5. **Information-sharing needs**

   CPFR as a process requires information sharing between all of the trading partners involved in the process. It is required to clearly identify the kind of information that will be shared (shipping data, point-of-sale data, etc.), time period for sharing information, mode of exchange of data, and the response time for sharing information.

6. **Commitment from trading partners**

   To ensure the success of CPFR, it is very important that there is a strong commitment from the senior management. The resources pledged for the CPFR process from different business functions by the trading partners should also be committed in terms of availability and work processes. Finally, a framework should be developed with a clear definition of the order and delivery commitments between the trading partners with service level agreements.

7. **Conflict resolution and review**

   This activity involves the framing of rules that govern any disagreement or differences between the trading partners. It should also consist of the procedure for problem resolution and the time frame for reviewing this CPFR agreement for continuous improvement.

8. **Publish frontend agreement**

   The frontend agreement jointly developed by the trading partners becomes binding for all of the participants in the process. This agreement can be updated for any changes based on the time period set for review in the previous process.

Step 2: Develop Joint Business Plan

In the second step of the CPFR process, trading partners develop a business plan that takes into account the goals and objectives of the individual organizations. They finalize the items, product groups, and category group that are to be considered for collaboration planning and replenishment. The joint business plan also includes the frequency of ordering and minimum order quantity for the items considered, lead time for replenishment, and inventory norms for various product and location combinations. The business plan forms the platform to finalize the special events that are planned to increase the sales and the promotions.

7.2.2 Stage 2: Forecasting

The second stage of the CPFR model details the forecasting process. It includes two types of forecasting: sales forecasting and order forecasting. The sales forecasting process consists of steps 3 through 5, and the order forecasting process consists of steps 6 through 8.

Step 3: Create Sales Forecast

The point of sales (POS) data obtained through data sharing from the trading partner and planned special events and promotions forms the input for developing the sales forecast. The new product introduction, phase in and phase out of products, and effect of causal factors on future retail sales based on historical events and the resulting sales impact are also incorporated into the sales forecast. The sales forecast should be more or less in line with the joint business plan. The information in the sales forecast is then shared with the trading partners.

Step 4: Identify Exceptions for Sales Forecast

In this stage, all of the products that represent exceptions or deviate from the set limit are identified. These exceptions are based on the criteria determined for each product during the formulation of the frontend agreement for collaboration.

Step 5: Resolve and Collaborate on Exception Items

This stage involves the resolution and clarification of the items for which the exceptions are raised from the sales forecasting. This is done through real-time communication and data sharing between the trading partners. The changes or the modified forecast after the resolution of exceptions are immediately updated to the original forecast, as a result of accelerated communication using collaboration tools, so the final sales forecast is more reliable and closer to reality.

Step 6: Create Order Forecast

The POS data is linked to the individual item's inventory strategies and the safety stock norms maintained by the partner, to generate a specific order forecast for the item. The joint business plan and the final sales forecast also form the input for generating the order forecast. The quantity of the order forecast generated for each individual item depends upon the inventory target chosen for that particular item by the trading partner and upon the lead time required for replenishment. The lead time consideration includes not only the production lead time, but also the transportation lead time and other logistics and handling lead times. The short-term order forecast is used to generate the actual orders, and the long-term order forecast is used for planning.

Step 7: Identify Exceptions for Order Forecast

Based on the ability of the manufacturer to supply the item, the order forecast is constrained. The order forecast value for each item is compared to the constraint value. If the values fall outside the constraint value, then those items are identified as exceptions. These exceptions are based on the criteria determined for each product during the formulation of the frontend agreement for collaboration.

Step 8: Resolve and Collaborate on Exception Items

This step involves the resolution and clarification on the items identified for which the exceptions are raised from the order forecasting. Here the data is gathered from both manufacturer and distributor through real-time communication and data sharing between the trading partners. The exceptions are researched using the shared information about promotions and special events and supporting information such as sales forecasting and the business plan.

If research does not yield satisfactory forecast changes or does not resolve the exception, then the issue is resolved using the set rules for conflict resolution.

If research changes the forecast and/or resolves the exceptions, changes to the order forecast are made and updated immediately.

7.2.3 Stage 3: Replenishment

The third and final stage of the CPFR model details the replenishment process. This process consists of generating the orders.

Step 9: Generate Order

This step involves the creation of actual orders based on the short-term final order forecast. The order generation can be done by the trading partner's buyer or seller depending upon the system capability of the partners.

7.2.4 CPFR: Revised Model

In the collaborative environment, information about forecast and inventory requirements is shared between the trading partners. All such collaboration across the supply chain might not necessarily fall under the formal nine steps of the CPFR process laid down by VICS. After many pilot implementations of CPFR, VICS revised its CPFR model, maintaining the initial nine step process as one of the options, but bringing in more flexibility to the overall CPFR model to accommodate the growing specific needs of collaboration from different trading partners.

The revised CPFR reference model provides a general framework for the collaborative aspects of planning, forecasting, and the replenishment processes that can be applied to many industries. In the revised model depicted in Figure 7.2, a buyer and a seller, as collaboration participants, work together to satisfy the demands of an end customer, who is at the center of the model.

The trading partner, who participates in the CPFR process, can be either be a buyer a seller, or both depending upon the context of the business function and the industry vertical.

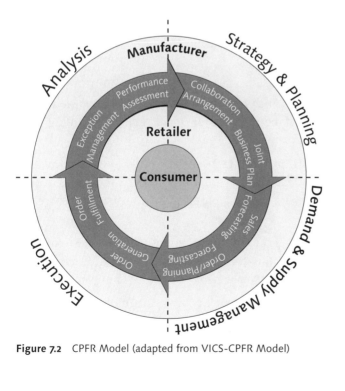

Figure 7.2 CPFR Model (adapted from VICS-CPFR Model)

As illustrated in Figure 7.2, the revised CPFR model consists of four major activities, which are broken down as follows.

- **Strategy and planning**

  Strategy and planning encompasses activities such as establishing the ground rules for the collaborative relationship, determining product mix and placement, and developing event plans for the period. Within the strategy and planning activity, various tasks are listed. Collaboration arrangement involves setting business goals for the relationship, defining the scope of the collaboration, and assigning roles, responsibilities, checkpoints, and escalation procedures. The joint business plan identifies the significant events that affect supply and demand in the planning period, such as promotions, inventory policy changes, store openings and closings, and product introductions.

- **Demand and supply management**

  Demand and supply management encompasses activities such as projecting consumer (POS) demand and order and shipment requirements over the planning horizon.

  The demand and supply management activity in turn consists of tasks such as sales forecasting, which projects consumer demand at the POS, and order planning and forecasting, which determines future product ordering and delivery requirements based upon the sales forecast, inventory positions, transit lead times, and other factors.

- **Execution**

  Executions include activities such as placing orders, preparing and delivering shipments, receiving and stocking products on retail shelves, recording sales transactions, and making payments.

  The execution activity in turn includes tasks such as order generation, which transitions forecasts to firm demand, and order fulfillment, the process of producing, shipping, delivering, and stocking products for consumer purchase.

- **Analysis**

  Analysis includes activities such as monitoring planning and execution activities for exception conditions, aggregating results, calculating key performance metrics, sharing insights, and adjusting the plans for continuous improved results.

  Analysis tasks include exception management, the active monitoring of planning and operations for out-of-bounds conditions, and performance assessment, the calculation of key metrics to evaluate the achievement of business goals, uncover trends, or develop alternative strategies.

Whereas these collaboration activities are presented in logical order, most companies are involved in all of them at any time. There is no predefined sequence of steps. Execution issues can impact strategy, and analysis can lead to adjustments in forecasts.

Collaboration may also focus on just a subset of the four activities (such as strategy and planning), whereas the rest of the process is performed through conventional enterprise processes.

7.3   Comparison of VMI and CPFR Processes

In a VMI scenario, the target level for the inventory is set for each partner location (the partner can be a manufacturer, distributor, retailer, etc.), and the supplier manages to replenish the stocks to those levels while the partner monitors to ensure that the targets are being met. If you take a closer look at the VMI process, you'll find that it is more or less focused on the execution aspect of the demand fulfillment process. The partner sends demand information to the supplier. So, the VMI process is not adequate enough to handle the varying demands of partner. In reality there is a time lag in the communication from the partner, and the VMI suppliers often find themselves on the losing end of an inventory imbalance. The absence of a joint business plan and lack of visibility of both the mid-term and short-term forecasted demand are the primary reasons for these inventory imbalances at the partner location.

You have to look beyond the basic customer-supplier replenishment process that takes customer relationship management to the next level, which is one of a shared business plan and forecasted demand for future. Using principles similar to VMI, CPFR can be thought of as an evolved version that addresses the shortcomings of VMI. The CPFR process begins with collaboration. Traditionally, suppliers and retailers developed their own independent forecasts. Using CPFR, retailers and suppliers submit their own individual forecasts, and then both evolve into one shared, agreed-upon forecast. The joint forecast is created through the sharing of POS information, existing inventory, stock-out information, promotions, and supplier production constraints. After the trading partners have arrived at the joint demand plan, the replenishment orders are created, taking into consideration the likely fluctuations in the future forecasted demand. So, the CPFR process incorporates the planning and forecasting that happens in collaboration with the customer. This forms the input for the replenishment of the inventory in CPFR, and in true sense VMI process can be considered the tail end of the CPFR.

Ultimately, both VMI and CPFR processes benefit not only the supplier but also the partners and the end customer. Through these collaborative planning processes, the response time to actual demand is lower because the order generation happens through the collaborative means. The visibility of actual orders to all of the trading partners' results in optimized turnaround times, which improves product availability and partner satisfaction.

The CPFR process enables the sales forecast to be generated jointly through collaboration of various partners. Because of this, the forecast gains in reliability. Independent of their position in the supply chain, or their activities there, the partners can bring their differing perspectives, consumer data, experiences, and research into the forecasting. This combined knowledge is the basis for high reliability in sales forecasting.

The establishment of direct communication channels between the supply chain partners raises the level of exchange between phases of the value chain. Next to the continual exchange of sales data, unique developments (increased or diminished demand due to weather or stepped-up advertising etc.) can be readily considered. The cooperation of all of the partners in the process of planning, forecasting, and replenishment dramatically reduces out-of-stock situations and dramatically reduces out-of-stock situations which cause loss-of-sales, while all partners profit.

The implementation of collaborative planning processes such as VMI and CPFR has its own challenges that have to be overcome attain the full benefits. First, the trading partners, who want to collaborate, need to access both their internal capability and readiness and the partners' capability to collaborate in creating a common business goal and objective. For a successful implementation there should be a high degree of organizational fit and potential for mutual benefit through collaboration between the trading partners. Otherwise, there is no point in attempting such initiatives.

However, if mutual benefits are identified for the collaborating organizations, there should be strong sponsorship from the senior management for these collaborative processes to succeed. Senior management should be involved in allocating the resources in terms of availability and number of resources identified from different business functions. Also, the involvement of senior management in conflict resolution and review of agreement from time to time is very important.

The basis for both VMI and CPFR processes is the shared information between the partners. To take full advantage of the benefits, trading partners need to create relationships founded on trust. Sharing sensitive data and close collaboration demands reliability and openness from the trading partners. The partners should focus on the relationship between two companies, and need to find comparable data from multiple organizations. In particular, best practice would be to collaborate at the lowest data level: sharing promotional plans, forecasts, and replenishment orders per trading unit and per POS.

Successful implementation requires efficient exchange of clean business data. Developing standards for enabling data exchange for the CPFR process is the key to seamless data flow between trading partners. The technology platform chosen for enabling CPFR should be scalable, compatible to use standards, and provide data security during collaboration.

7.4   Collaborative Planning Process in SAP APO

The basis of collaborative planning processes like VMI and CPFR is the shared information across the boundaries of the trading partners' organizations. Collaboration among these partners happens regularly with the sales and inventory data shared on a daily basis. Thus, the system enablement and automation of the whole collaboration process becomes a key success for the implementation of these processes. SAP APO Collaborative Planning (CLP) helps enterprises engage in collaborative supply chain planning activities with their business partners. SAP APO provides a common platform to the trading partners for sharing information regarding sales and forecast data and enables them to collaborate and arrive at a consensus demand plan. You can generate optimized supply plans using SAP APO by gathering partners' shared information across the supply network.

The Internet is one of the most outstanding innovations in the history of mankind, and the foremost target of the Internet has always been communication and increased information sharing. The Internet and associated technologies such as XML have revolutionized interenterprise business processes by enabling seamless information exchange between partners. The economical manner in which the data can be exchanged through the Internet has been a boon for all of the business partners, even those with minor stake in the entire supply chain. Interactive online access to each other's systems can be achieved easily via a conventional Internet browser.

SAP APO CLP is the building block that enables enterprises to collaboratively plan all logistics activities ranging from forecasting to shipment planning, together with their business partners. Collaborative planning in SAP APO includes all of the relevant trading partners such as suppliers, manufacturers, and retailers in the supply chain and enables them to plan across the network in a cost-effective manner, thereby increasing the value delivered to the customer. With SAP APO CLP, the trading partners exchange the relevant information required for developing the business plan and the forecast. It also provides the business user with the ability to view other partners' data and, if required, make modifications within the agreed limits. However, all business users do not have authorization to perform all of the functions in collaborative planning using SAP APO. Access is restricted based on the role and authorization profile assigned to each the business user. SAP APO CLP supports gathering information from various trading partners and hence enables the partners to create a consensus plan and alerts them if there is any exception in comparison to the set of agreed upon rules.

There are two basic options for using SAP APO CLP:

▶ Collaboration Engine (CE) within and between SAP APO systems
▶ Interactivity with Internet Transaction Server (ITS)

Figure 7.3 provides an overview of the architecture behind the SAP APO Collaborative Planning solution and various means by which communication takes place between different systems.

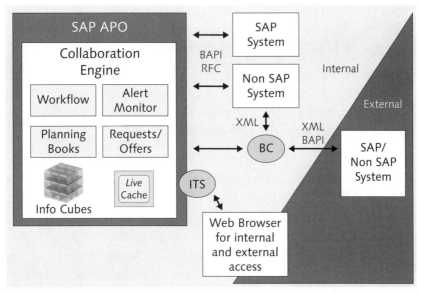

Figure 7.3 Architectural Overview of SAP APO CLP

There are two ways in which data can be transferred between the supplier and the retailer system:

▶ **Automatic data transfer**
Automatic sharing of information between partner systems can happen through and inbound-outbound interface to transfer time series and orders via electronic data interchange (EDI), business application programming interfaces (BAPIs), and XML. For XML, an SAP middleware technology connector is needed to exchange data and make Internet linkage possible.

▶ **Manual data transfer**
The collaboration between partners happens by means of data maintenance via a browser interface. Only Internet access is needed for such manual transfer of data. SAP APO CLP makes this possible by the use of SAP middleware technology for Internet applications: SAP Internet Transaction Server (ITS).

7.4.1 Collaborative Demand Planning Process in SAP APO

Collaborative demand planning between manufacturers and their retailers in SAP APO CLP allows both partners to streamline their demand planning processes and ultimately benefit from a more accurate forecast, better market transparency, greater stability, reduced inventory, and better communication.

With collaborative demand planning, the buyer and seller develop a single forecast and update it regularly based on information shared over the Internet. The sales- and inventory-related data is exchanged between the partners on a frequent basis.

On the basis of the CPFR philosophy, both the supplier and the retailer collaborate to generate a consensus forecast based on combined promotion calendars and analysis of POS data and causal data. The consensus forecast is then reviewed for exceptions, taking into consideration the current stock levels in each store adjusted for changes, such as promotions.

The collaboration of external partners for developing the consensus demand is made possible using a web browser. In a collaborative planning process, the external partner accesses the manufacturer's SAP APO system for viewing and modifying the forecast data across different characteristics, creating the forecast data manually by entering the data in the specified key figure. The external partner can also execute macros to aid in identifying the exceptions in the consensus forecast based on the set criteria.

User access for the external partners is restricted to authorized data and activities that are based on the roles of the business user accessing the system. User settings and authorizations for the business users are defined in SAP APO. The collaborative supply and demand planning web interface changes according to user authorization for performing certain activities. For example, the drill-down icon is only visible if the user is authorized to use the drill-down function.

The external partners can access collaborative demand planning by logging in to the browser and specifying the planning book, data view, and selection details.

As shown in Figure 7.4, in the characteristics overview, the external partner can view all of the characteristics that correspond to the planning book, for example, location, planning version, and product. If the user is authorized to use the drill-down function, the drill-down icon appears next to the respective characteristic. The planning book details are present in the lower section of the screen. The data in the forecast key figure can be displayed and changed, both at the aggregated level and at the individual characteristic level based on the authorization to the drill-down option. The external partner shares the data by either modifying the forecast values of the manufacturers in a separate key figure or entering the new values of the forecast in the key figure by choosing the edit mode. Thus, both the external partner and the manufacturers collaborate via web browser using SAP APO CLP to arrive at a consensus forecast, after which the data is saved.

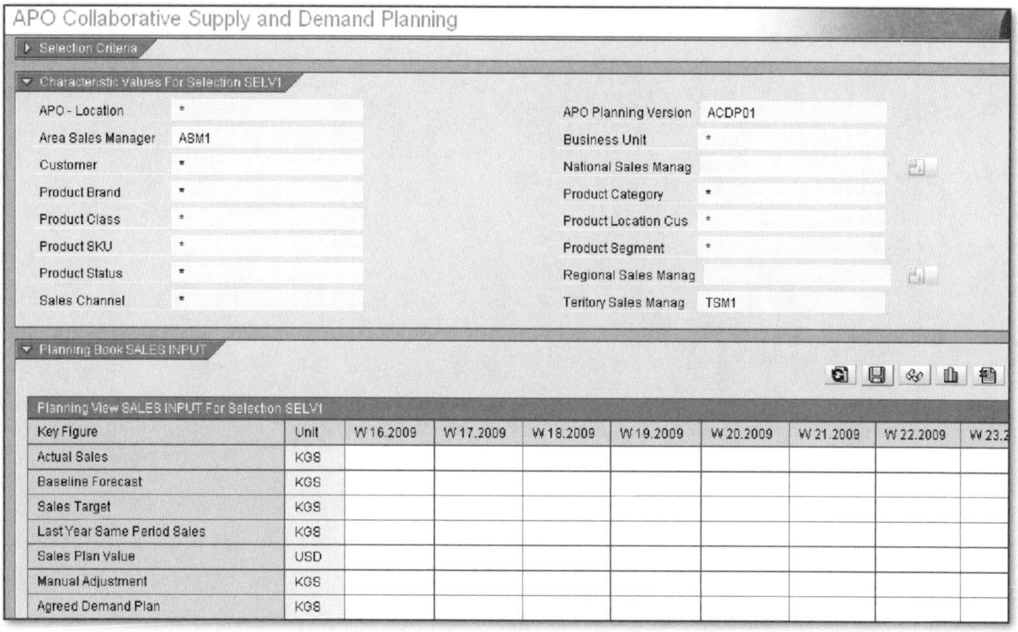

Figure 7.4 SAP APO Collaborative Demand Planning Book

7.4.2   Settings for Collaborative Demand Planning in SAP APO

The user settings for an external partner, who accesses collaborative supply and demand planning using a web browser, can be configured in SAP APO, and this determines the layout of the Internet planning book and which options are available for the user.

You make the settings for the user in the SAP SCM system, by accessing the SAP Easy Access screen and following the menu path SUPPLY CHAIN COLLABORATION • ENVIRONMENT • CURRENT SETTINGS • USER SETTINGS FOR COLLABORATIVE SUPPLY AND DEMAND PLANNING.

Figure 7.5 illustrates the user settings in a collaborative planning scenario. If you make user-specific settings, then you must specify the user name in the User field. To maintain general settings for all users, enter "*" in place of the user.

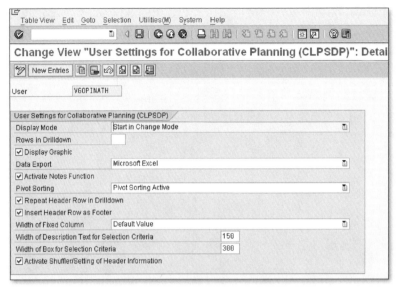

Figure 7.5 User Settings for Collaborative Planning

You can use the shuffler to create, change, or delete selections directly in the collaborative supply and demand planning screen. Unlike the shuffler in interactive planning, selection management is not available to the user in collaborative planning. This means the selection is automatically assigned to the user and is saved directly under the user. You make the shuffler function available to the user by selecting the Activate Shuffler/Setting of Header Information checkbox. The Display Mode field settings specify whether collaborative supply and demand planning is to be started in the change mode or the display mode when the user calls it. Select the Display Graphic checkbox if the user is to be provided with the option of graphical display of the data.

In the Data Export field, you specify whether or not the user can export data, and if so, how (Microsoft Excel or other software). In the Internet planning book, the user can then export data by choosing the option of Download Planning Book.

The procedure for maintaining the settings for collaboration partners consists of the following:

▶ Determine the collaboration partner.

▶ Define the communication settings for each collaboration scenario.

▶ Assign user names to collaboration partners.

You can make the settings for the collaboration partners in the SAP SCM system by accessing the SAP Easy Access screen and following the menu path SUPPLY CHAIN COLLABORATION • ENVIRONMENT • CURRENT SETTINGS • COLLABORATION PARTNERS.

You can define a partner in the system by choosing new entries in the maintenance screen for collaboration partner settings. The names and descriptions of the partners who will participate in the collaboration process are defined along with their addresses in the maintenance screen. After you've completed the settings, the name of the partner that is defined appears in the list of partners.

As shown in Figure 7.6, the communication settings for the partners screen, consists of the maintenance of parameters such as determining the collaboration scenario. In this setting, you maintain options for various collaborative planning scenarios, such as transportation planning and demand and supply planning. From the given options, you select the scenario relevant for the business context.

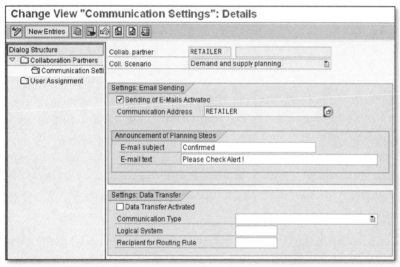

Figure 7.6 Settings for Collaboration Partners and Communication

If a workflow is used for collaborative demand planning, you can select the Sending of E-Mails Activated checkbox. You must specify the address to which the emails have to be sent. In SAP APO CPL, workflow messages can be sent to an internal user, to a distribution list, or to an external email address. If the standard text is to be posted in the mails, then those texts can be maintained along with the subject in the announcement of planning steps in the email area.

To exchange the time series data with the external partner, select the Data Transfer Activated checkbox. In the Communication Type field, specify the mode in which the time series document is sent, and in the Logical System field, specify the target system to which the data has to be sent. In the User Assignment node, you assign the collaboration partner with the user for which the necessary settings are already maintained.

Planning book data can be exchanged directly between your SAP APO system and your partner's SAP APO system. This type of data transfer can happen in collaborative scenarios such as CPFR, consensus-based forecasting between manufacturer and customers, and exchange of inventory data between manufacturer and supplier. *Send time series* is the function that is used for the transfer of planning data from the planning book of one system to another system. The data can be exchanged through bucket-oriented key figures between either two SAP APO systems or between an SAP APO system and a third-party system.

The settings for the exchange of time series can be made in the SAP SCM system by accessing the SAP Easy Access screen and following the menu path SUPPLY CHAIN COLLABORATION • COLLABORATIVE SUPPLY AND DEMAND PLANNING • SEND TIME SERIES.

Figure 7.7 shows the parameters that are to be maintained for the exchange of data from the manufacturer's system to the external system. The source-system-related settings that have to be maintained are the planning book, selection, partner ID of the data source system, and the key figures from which the data has to be sent from the source system. The target-system-related settings that have to be maintained are the planning book, selection, and partner ID of the data target system to which the data has to be sent.

In the Characteristics field, the choice of characteristics that is given as input determines the level at which the data is exchanged. Based on the different characteristic combinations maintained in this field as input, the key figure data that is defined in the data source is aggregated and transferred to the target system. For example, you can transmit the forecast values for a location that is grouped according to its products. This means the system shows the forecast for each individual product at this location. If no characteristics are maintained, then the data is completely aggregated and is transferred as one value per bucket and key figure. Depending on the disaggregation settings in both systems, this can result in the values at the detail level being different in both systems

Data Source (Own System)		
Planning Book	MONTHLY FORECAST	
Selection	PROD_LOC	
Partner	VGOPINATH	
Key Figures	FORECAST	⇨

Optional: Restriction of Period Relatively			
Number of Weeks		Offset	
Number of Days		Offset	

Data Target (External System)	
Planning Book	SALES INPUT
Selection	SELV1
Partner	DP_CUST01

Characteristics for Data Aggr. in Source System	
Characteristics	PRODUCT

Optional: Mapping of Key Figures Between Source and Target System			
Source Key Figure 1		Target Key Figure 1	
Source Key Figure 2		Target Key Figure 2	
Source Key Figure 3		Target Key Figure 3	
Source Key Figure 4		Target Key Figure 4	
Source Key Figure 5		Target Key Figure 5	

Optional: Mapping of char. names between source + target systems			
Source Char. 1		Target Char. 1	
Source Char. 2		Target Char. 2	
Source Char. 3		Target Char. 3	

Figure 7.7   Settings for Time Series Exchange

Values in these fields of the key figure mapping denote if the data should be stored in other key figures in the target system as compared with the source system. This can be used, for example, to read the planned distribution demand from one system and save it as the forecast in the other system.

Values in these characteristic mapping fields denote if the data should be stored in other characteristics in the target system rather than in the source system. The same characteristic value combinations should be available in both systems. An information message is stored in the application log for each characteristic combination that does not exist in the target system. This means that even if you change the name of the characteristic, its value must remain the same in both systems.

7.4.3 VMI Process in SAP APO

In a VMI process, there is tight collaboration between the customer and the supplier, with a high volume of data exchange. The customer sends stock and sales data from his SAP ERP system or any legacy system to the vendor. This forms the basis on which the vendor independently replenishes the stocks at the customer's warehouse.

The following are the steps are required to exchange data:

1. The vendor uses the statistical forecasting methods available in the demand planning functionality of SAP APO to generate planned independent requirements, and the customer's historical sales data forms the basis for the forecast generation.

2. The vendor defines a short- to medium-term plan on the basis of the demand plan, also taking into account the current stock figures at the customer location provided by the customer.

3. The vendor creates optimized distribution plans using the deployment function in Supply Network Planning, defining when and how the products available at the vendor location are to be delivered to the VMI customers.

4. In the Transport Load Builder (TLB), the vendor groups the transport recommendations generated for individual products during deployment into TLB shipments of multiple products to optimize the utilization of transport capacities. The vendor's SAP ERP system automatically creates sales orders based on the confirmed TLB shipments.

5. The SAP ERP system transfers the sales order number to SAP APO during change transfer.

6. The vendor sends an order confirmation (message type ORDRSP with message code VMI) to the customer through EDI or application link enabling (ALE) during the change transfer between SAP ERP and SAP APO. In the standard system, the order confirmation for the sales order is generated as a message of type BAV0. The customer's SAP ERP system automatically creates a purchase order on the basis of the order confirmation. If the purchase order number has not been assigned in SAP APO, it is transferred to the vendor's SAP ERP system by IDoc (message type ORDCHG with message code VMI) and entered in the sales order as a reference.

7. After processing the sales order, the vendor creates an outbound delivery in SAP ERP.

8. The vendor reduces the VMI sales order and generates a delivery in SAP APO.

9. The vendor posts a goods issue for the delivery in SAP ERP, and then reduces the delivery and generates stock in transit at the customer location in the SAP APO system.

10. The vendor can send a shipping notification (DELVRY03 IDoc with message type DESADV) to the customer's SAP ERP system if desired. In this case, the customer's SAP ERP system automatically creates an inbound delivery. Otherwise, the customer creates the inbound delivery manually.

11. The customer posts a goods receipt in its SAP ERP system and sends a proof of delivery to the vendor's SAP APO system (DELVRY03 IDoc with message type STPPOD). In its SAP APO system, the vendor reduces the stock in transit at the customer location. Alternatively, they can reduce the stock in transit using a product activity notification IDoc, based on information about open purchase order quantities.

The following are the settings that have to be maintained in SAP APO for enabling the VMI process. The customer location master data is transferred from the vendor's SAP ERP system to the vendor SAP APO system. The assignment of the VMI customer to the VMI location is maintained in the SAP APO system. This assignment takes place via the SAP menu path ADVANCED PLANNING AND OPTIMIZATION • MASTER DATA • LOCATION • LOCATION.

As shown in the Figure 7.8, in the Location for Sold-To Party field in the location master, you maintain the SAP APO location number of the sold-to party. The customer location itself can be a ship-to party. In the Ext. Location Short Text field, you specify the name that the VMI customer uses for this sold-to party location. The ATD field in the location master is filled because the deployment functionality of APO uses this field, and if the scenario demands the inclusion of a shipping calendar, it can be assigned to the supply location in the location master.

The SAP APO system automatically creates location products for the customer materials transferred from the vendor's SAP ERP system. The material master transferred from the vendor's SAP ERP system at the plant location is verified in the APO system for promotion lead times, customer product names, Goods Receipt/Goods Issue lead time, and forecast horizon.

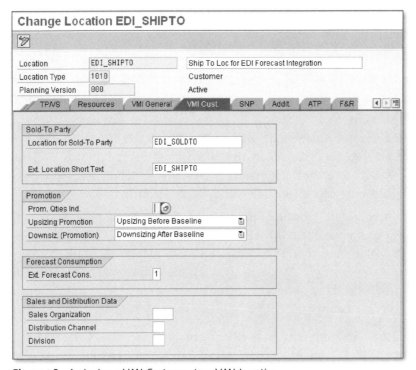

Figure 7.8 Assigning a VMI Customer to a VMI Location

The transportation lanes are created between the supply location and the customer location. In the transportation lane, you assign the means of transport and the transportation calendars.

To save the sales and forecast data of the VMI customer, you make settings such as creation of a planning object structure and a planning area. The planning object structure created should contain at least two characteristics (location and material). At least two key figures should be available in the planning area for saving the sales and/or forecast data of the VMI customer. A planning book is also created based on the planning object structure and the planning area.

You map the external time series data to a key figure in the planning area by following the menu path ADVANCED PLANNING AND OPTIMIZATION • DEMAND PLANNING • ENVIRONMENT • CURRENT SETTINGS • MAINTAIN MAPPING OF EXTERNAL TIME SERIES TO PLANNING AREAS (see Figure 7.9).

New Entries: Overview of Added Entries

External Time Series for Location Product: Assgmt in SDP					
Q	Location	Plng area	Plng versn	InfoObject	
003	EDI_SHIPTO	ZADP01	000	ZSALES	▲
		☑	☑	☑	▼
		☑	☑	☑	

Figure 7.9 Mapping External Time Series to Planning Areas

The key figure of the planning area is assigned to the external time series and the associated *qualifier* (003 for sales quantity, 004 for forecast sales quantity).

The calculation and result key figures are defined for the forecast in the Demand Planning book, and if necessary, a mass processing job is created for the release from Demand Planning to Supply Network Planning.

To create a mass processing job for release from Demand Planning to Supply Network Planning the following steps are required:

▶ **Step 1**
The user needs to create an activity. In SAP APO you create an activity using the menu path DEMAND PLANNING • PLANNING • DEMAND PLANNING IN BACKGROUND • DEFINE ACTIVITIES FOR MASS PROCESSING. The user needs to enter the Activity and Description and click on the Create button as shown in Figure 7.10.

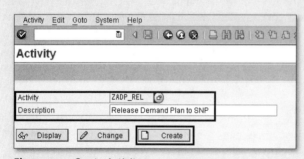

Figure 7.10 Create Activity

▶ **Step 2**
In the Activity window in the Header Setting Box, add the Planning Book and Data View as shown in Figure 7.11. Also, in the Release Prfl tab, click on the button for release profile to create a Release Profile.

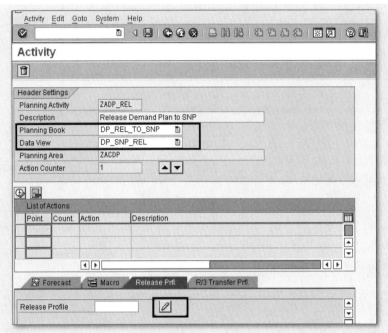

Figure 7.11 Add Planning Book and Data View; Button to Create Release Profile

▶ **Step 3**
In the Release Profile Window, fill in the Planning Area, Key figure, Trgt Plng Vers. Category, Product. Char, and Location Char. as shown in Figure 7.12. Save the Release Profile.

▶ **Step 4**
Click on the Adopt button to adopt the release profile in the Activity window, as shown in Figure 7.13. Save the Activity.

▶ **Step 5**
Create a Planning Job for releasing from Demand Planning to Supply Network Planning. In SAP APO you create a background job for mass processing via the menu path DEMAND PLANNING • PLANNING • DEMAND PLANNING IN BACKGROUND • CREATE DEMAND PLANNING IN BACKGROUND. As shown in Figure 7.14, in the Create Planning Job window, enter the Job Number and Job name and click on the Execute button.

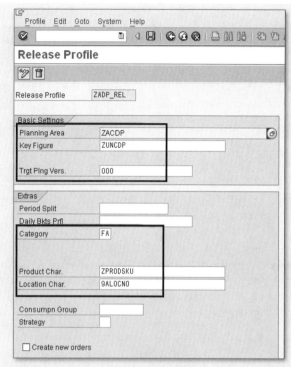

Figure 7.12 Creation of Release Profile

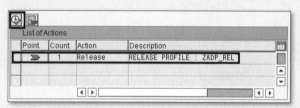

Figure 7.13 Adopt Button to Adopt Release Profile to the Activity

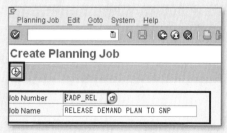

Figure 7.14 Enter Job Number and Job Name

▶ **Step 6**

In the next window, shown in Figure 7.15, add the Planning Book, Data View, and Version and click on the Execute button.

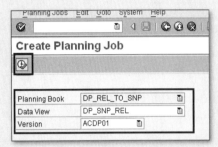

Figure 7.15 Maintain Entries for Planning Book, Data View, and Version

▶ **Step 7**

In the Create Planning Job window, select the Activity, select the Selection ID, click on the Aggregation Level button, and select Product and Location characteristics and save to create the mass processing job to release from Demand Planning to Supply Network Planning, as shown in Figure 7.16.

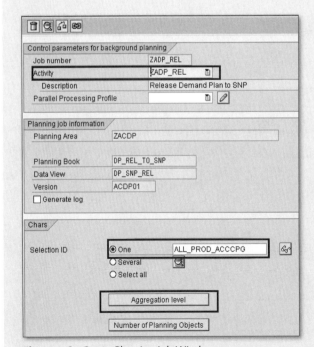

Figure 7.16 Create Planning Job Window

> The other setting to be maintained for enabling the VMI process is the TLB profile. To enable the transfer of TLB shipments to SAP ERP, include the sales order publishing type for the supplying plant or distribution center in the distribution definition.

7.5 Consumption Data and the Vision Chain Demand Signal Repository

Vendor-managed inventory and CPFR both offer demand signals back to the manufacturer or distributor, which tend to focus on the movement of product out of a customer's warehouse. In some supply chains, these *demand signals* are synonymous with consumption as the product, for example, semiconductors, is being built into a finished product. In other cases, such as retailers shipping products from their warehouses into their retail outlets or distributors sending products to original equipment manufacturers, the product has not been consumed.

Until the product is consumed, there is a possibility that it is being held in inventory either in a back room or at a downstream warehouse. Inventory buffers can camouflage actual consumption of the product because it is ordered either in large batches or from strategic movements such as buying on deal or ahead of a price increase. In these cases, demand might seem to be increasing because of the large shipment. If a planner looks at the shipment data, he might assume that it is a legitimate trend and increase production and/or inventory buffers, only to find that not only is it not an increase, but there is a drop in demand as consumption, which has remained consistent the whole time, slowly works through the stockpiled inventory.

The unfortunate planner, having been burned once, might now assume that this slowdown in demand is also a trend (especially if his exponential smoothing is set to be very responsive to recent changes). This could cause a company to overcompensate again, but in the opposite direction, reducing production and drawing down inventory buffers. This back and forth whipsawing is known as the *bullwhip effect* (Figures 7.17 and 7.18) and has been known to students and practitioners of supply chain management for decades.

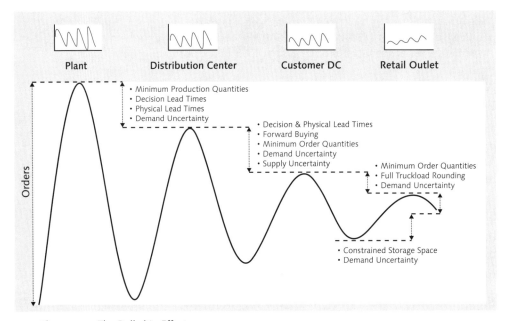

Figure 7.17 The Bullwhip Effect

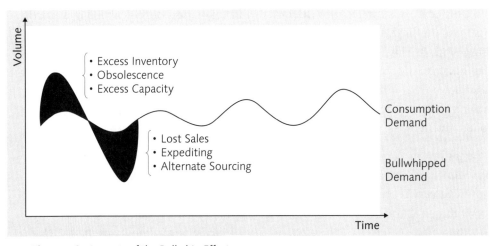

Figure 7.18 Impacts of the Bullwhip Effect

One solution to the bullwhip effect is to gain end-to-end supply chain visibility of consumption data so that production and distribution can better match demand from the ultimate consumer. Of course, as we'll discuss in Chapters 8 and 9, organizations can engage in activities designed to temporarily impact demand (like the aforementioned deal) and disturb downstream demand. But assuming that these impacts are anticipated and communicated by the sales and marketing executives within the organization, consumption data can significantly increase a company's visibility of downstream demand and in doing so, increase its ability to project demand.

Gathering downstream demand data, such as retailers' aggregated POS information from their cash registers, is a fairly simple concept to grasp, but becomes complicated at scale. The number of locations in which an organization's products are consumed can be between 10 and 1000 times larger than the number of customer locations to which they initially ship their products.

Consumption data also tends to be more granular. Where shipments to customers may occur every few days, weekly or monthly consumption happens every minute of every day, and some major retailers are able to identify and refresh their consumption information in less than 10-minute increments. Given that most companies run forecasts monthly, with the best doing so weekly, collecting, storing, and analyzing 10 to 1000 times the information 10 to 100 times more frequently can be very challenging.

A demand signal repository (DSR) is a single, broad collection of transactional and contextual data that is real-time, granular, and historical, regarding purchases and past, present, and future inventory. This bulk of the data in a DSR comes from a retailer and is shared with the product manufacturer. The manufacturer owns and houses the DSR and uses the DSR to answer questions about sales and inventory by item, store, and day combinations. More advanced DSR systems tie to the retailer POS and inventory figures other data such as syndicated demand, product, or location master data; internal data such as shipments; and other pertinent, enriching information. The DSR does not include loyalty card or direct consumer information, because the retailer keeps this information away from their suppliers, owing to privacy, legal, and other restrictions.

To spare their ERP and demand management solutions from being overwhelmed by this information, organizations turn to high-volume repositories with the ability to store and analyze consumption demand signals. Whereas these DSR organizations can receive consumption-related data from collaborative partners through EDI, the majority of the information exchanged does not align with standard fields in the predefined transaction sets (i.e., EDI 852, EDI 830, etc.) Indeed, in the case of retailers, nearly every partner is completely different in terms of what they share and how they share it. This can be a challenge for any organization, making the "onboarding" of each new collaborative partner a new project with little in the way of economies of scale or learning curve that might be the case with more standardized data sets in the case of VMI or CPFR.

What is in a DSR?

▶ Some of the data the in a DSR includes:
  ▶ Item attributes (e.g., size, flavor, bar code, UPC, color)
    ▶ Store attributes (e.g., zip code, number of square feet)
  ▶ Retailer-provided consumer attributes (e.g., age, ethnicity)
  ▶ Other attributes (e.g., replenishment variables, seasonality index, new item flag, or time attributes such as fiscal and supplier calendars)
  ▶ Sales and quantity in international local currency and/or U.S. dollars
  ▶ Returns
  ▶ Inventory at each node in the supply chain
  ▶ Supplier shipments or, in some cases, purchase orders
  ▶ For each store item combination, planogram, or modular data
  ▶ Sometimes more advanced enhancing information, including:
    ▶ Supplier forecast
    ▶ Retailer forecast
    ▶ RFID reads
    ▶ Promotion information when not a temporary price reduction (TPR)

In the process of transmitting consumption data, especially at daily or higher frequencies, it is possible for technical issues to occur. This can result in gaps in visibility for a given product or consumption point. Although algorithms exist to extrapolate the correct values, this becomes a self-fulfilling prophecy given that these extrapolation techniques are often related to the univariate statistical algorithms that organizations would be applying these numbers to anyway.

Extrapolation can also be a crutch for syndicated data providers (such as Nielsen and IRI in the consumer products industry) because it enables them to offer data for locations from which they do not want to collect data. In general, from a demand management perspective, it is better to leave the time period empty for the product and location in question and let outlier correction account for it when the forecast is generated.

Furthermore, a zero consumption value can be very real if the location in question is experiencing an out-of-stock, meaning that whereas there may be demand, there is no inventory of the product available. This could be very relevant for an organization because a missed opportunity for a downstream trading partner to sell the product to an ultimate consumer or embed it in a finished product translates to a missed opportunity to replenish that product with a sale to that trading partner. In this case you can develop your own diagnostics to review recent inventory and demand reports to winnow out the potential out-of-stock situations from the data transmission errors.

To accommodate the eccentricities of individual trading partners and data transmission errors, not to mention master data harmonization issues (such as customers calling your products something different from what you call them), demand signal repositories are often preceded by adapters and harmonization engines that leverage business logic to make the data within the DSR as clean and reliable as possible. With this prophylactic middleware, the DSR becomes an excellent tool for data mining and analysis, offering organizations earlier, more granular visibility of demand. In many cases the organization can project changes in demand before it begins to impact their customers' ordering patterns. This is known as *demand sensing,* and when used to augment other demand sources, it can significantly improve near-term forecast accuracy.

7.6 Customer Collaboration with SAP SNC

VMI and CPFR are traditional, fairly well understood planning methods that have been around for more than a decade. They were developed in a time when plans were updated monthly and normally at an aggregated level owing to computer hardware and software limitations. Moore's law and the global build-out of higher bandwidth transmission lines now enable multiple subdaily updates on customer sales and stocks in some industries. For many organizations that have evolved well-tuned monthly or even weekly demand management cycles, trying to accommodate daily or subdaily updates can be ruinous, but so can ignoring the data when their competitors begin to take advantage of it.

One answer is to adopt a nested cycle of responsive replenishment planning. Where traditional VMI and CPFR planning and even long- and mid-term planning based on consumption data can continue to guide longer-term decision making, short-term demand projection based on daily or subdaily input from trading partners can drive immediate decisions — if, that is, the organization has the flexibility to be responsive with their production and distribution assets.

From the cockpit of a supertanker there is no way to see directly in front of the ship. This is not a limitation because once the ship is in motion it takes hundreds of yards to appreciably shift its course. The same can be said for some production and distribution operations. If set-up times are so long or logistics contracts locked in so far in advance, then it doesn't really matter how demand is changing at the customer's location this afternoon because it will be a week or two before the company can react to it anyway.

For companies investing in manufacturing and logistical agility, though, short-term collaborative data from their customers' locations can be actionable. Shipments can be changed, and production schedules can be updated. In these cases, short-term forecasting algorithms coupled to replenishment planning that includes an inventory availability check can enable companies to anticipate a customer order, possibly before the customer recognizes their own need for replenishment.

For these companies, SAP Supply Network Collaboration (SAP SNC) provides a fully integrated environment where plans can be more easily developed, shared, transitioned to execution, and monitored in a single environment. SAP SNC provides a web-based user interface to improve demand planning through enhanced customer collaboration. Although the tool also supports multiple collaboration scenarios with a manufacturer or distributor's suppliers, we'll focus only on the customer collaboration capabilities for the purposes of demand management.

7.6.1   Generating Forecasts in SAP SNC

SAP SNC provides users with various statistical forecasting tools to generate an accurate demand at a customer product level. The forecast overview function provides you with an option to view multiple location products and to perform forecasting operations such as run a statistical forecasting model, manually moderate the system-calculated forecast, and so on. The menu path to access the forecast overview in the SAP SNC web interface is DEMAND • STATISTICAL FORECASTING • FORECAST OVERVIEW.

As shown in Figure 7.19, a selection panel is provided in the forecast overview screen of SAP SNC to identify multiple location products. The location products are identified by providing the customer location number, the product number, or the SAP SNC planner associated with the planning activities. Planners can provide more than one of these inputs, but providing one of them in the selection panel is mandatory for the system to identify the location products.

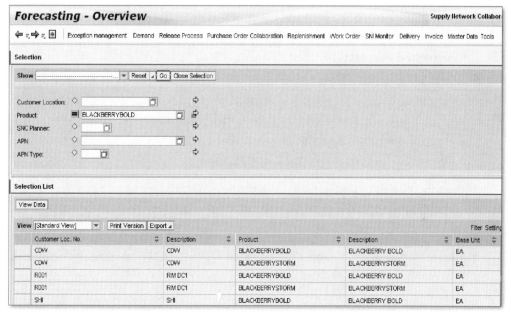

Figure 7.19 Forecasting Overview Selection Panel

After this data is input in the selection panel, you can perform a search to identify the location product by selecting Go. The required location products are then shown in the selection list panel below the selection panel. In the selection list panel, you can select one or more location products and populate them in the statistical forecast panel for performing the forecast operations.

As shown in Figure 7.20, the forecast overview function consists of the following key figures in the statistical forecast panel:

▶ **History**
This key figure stores the sales data for a particular product at a given location over a particular period.

▶ **Corrected History**
This key figure stores the value that the user has modified from the original history, in order to correct the outliers in the history. The outliers in the history can be due to external factors or special events.

▶ **Forecast**
This key figure stores the future sales projection for a product that is calculated based on different statistical models.

▶ **Corrected Forecast**
This key figure stores the value of the forecast that is manually corrected.

After the history data is loaded in the statistical forecast panel for a location product, you can execute a forecast run from the forecast overview screen by selecting the option Run Forecast. The forecast values calculated by the system are then moderated to add the marketing and sales inputs.

The forecast detail function shown in Figure 7.20 provides users an option to view a single location product and to perform forecasting operations at a detailed level. Additional information includes the ex-post forecast, seasonal index, and trend.

The menu path to access this forecast detail function in the SAP SNC web interface is DEMAND • STATISTICAL FORECASTING • FORECAST DETAIL.

In the forecast detail screen, on the bottom panel, Master Record and Profile information is displayed, depending on the tab selected. Users interactively make changes to the parameters as required and save data. The forecast run then can be carried out with the changed parameters.

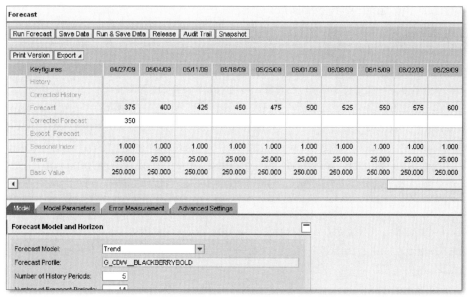

Figure 7.20 Forecasting Overview Statistical Forecast Panel

7.6.2 Collaborative Sales Forecasting (CSF)

This function in SAP SNC allows suppliers and customers to collaborate on sales forecast data. The supplier baseline forecast and the customer baseline forecast forms the basis on which the collaboration takes place.

The system generates the supplier baseline forecast through statistical tools and techniques. This forecast can be created either using the forecasting functionality available in SAP SNC at the customer product level or using SAP APO demand planning at a different planning hierarchy than the one included in the demand planning system. Customer forecast details are obtained from the customer and sent to the SAP SNC system through XML messages, namely, the product forecast notification (PFN) and the product forecast revision notification (PFRN) messages.

The supplier and customer then use the consensus-finding functionality in SAP SNC to compare forecast data and come to an agreement about the sales forecast for a particular product in a specific time period. CSF uses baseline data only and calculates the absolute differences and percentage differences between supplier and customer data and proposes a final consensus sales forecast.

Two process variants are available:

- A customer-led variant based on daily forecast data
- A supplier-led variant based on weekly forecast data

In both processes, the supplier bears the overall responsibility for replenishment, although the customer is still involved and can control consensus finding. Suppliers can manually change the system proposal if the data does not correspond to expected or acceptable values. Suppliers can send outbound XML messages to customers to share the results of the consensus finding, or release final consensus forecast data to short-term forecasting before the data is released to replenishment planning.

Various steps are involved in setting up the CSF. The first step is to create and assign the profiles for CSF. In the CSF profile various horizons are maintained, such as:

- Display horizon
- Planning horizon
- Release horizon
- Publish horizon

A profile for CSF is created in Customizing for SAP SNC, by following the menu path DEMAND • COLLABORATIVE SALES FORECASTING • CREATE PROFILES FOR COLLABORATIVE SALES FORECASTING.

As shown in Figure 7.21, data storage maintained in the CSF profile determines whether the display, planning, and release horizons are weekly or daily. Data storage also determines the type of XML messages that SAP SNC accepts and the time and logic of the disaggregation of the final consensus data. For a supplier-led CSF process variant, data storage is set weekly. For a customer-led CSF process variant, data storage is set daily. To define whether the publish horizon is weekly or daily, the publish bucket size should be maintained.

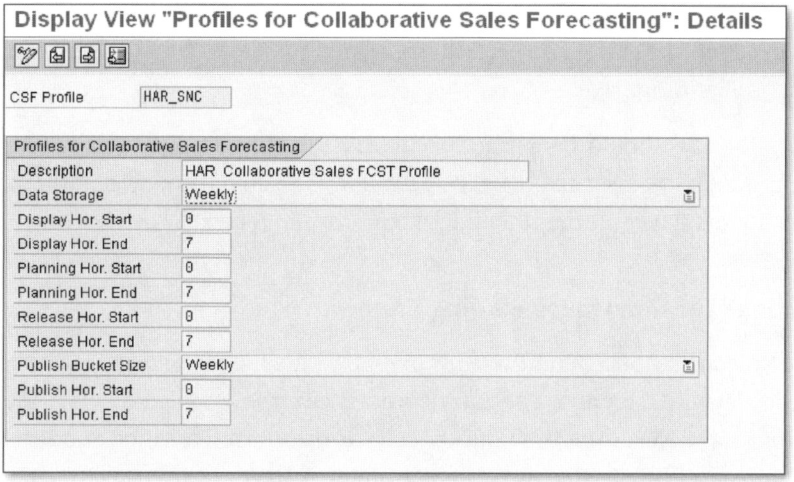

Figure 7.21 Maintaining Profile for Collaborative Customer Sales Forecast

As shown in Figure 7.22, the other important setting for CSF is that in the forecast master record, the status flag should be set to G, which prevents the forecasted data to be sent to short-term forecasting directly from the statistical forecast, before a consensus finding has been run in CSF.

You create the forecast master record setting in Customizing for SAP SNC, by following the menu path DEMAND • FORECASTING • UPDATE FORECAST MASTER DATA.

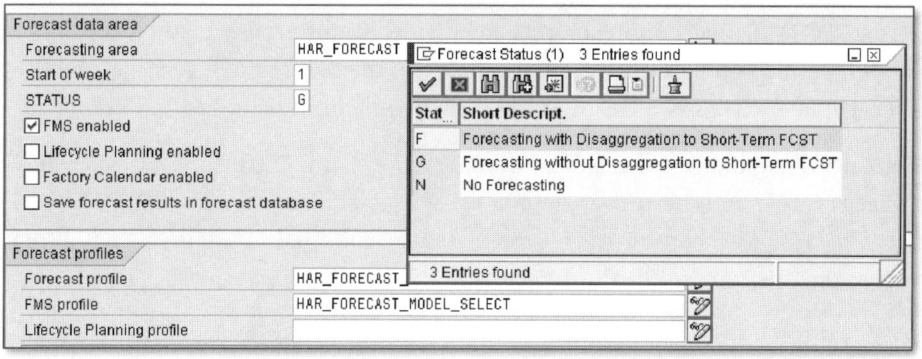

Figure 7.22 Updating Forecast Master Data

You define alert profile settings in the customizing for SAP SNC under DEMAND • DEFINE ALERT PROFILES FOR CSF AND OFM. Alert profiles define the alert levels that the system issues for predefined situations. An alert can be configured as either a warning or an error. The system displays alerts related to CSF in the Alert Monitor on the Demand Planning page.

Color profiles for CSF should be defined in the Customizing for SAP SNC under DEMAND • DEFINE COLOR PROFILES FOR CSF AND OFM. The color profiles determine which colors are displayed in the time bucket cells of the relevant key figures.

7.6.3 Settings for Consensus Finding Framework

CSF of SAP SNC consists of different screens in which data for the selected location products is displayed differently. The Sales Forecast Overview screen displays the forecast status as a color in the time bucket cell for the chosen location products after a consensus finding. The status is based on the key figure Consensus Baseline Sales Forecast – Final.

The SALES FORECAST DETAILS • PRODUCT VIEW screen displays the detailed information of the CSF profile, key figure calculations, and rule and tolerance parameters for the specific location product that is chosen. In the menu path SALES FORECAST DETAILS • PRODUCT VIEW, to calculate the tolerance value for differences, CSF uses the CD_QTY_DIFF0 consensus rule.

To create a consensus rule in customizing for SAP SNC, follow the menu path BASIC SETTINGS • CONSENSUS FINDINGS • MAINTAIN CONSENSUS RULES.

The CD_QTY_DIFF0 consensus rule calculates the difference between customer quantities and supplier quantities. As shown in the Figure 7.23, CFS uses the CD_QTY_DIFF0 consensus quantity profile for the tolerance values for differences.

For calculating the consensus baseline sales forecast, CSF uses the CD_QTY_AVG consensus rule and the corresponding consensus quantity profile, CD_QTY_AVG. The CD_QTY_AVG consensus rule calculates the consensus baseline demand forecast as the average of the sales forecasts of the customer and the supplier.

In the customer forecast collaboration, the default settings in the consensus quantity profile can be changed to the user-specific settings. You do this in customizing for SAP SNC, by following the menu path BASIC SETTINGS • CONSENSUS FINDINGS • CONSENSUS PROFILE.

Forecast data area

Forecasting area	HAR_FORECAST
Start of week	1
STATUS	G
☑ FMS enabled	
☐ Lifecycle Planning enabled	
☐ Factory Calendar enabled	
☐ Save forecast results in forecast database	

Forecast Status (1) 3 Entries found

Stat..	Short Descript.
F	Forecasting with Disaggregation to Short-Term FCST
G	Forecasting without Disaggregation to Short-Term FCST
N	No Forecasting

3 Entries found

Forecast profiles

Forecast profile	HAR_FORECAST..
FMS profile	HAR_FORECAST_MODEL_SELECT
Lifecycle Planning profile	

Figure 7.23 Maintain Consensus Rule

In the quantity profile for consensus finding, as shown in Figure 7.24, in the Overdeliv. Tol. fields, you can specify which positive quantity tolerance is allowed for the differences. In the Underdeliv. Tol. fields, you can maintain which negative quantity tolerance is allowed for the differences.

Change View "Quantity Profile for Consensus Finding": Details

New Entries

Quantity Prof.	CD_QTY_DIFF0

Quantity Profile for Consensus Finding

Description	Cons. Det. Quantity Difference
Data Type	C
Overdeliv. Tol. (%)	
Overdeliv. Tol. Qty	15
Overdeliv. Tol. UoM	EA
Underdeliv. Tol. (%)	
Underdeliv. Tol. Qty	15
Underdeliv. Tol. UoM	EA

Figure 7.24 Maintain Quantity Profile for Consensus Finding

If the data type is maintained as R, consensus finding calculates the quantity tolerance as the difference between the customer quantity and the supplier quantity. If the data type is C, the consensus finding calculates the quantity tolerance as the difference between the supplier quantity and the customer quantity.

Using condition techniques is not a standard configuration. This is used only when user-specific consensus rule have to be used and to override the default settings. The condition techniques are defined based on parameters such as:

- ▸ Customer

- ▸ Supplier

- ▸ Product

- ▸ Order document type

- ▸ Ship-to location

As mentioned above, SAP SNC uses the standard CD_QTY_AVG consensus rule to calculate the consensus baseline demand forecast as the average of the sales forecasts of the customer and the supplier. However, when by design or through observation, the customer forecast is found to be more accurate than the supplier forecast or vice versa, then instead of calculating the plain average of the two through rule CD_QTY_AVG, a user-defined rule can be formulated using condition techniques based on the above-mentioned parameters to improve the accuracy of the consensus forecast.

Condition records are to be created and then assigned to consensus rules for the parameters listed above. Consensus finding then uses the condition technique to determine the appropriate consensus rules.

7.6.4 Collaborative Sales Forecasting Process

The CSF process in SAP SNC consists of various steps. The initial step is that a customer sends daily or weekly forecast data in the form of a PFN or PFRN XML message to CSF of SAP SNC, and sends a product activity notification XML message indicating the daily sales forecast data.

In the supplier-led process variant, the customer's daily forecast data is aggregated and stored as weekly time buckets upon receipt in CSF. In the customer-led process variant, the customer's daily forecast data is stored as daily time buckets upon receipt in CSF. The forecast data sent by the customer forms the customer baseline forecast in CSF. The key figure Customer Baseline Sales Forecast displays the customer forecast data.

The forecast calculated through the forecasting functionality of SAP SNC using the statistical tools and techniques is then released to CSF as the supplier baseline forecast. The key figure Supplier Baseline Sales Forecast displays the supplier forecast data.

The menu path to access CSF in the SAP SNC web interface is DEMAND • COLLABORATIVE SALES FORECASTING • SALES FORECAST DETAILS-PRODUCT VIEW (SUPPLIER) if you want to view the supplier variant or PRODUCT VIEW (CUSTOMER) if you want to view the customer variant.

The system automatically calculates the difference between the supplier and the customer forecasts based on the quantity profile for the consensus finding, in both quantity and percentage terms, and stores it in the Baseline Sales Forecast Difference key figure.

The next step is to execute the consensus finding. As shown in Figure 7.25, the consensus finding can be executed by selecting Run Consensus Finding in the web user interface of the CSF. The system displays the results of the consensus finding in the key figure titled Consensus Baseline Sales Forecast – Calculated. Based on the settings made for the tolerance levels and the color profile, the color of the cells is modified, which denotes the status of the consensus finding.

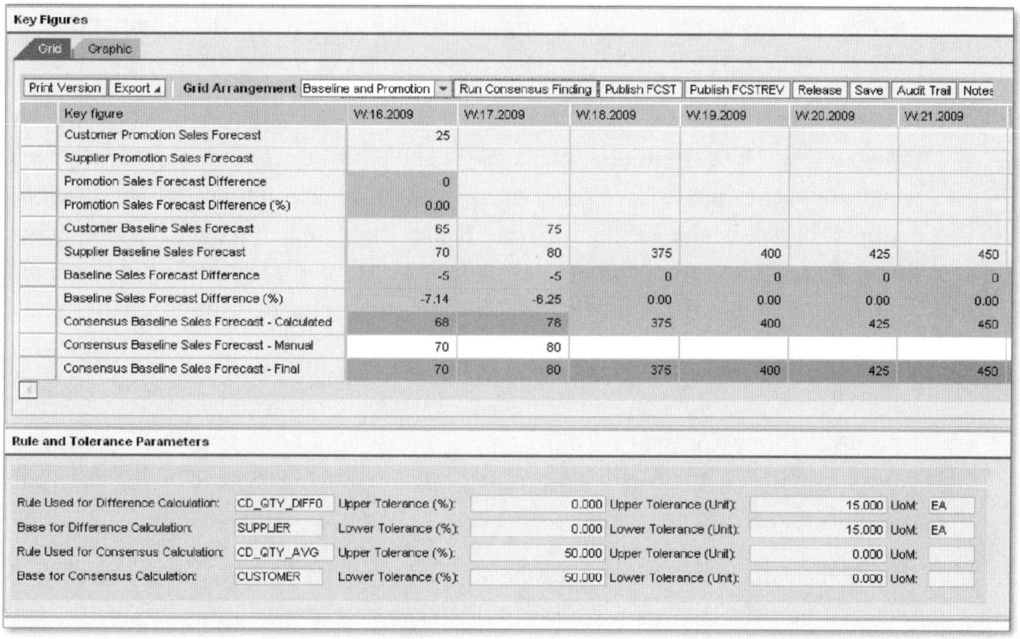
Key Figures

Grid | Graphic

Print Version | Export | Grid Arrangement: Baseline and Promotion | Run Consensus Finding | Publish FCST | Publish FCSTREV | Release | Save | Audit Trail | Notes

Key figure	W.16.2009	W.17.2009	W.18.2009	W.19.2009	W.20.2009	W.21.2009
Customer Promotion Sales Forecast	25					
Supplier Promotion Sales Forecast						
Promotion Sales Forecast Difference	0					
Promotion Sales Forecast Difference (%)	0.00					
Customer Baseline Sales Forecast	65	75				
Supplier Baseline Sales Forecast	70	80	375	400	425	450
Baseline Sales Forecast Difference	-5	-5	0	0	0	0
Baseline Sales Forecast Difference (%)	-7.14	-6.25	0.00	0.00	0.00	0.00
Consensus Baseline Sales Forecast - Calculated	68	78	375	400	425	450
Consensus Baseline Sales Forecast - Manual	70	80				
Consensus Baseline Sales Forecast - Final	70	80	375	400	425	450

Rule and Tolerance Parameters

Rule Used for Difference Calculation:	CD_QTY_DIFF0	Upper Tolerance (%):	0.000	Upper Tolerance (Unit):	15.000	UoM:	EA
Base for Difference Calculation:	SUPPLIER	Lower Tolerance (%):	0.000	Lower Tolerance (Unit):	15.000	UoM:	EA
Rule Used for Consensus Calculation:	CD_QTY_AVG	Upper Tolerance (%):	50.000	Upper Tolerance (Unit):	0.000	UoM:	
Base for Consensus Calculation:	CUSTOMER	Lower Tolerance (%):	50.000	Lower Tolerance (Unit):	0.000	UoM:	

Figure 7.25 Collaborative Sales Forecasting Screen

Depending upon the value displayed in the cells of the consensus finding key figures, one of the following operations can be performed. If all values show expected or acceptable values, then the calculated consensus forecast can be saved, and the system then copies the data into the key figure Consensus Baseline Sales Forecast – Final.

If values are over or below the expected or acceptable tolerance levels, the values are manually modified in the key figure Consensus Baseline Sales Forecast – Manual and Saved. The customer can give their inputs during the moderation of demand to obtain a more realistic demand value. The system then copies the modified data into the final CSF key figure.

7.6.5 Short-Term Forecasting Process

The short-term forecasting process is executed mainly to include any current or recent past conditions that form a basis for, or an enhancement to, the forecast. In SAP SNC, the results from the key figure Consensus Baseline Sales Forecast – Final are released to short-term forecasting, where the system displays forecast data in daily time buckets.

In the supplier-led process variant, the forecast data received from CSF is in weekly time buckets. The system disaggregates the data during release using the demand weighting factor of the forecasting process. The distribution pattern for disaggregation is based on the key figure Time Based Disaggregation Factors. The values for disaggregation are calculated based on the customer sales history data. These values can be modified manually to suit the user-specific distribution pattern.

In the customer-led process variant, forecast and planning is done on a daily time bucket level. Therefore, no additional disaggregation takes place when the final consensus forecast is sent to short-term forecasting. Short-term forecasting provides an interface that assists users to perform short-term forecasting for individual locations and products.

The menu path to access short-term forecasting in the SAP SNC web interface is Demand • Short Term Forecasting • Short Term Forecasting.

As shown in Figure 7.26, short-term forecasting consists of the following key figures:

▸ **History**

This key figure stores the sales data for a particular product at a given location over a particular period.

▸ **Stock-Outs**

This key figure can be calculated either by the system by executing the postprocessing framework, or the customer can send in the details in their product activity notification XML message. This key figure compares the sales data with the forecast, taking into consideration the inventory position at the customer location. If the forecast for a location product is higher than the sales, and if no inventory is maintained for that location product, then there is a stock-out situation.

▸ **Calculated History**

Calculated history is the sum of the sales data and the stock out value.

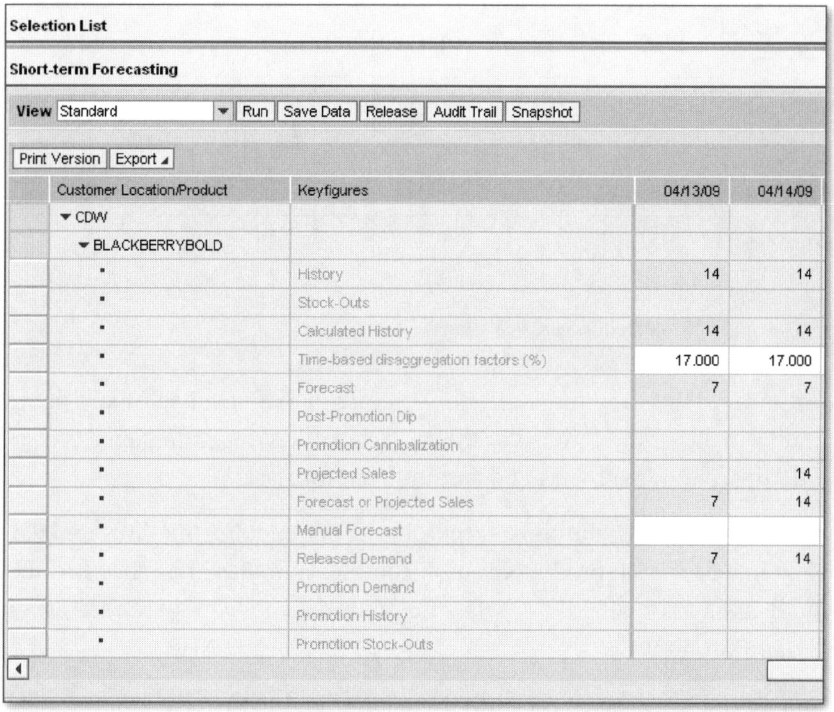

Selection List			
Short-term Forecasting			
View Standard ▼	Run	Save Data	Release	Audit Trail	Snapshot		
Print Version	Export ◢			
Customer Location/Product	Keyfigures	04/13/09	04/14/09
▼ CDW			
▼ BLACKBERRYBOLD			
▪	History	14	14
▪	Stock-Outs		
▪	Calculated History	14	14
▪	Time-based disaggregation factors (%)	17.000	17.000
▪	Forecast	7	7
▪	Post-Promotion Dip		
▪	Promotion Cannibalization		
▪	Projected Sales		14
▪	Forecast or Projected Sales	7	14
▪	Manual Forecast		
▪	Released Demand	7	14
▪	Promotion Demand		
▪	Promotion History		
▪	Promotion Stock-Outs		

Figure 7.26 Short-Term Forecasting Screen

In short-term forecasting, the projected sales key figure is calculated as the result of comparing the sales history (received in the data import controller) and the forecast values of the previous short-term forecast subperiods in the overall forecast period. The projected sales are based on the history and forecast key figure. In the short-term, sales are more reliable than the forecast.

The system calculates the projected sales for the location product in the following way: Initially, the system calculates the ratio of the cumulative sales and cumulative forecast. Then, starting with the current short-term forecasting period, the system multiplies the ratio calculated above with the corrected forecast of the short-term forecasting period. Figure 7.27 shows an example of how a projected sale is calculated.

	Total	Monday	Tuesday	Wednesday (Today)	Thursday	Friday
Corrected forecast	500	130	110	90	120	140
Sales		116	100			
Cumulative sales/ Cumulative forecast			0.9 (216/240)			
Projected Sales				81	108	126

Figure 7.27 Example of Projected Sales Calculation

In the short-term forecasting function, the Forecast or Projected Sales key figure stores the value of either the forecast or the projected sales, depending on a threshold and ratio of accumulated sales and accumulated forecasts.

As shown in Figure 7.28, in the short-term forecast parameters, the threshold values are maintained for each product-location combination. Based on the ratio and the threshold value maintained, the system determines the key figure forecast or projected sales as follows.

If the absolute value of 1 minus the ratio is greater than the threshold value maintained, the key figure Forecast or Projected Sales equals the projected sales. If the absolute value of 1 minus the ratio is less than or equal to the threshold value maintained, the key figure Forecast or Projected Sales equals the forecast.

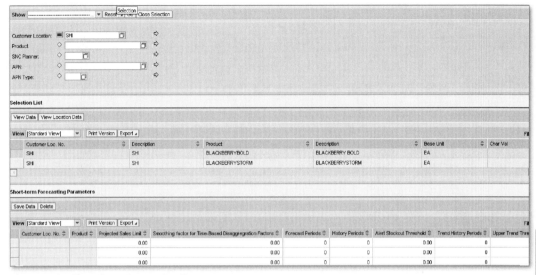

Figure 7.28 Short-Term Forecasting Parameters

The manual adjustment to the short-term forecasting is made in the key figure Manual Forecast. The forecast from short-term forecasting is released for the replenishment calculation. The quantity of demand in the key figure Released Demand is used for releasing the demand to the replenishment engine. If a manual forecast is maintained for a particular period, then the manual forecast gets copied to the released demand. If no manual forecast is maintained, then the forecast or projected sales quantity is taken. If nothing is entered, then SAP SNC takes this as a zero.

7.6.6 Replenishment Planning

In a replenishment planning scenario, the supplier is responsible for planning the inventory at the customer location and replenishing the stock according to the set norms in a timely manner. In SAP SNC, the supplier can use the replenishment planning functionality to determine the quantity of products that has to be delivered periodically from the supplier location to the customer location to cover the demand at the customer on time. The input for the replenishment planning is the data that is obtained from the customer such as stock, customer forecast, and customer sales data.

As a result of the replenishment planning by the supplier in the SAP SNC system, planned receipts are created. The Planned Receipts key figure represents the quantity of product that is to be delivered at the customer location for every period until the end of the period considered in the replenishment planning run. The system proposes planned receipts (depending on the replenishment planning method) so that the project stock reaches a certain value and the planned receipts are stored in the planned receipt key figure.

The Projected Stock key figure provides information about the demand-stock balance for a customer location and product in a period. It represents the product quantity that, according to planning, is available at the end of every period at the customer location. The projected stock considers the current stock on hand and various demands and receipts. The supplier must plan the planned receipts in such a way that the projected stock represents the replenishment requests of the customer.

The replenishment planning run in SAP SNC can be executed by the supplier, using a replenishment service, periodically in the background with a planning service manager (PSM) run. The planned receipts that are created as a result of the planning run are saved in SAP SNC as planned replenishment orders (orders of the order document type DRPV). The supplier can use the TLB service to be able to load means of transport according to certain criteria. From the planned replenishment orders, the TLB service creates TLB shipments (orders of the order document type TLBO), which are assigned corresponding replenishment orders (orders of the order document type VGOR).

When the supplier publishes a replenishment order in SAP SNC, SAP SNC sends the replenishment order to the supplier backend system (optional) and to the customer backend system. Based on the replenishment order, a purchase order is created in the customer backend system, and a sales order is created in the supplier backend system. These orders are the binding basis for finalizing the replenishment process in the backend systems (for example, for the goods issue and for the goods receipt). For replenishment planning in SAP SNC, the replenishment order represents a firm receipt at the customer location.

7.7 Summary

Chapter 7 concludes the portion of the book dedicated solely to projecting demand. We examined statistical algorithms applied to historical demand data, leading indicators, and downstream demand data. We covered a number of customer collaboration scenarios in this chapter and reviewed a number of SAP solutions that can be used to address the various scenarios. In Chapter 10 we'll see how these can all be brought together.

Before bringing everything together, though, we need to look at how organizations attempt to impact demand with marketing and sales activities. These will be the subjects of Chapters 8 and 9, respectively.

In this chapter, you'll learn that SAP APO acts as an enabler for the marketing function to carry out the promotion planning process.

8   Marketing

In the previous chapters of this book, we concentrated on tools and methods to more accurately project the future shape of a market for a product over a period of time. In this chapter, we'll consider the planning and results of activities that organizations can undertake to influence the size and shape of this market.

A demand projection based on historical demand data and augmented with causal analysis of leading indicators, as well as visibility of downstream demand, can be a fairly good prediction of sales volumes. However, as you'll learn in Appendix A, the actual size and shape of the market for a company's products does not always correspond to the expectations by stakeholders and potential investors of the company's revenues and margins.

For corporate management teams who want to remain management teams, this means influencing demand to increase revenue, margin, or both to fill the gap between what demand projections predict they'll be and what stakeholders expect.

Because it's fairly simple to sell less or spend more, it doesn't really warrant a chapter in a book on demand management to cope with expectations that are short of current demand projections.

This leaves the rest of the chapter, then, to discuss methods by which you can impact demand by leveraging one or more of a number of techniques. There are probably as many techniques as there are management philosophies, so this list is not exhaustive, but it is representative.

8.1   The Gap Between Projections and Expectations

Revisiting Chapter 1 and our ill-fated hot dog cart vendor, the purpose of marketing is not to whip customers and consumers into a frenzy, driving them to buy as much of a product as they possibly can. Marketing encompasses multiple techniques that can help companies impact demand in such a way as to close the gap between current projections and expectation targets.

8.1.1   Pulling Demand Forward

The easiest method of increasing short-term demand is to borrow it from the near future, but as with borrowing money, an organization that does this generally pays for it with interest in the future. Figure 8.1 accurately captures this phenomenon. The straight line represents demand as it would naturally occur. Think about a product with a fairly stable demand such as store-brand diapers. Population growth causes an upward trend, but demand is stable. However, if a manufacturer were to offer a discount to a retailer or directly to consumers, they might stock-up their respective warehouses or closets, temporarily increasing demand. However, because babies aren't going through diapers any faster just because of a discount, it takes a while for the extra diapers stored in warehouses and closets to be "consumed." During that time, no one is buying diapers, which causes the drop in demand because that future demand was "cannibalized" by the earlier artificial increase. Any tactic that increases sales without increasing ultimate consumption will likely result in this predictable pattern of a temporary increase and a temporary drop.

To make up a $700 million projected shortfall in the first fiscal quarter (Q1), an organization offers its customers a 30% discount on $1 billion worth of product if they buy it before the end of the quarter. Customers with enough capital to afford the deal buy, but because nothing has been changed to increase the customers' consumption of the product, they need $1 billion less in the second quarter. As Figure 8.2 shows, pulling the demand forward a quarter costs the organization $300 million ($1 billion – $700 million) in revenue within the next quarter, expanding that quarter's projected revenue gap.

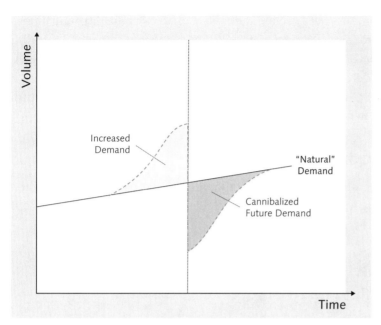

Figure 8.1 Pulling Demand Forward

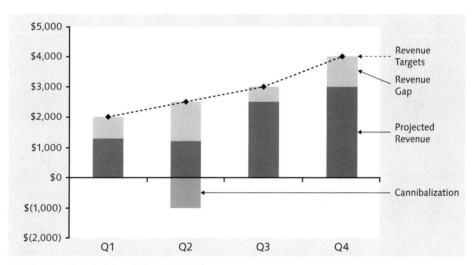

Figure 8.2 Cannibalizing Future Demand

This is, of course, a gross over-generalization. It could be that the discounted price actually made it profitable for customers to do any number of things on their own to impact their demand (which our manufacturer or distributor would see as consumption). It is rarely as simple as our initial example makes it out to be, but it tends to be true in a karmic sort of way that if all a company does is pull forward future demand, it will pay for it at some point in the future.

8.1.2 Increasing Your Market Share

In attempting to pull forward demand, it's possible that an organization could also increase its share of the market for one or more products at the expense of competitors (Figures 8.3).

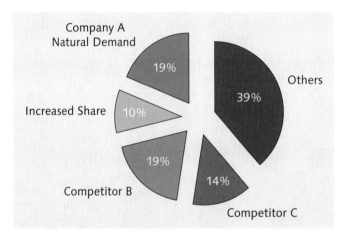

Figure 8.3 Increasing Market Share at the Expense of a Competitor

Customers may choose to buy more of your products at the lower price and fewer of your competitors' similar products. Whereas this is preferable because it reduces the amount of cannibalization from the next quarter (or whatever time period you might be pulling demand into), there are repercussions. Offering discounts that impact competitors' market shares can trigger price wars in which revenue spirals down in a destructive cycle, as shown in Figure 8.4.

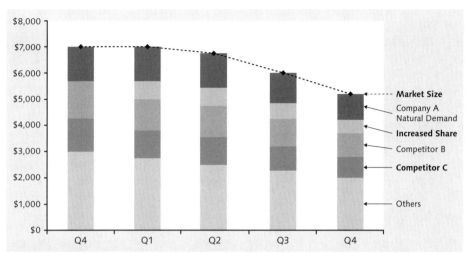

Figure 8.4 Destructive Price Discounting Cycle

Although driving a market into a discounting spiral can be a legitimate strategy for organizations with a significant cost advantage, it is unlikely that the eventual victor will be able to regain earlier price premiums. Logically, revenue gains made by increasing market share are more sustainable if they are the result of leveraging an organization's strategic advantage, such as a higher in-stock percentage resulting from better demand management processes, enhancements in sales techniques, or improvements in marketing activities.

Growing the Market for Existing Products

Supply chain, sales, and marketing techniques can also be used to increase the size of the overall market being served by a company and its competitors. In this case, the size of the entire market grows as new customers are indentified or new uses for products are brought to light. Figure 8.5 depicts the "rising tide" of an expanding market lifting the "boat" of each company competing in it.

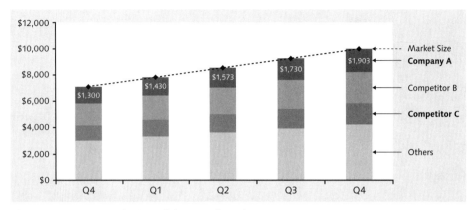

Figure 8.5 Increasing the Size of the Overall Market

In the example of a new use for existing products, the sales of one company's moisturizing cream exploded years back when common wisdom came to realize that it also repelled mosquitoes and other insects. This is a fairly unique case where the product transcended its initial market (skin care) and expanded into a completely different market (insect repellent). It is more likely that a company brings its products to a new geographic region such as opening outlets in Russia or begins to operate through a new channel such as Internet sales. In both of these cases, the organization is able to reach customers who had previously not known of or not had access to such products.

Expanding the Product Portfolio

New products are the growth engines of some companies and indeed of entire industries. Media, high-tech, and consumer products are examples of industries whose growth is driven by innovation. This could be growth in the market by creating an entirely new segment, as high tech has seen with the advent of inexpensive, smaller netbook computers, or it could be growth in individual market share by finding an interesting new flavor such as chipotle (smoked, dried jalapeno chili) for your products. Figure 8.6 shows a product portfolio being continuously expanded to meet revenue targets.

Innovative bundling of existing products can also help increase sales or potentially rejuvenate lagging sales of existing brands. Video game manufacturers often package aging console platforms together with a number of popular games to spur sales. Figure 8.7 is a simplistic example of growth through product bundling.

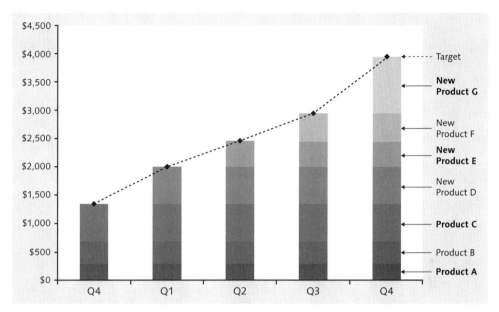

Figure 8.6   New Products Driving Growth Revenue

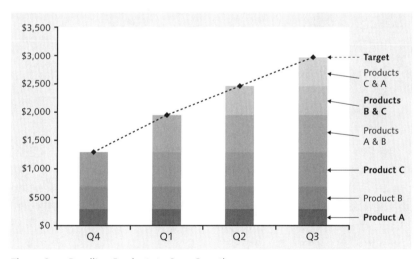

Figure 8.7   Bundling Products to Spur Growth

To make the prior two examples more realistic, though, we need to add an element of cannibalization. When a company launches a new product, it frequently steals demand away from some of that company's other products in addition to increasing sales.

To use a breakfast cereal example, whereas each new flavor of Cheerios® attracts new customers, it likely also draws some customers away from the other flavors. Figure 8.8 illustrates the impacts of cannibalization.

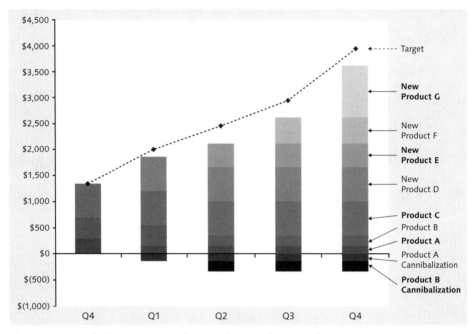

Figure 8.8 Cannibalization Impacts the Contribution of New Products

Outside of the expenses in research and development along with marketing incurred by launching a new product, organizations also need to contend with the impact of an ever-increasing number of items that this product proliferation brings to their demand management processes. Each new product requires its own forecast and all of the data maintenance, statistical algorithms, and collaboration that comes with it.

This challenge is compounded when each new product is not just a single product, but an entire line of new products. A new flavor of soda is not just a single new product, but a legion of them. It is a new flavor multiplied by all of the existing sizes (10 oz. can, 12 oz. bottle, 2 liter bottle, 500.mL can, fountain canister, etc.) packaged in all of the languages required where it will be sold. Demand projections for each of these products, or stock keeping units (SKUs), as they are called in the consumer products industry, must also be made for each channel (restaurant, convenience store, grocery store, mass merchant, etc.), and each of these characteristics value combinations can impact one or more others for existing products through cannibalization.

Beyond the time and expense associated with demand management for new products, incremental supply chain expenses are associated with them as well. Each new product requires additional buffer inventories of safety stock to compensate for variance (forecast error) between the demand projection and the actual sales. Many new products, at least those that are extensions of other products, create less demand than the existing product on which they were based. Coupled with the cannibalization they cause those base products, the number of orders and size of orders for both the new and base product are smaller than those of the original base product. Lower volumes and a smaller set of data points can reduce the statistical significance of demand projections, which leads us to a conclusion already intuited by demand managers the world over: Each new product, especially when it is an extension of an existing product, increases costs at a greater rate than the one before it.

Of course, expenses have nothing to do with revenue growth. Organizations willing to increase expenses disproportionately will most likely be able to "buy their way" to increased revenues — at the expense of their profit margins. Although this can be a legitimate business strategy for any number of reasons (including trying to get to a critical mass in order to enjoy economies of scale, attempting to secure a spot in an explosive new market experiencing a "land rush," etc.), more often than not, it is short-sighted. To balance revenue and margin growth, organizations need to not only engage in the strategies mentioned so far in this chapter, but to simultaneously improve demand management and other corporate processes.

Changing the (Product) Sales Mix

Alternatively, there are strategies organizations can use to focus on increasing profit margin. One of these strategies is to manipulate the amounts of individual products that are being sold. By changing the product sales mix, companies can sell more of the products that offer higher profit margins and fewer of the products that offer lower margins or even cost money to produce.

Choosing to sell less of any product can negatively impact a company's ability to grow its revenue, but in some cases where the product involved is consuming manufacturing or distribution capacity, which could be used to bring higher value products to market, it can lead to growth in both margin and revenue.

Another benefit of manipulating the sales mix is that it allows for the reduction or elimination of unprofitable or less profitable products, which slows the proliferation of new products and its associated complexity and expense. However, the long-term possibilities must be balanced with the short-term impacts. Some new products, especially those forging new market segments or opening new geographic regions, are strategic for their organizations. These products must be kept in the market, even when sold at a loss, to ensure a pipeline of future revenue.

Improve Margin with Customer Profitability

Like products, some customers are more profitable than others. The profitability of a customer is dependent on a number of characteristics. Customers who frequently order small volumes of large numbers of products through nonstandard or premium protocols and constantly return excess, obsolete, or damaged products are likely to be far more expensive than customers who order full containers of single products with advanced notice through automated means.

Using analytical tools applied to customer relationship data, some organizations can even identify groups of customers that cost more money than they bring in. As with sales mix, this analysis can be facilitated by a companywide ERP system and processes like activity-based costing to correctly attribute and capture costs associated with making and delivering these products and serving these customers.

Similar to removing products from the sales mix, culling customers is an activity that must take into account marketing strategy in addition to the more tactical customer profitability. Customers that offer unique access to strategic market segments or customers poised to grow (whether organically or through mergers and acquisitions) may be worth serving even at a loss for a time.

Mergers, Acquisitions, and Divestitures

Mergers and acquisitions are yet another means by which companies can change their revenue and margin outlooks. Target organizations can be sought for their existing product portfolio, access to and command of key markets, new product pipeline, or any other of a number of reasons. Regardless of the motivation, once the companies have been brought together, it is likely that many if not most of the other strategies listed above will be executed to promote the best of both.

Partnerships

Whereas we have discussed leveraging the sales of complementary products to better project sales of our own products, actively working with partners to jointly promote the sale of such products is slightly more advanced. Partnerships like this can be used simply to take advantage of the strong mind share and or market share of a certain component product (such as the Intel® chips made famous by Intel Inside® advertising or cake mix that gets a marketing boost by being able to boast that it is made with Jell-O® pudding), or it could actually provide synergistic benefit. A set of juggling balls sold together with a book on juggling might be such an example. Partnerships like this involve collaborative planning, similar to what we discussed in Chapter 7.

8.2   The Four Ps of Marketing

We've discussed the contribution of different products to a company's revenue, commonly known as the *sales mix*. In the early 1960s, a Harvard Business School professor named Neil Borden suggested a combination of activities or tactics that a company could perform to influence demand. In keeping with one of the marketing mantras of this era, Borden alliteratively named this a *marketing mix*, which he further described as the four Ps of marketing: product, pricing, placement, and promotion. Together, these have become the core of marketing in many, if not most, organizations today.

8.2.1 Product

A common marketing activity is to define the product being sold. It doesn't matter if this is done in a department called research and development reporting to a marketing vice-president, or product portfolio management reporting to a sales vice-president. Product is one of the 4 Ps that define marketing. It can be confusing that the proportion of certain products that a company sells is called the *sales* mix, even though it is a *marketing* activity; this apparent contradiction may explain why not all of us get into Harvard.

Regardless of what it is called, the process of defining and launching new products or tweaking the composition of existing products can be crucial to increasing market share, market size, or most of the other strategies for positively impacting demand. Even mergers and acquisitions can often revolve around a key selection of products. The textbook definition of product is a component of the marketing mix and includes the inherent services delivered with the product, such as product support, guarantees, and so on. It could be argued that for some products, improvements in spare parts availability or trained technicians could be perceived by the market as an improvement in the product.

Whereas aspects of a product can be quantitative (i.e., a 90-day warrantee versus a one-year warrantee), the majority of a product's aspects are qualitative. This makes manipulations of the aspects of individual products or the launch of extensions on an existing product line more difficult to quantify when it comes to projecting the impact of the change on future demand. Organizations with a broad product set and deep histories can compare similar modifications or extensions, such as assuming that chipotle tortilla chips might follow the same demand path as previously launched chipotle salsas. This was discussed in Section 5.4, Like Using Like-Modeling and Phase-In/Phase-Out to Support Product Planning Across Its Lifecycle.

8.2.2 Pricing

If product is seen as "what you get," then pricing can be understood as "what you paid for it." Whereas pricing is far from simple and very much an art and a science in and of itself, its nature is mostly quantitative, which makes it much easier to apply to demand management. Price increases or discounts can be known ahead of time, making them ideal leading indicators, as discussed in Chapter 6.

With the advent of enterprise resource planning solutions and the insights offered by business analytics tools, the prices of your products is becoming only a component in what your customers may see as the total cost of purchasing your product. Other implications that a customer might consider include the amount of buffer stock of your products that they need to hold as safety stock to prevent production line halting stock-outs and the lead time between order and delivery.

This redefining of price is unfortunate in that again it introduces qualitative measures and even subjective measures such as quality and "ease of doing business with," which are more difficult to model in projecting demand. The silver lining in this trend is, however, that for many customers price is no longer seen as the sole variable in the decision to purchase your product against a similar offering by a competitor. Organizations choosing to invest in improving their demand management, sales, and logistics capabilities can generate returns in the price premiums resulting from shorter order cycles and fewer out-of-stocks.

8.2.3   Placement

With a global information network making your products only a few clicks away and global (or at least very far reaching) parcel post logistics networks that bring more manufacturers' goods closer to more markets than ever before, placement might seem to be in danger of simply becoming the intersection of pricing and promotion (i.e., all products are available everywhere once they are promoted on the Internet, with only variances in their delivered costs.)

With today's shorter manufacturing cycles and lean inventories for customers and immediate gratification expectations from consumers, though, there is still some advantage to being "at arm's reach of thirst," which was once a goal, arguably now realized, of a popular beverage company. During the heightened security immediately following the terrorist attacks on the United States of September 11, 2001, automobile assembly lines that were normally within an hour's drive of their suppliers were forced to idle while waiting for components and materials to come across the border of the United States and Canada.

Whereas "on campus" placement, made popular by innovative companies like Dell, are long-term marketing decisions, organizations can execute strategies in the short term as well. Decisions to offer products in new geographic regions, such as developing countries or through new sales channels such as resellers or

Internet-based sales, can be made more quickly than building a new production or distribution facility. Even collaboration with customers that gives preferred placement within their warehouses or retail outlets can significantly impact demand, as anyone who has picked up a box of something that wasn't on their list but was at the end of the grocery aisle can attest to.

From a demand management perspective, projecting the impact of placement-based tactics can be assisted by leveraging like-modeling for similar regions or products that have already been offered through the new channels. For longer-term commitments, it is possible that customers will have committed to contractual minimums or otherwise be offering collaborative information to improve demand projections.

8.2.4 Promotion

"Whiter than White…," "New & Improved…," "Operators are standing by…." Promotion is the portion of the marketing mix that most people would identify as marketing. Advertising is just one component of promotion, which in turn is just one component of the marketing mix, but by its nature it is the most commonly recognized.

Advertising is replete with quantitative metrics that lend themselves well to demand projection. In an efficient market for advertising, $1 spent on radio should have an equivalent impact to $1 spent on the Internet, TV, or print, making incremental ad spending a good leading indicator of demand impacted. Other measures might be the number of "eyeballs," "click-thrus," or downloads.

Chapter 6 explored turning leading indicators like this into statistical projections of the impact on demand. Less ably modeled are promotion-related attributes such as brand, word of mouth, and product placement in popular media.

Whereas the branding of a product logically extends across a broad enough subset of other products that like-modeling can be applied, word of mouth and product placement can be unique to an individual product or even unique to a particular product within a unique market segment. Especially within highly networked markets such as consumer products in developed countries or exceptionally dynamic markets such as high-tech sub-components, word of mouth and product placement can lead to such discontinuities that they might best be used not to estimate impact but rather to direct downstream demand signal detection to watch for breakaway hits.

8.3 Promotions in SAP APO

Promotions in SAP APO are used to record the effect of promotions and other planned special events on the demand.

8.3.1 Promotion Planning Process: Overview

The first step in the promotional planning process is to review the market situation to understand the customers and the opportunity area for which the promotional activities can be carried out. The next step in the process is to set up the overall sales promotion budget along with the SMART (specific, measurable, achievable, relevant, and timely) objectives in place. The final step is to develop promotion strategies and schedule the promotional activities.

Certain key decision factors have to be considered during promotion planning.

1. How much should be spent on promotional activities, and for which markets and product lines?

2. At what level should the promotions be carried out — at the product and region level, at a brand level, at a product group level, or at some other level?

3. What is the definitive time period for which the promotional activities will be carried out?

4. What is the performance measurement criteria for a promotional activity with respect to the outcome and its impact on the other product lines?

In SAP APO Demand Planning, promotions and other special events can be planned separately from the rest of the demand forecast and can then later be reintegrated into the consensus demand plan. The promotion planning functionality can be used to record any type of promotional activities or events designed to impact demand. Examples of such activities include quarterly advertising campaigns, trade fairs, trade discounts, dealer allowances, product displays, coupons, contests, free-standing inserts, and so on.

8.3.2 Promotion Base

A *promotion base* in SAP APO specifies characteristics such as product, brand, product group, region, and location, which are used for planning promotions. Each promotion base should contain at least one characteristic, which specifies the level at which promotion planning is carried out and is known as the promotion level. The promotion base forms the basis for multiple promotions that are to be planned in the system. The system allows a user to define more than one promotion base, each with a specific start and end date, and assign each of these promotion bases to different individual promotional key figures.

You can access the promotion base in SAP APO Demand Planning by following the menu path DEMAND PLANNING • PLANNING • PROMOTION • SETTINGS • MAINTAIN PROMOTION BASE, as shown in Figure 8.9.

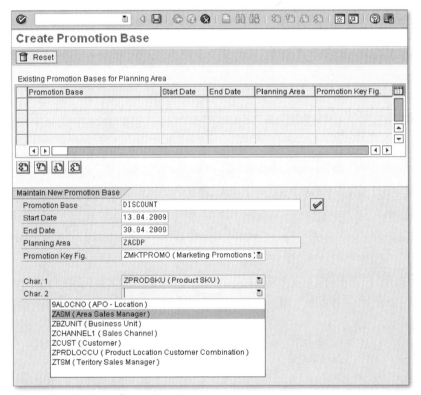

Figure 8.9 Creation of Promotion Base

The first step in the procedure for creating the promotion base in SAP APO is to name the promotion base that is to be created. The system automatically enters the planning area and promotion level. The next step is to add other fields such as validity dates for the promotion base. Validity dates specify the time period for which the defined promotion base will be active. Then the promotion key figure is assigned to the promotion base. There cannot be more than one identical promotion base in a planning area. This means the validity periods of two promotion bases cannot overlap if the same promotion key figure is used. However, it is possible to use a second key figure for identical characteristic combinations and identical or overlapping validity periods.

The final step in the process is to assign the characteristics that should be considered for promotion planning to the promotion base. The system automatically assigns the promotion-level characteristic to the promotion base, and this assignment cannot be deleted. In addition to the promotion-level characteristic, other characteristics from the planning area can be assigned to the promotion base using the dropdown box.

> **Note**
>
> You should only add characteristics that are relevant and are used in the promotion planning, and keep the number of characteristics less than 20 for performance reasons.

8.3.3 Cannibalization Group

As we discussed previously, cannibalization refers to a reduction in the sales volume, sales revenue, or market share of one product as a result of the introduction of a new product. Cannibalization is not limited to products but can be the result of overlapping sales territories as well, such as when a retailer opens outlets too close to each other. Much of the market for the new outlet is drawn from the existing outlet.

Cannibalization groups are used to model the impact of a promotion on sales of related products. The cannibalization group can be specified while creating a promotion for a product. The promotions for other products in the cannibalization group are calculated automatically. The prerequisite for using the cannibalization group is that the characteristic of the product is to be included in the planning book, and the products that are used in the cannibalization group should have the product master data in SAP APO. Figure 8.10 highlights the maintenance of cannibalization groups.

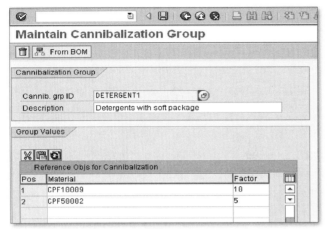

Figure 8.10 Maintain Cannibalization Group

In SAP APO, you can access cannibalization groups by following the menu path DEMAND PLANNING • PLANNING • PROMOTION • SETTINGS • MAINTAIN CANNIBALIZATION GROUP.

To maintain a cannibalization group, you need to create a cannibalization group ID along with its description as shown in Figure 8.10. In the table Reference Object for Cannibalization, enter the products whose sales are affected. The impact will be positive for some products and negative for others.

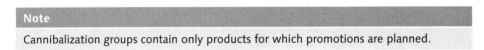

Cannibalization groups contain only products for which promotions are planned.

8.3.4 Create Promotional Planning in SAP APO

Certain prerequisites should be met before creating promotions in SAP APO. When you use Demand Planning Administration, key figures for storing the values of baseline forecasts and promotion plans should be included in the planning area. In SAP APO the key figures are added to the planning area during the initial planning area configuration using the menu path DEMAND PLANNING • ENVIRONMENT • ADMINISTRATION OF DEMAND PLANNING AND SUPPLY NETWORK PLANNING.

Select the Planning Area and move the promotion key figure (i.e., Marketing Promotion) as shown in Figure 8.11 to the left to include in the planning area.

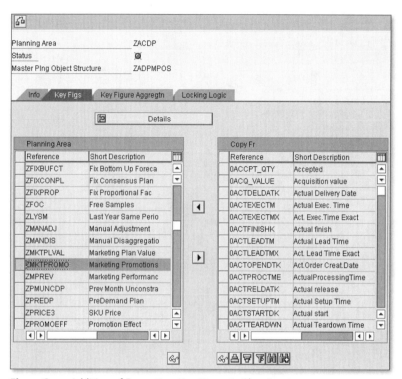

Figure 8.11 Addition of Promotion Key Figure in Planning Area

The promotional value is stored in the promotion key figure. If promotion is defined as a percentage, then the system converts it into an absolute number before storing it. To view the promotional values stored in the promotion key figure, the promotion key figure needs to be included as a row in a data view of the planning book.

The promotion key figure determines the key figure to which the promotion value is written after the promotion is activated.

The lowest level of detail, or the promotion level at which the promotion is saved, needs to be defined for each key promotion figure that is used in the planning area. In SAP APO the promotion key figure and level can be maintained using the menu path DEMAND PLANNING • PLANNING • PROMOTION • SETTINGS • MAINTAIN PROMOTION KEY FIGURES.

The Planning Area, Promotion Key Figure, and Char. for Promotion Level can be defined as shown in Figure 8.12.

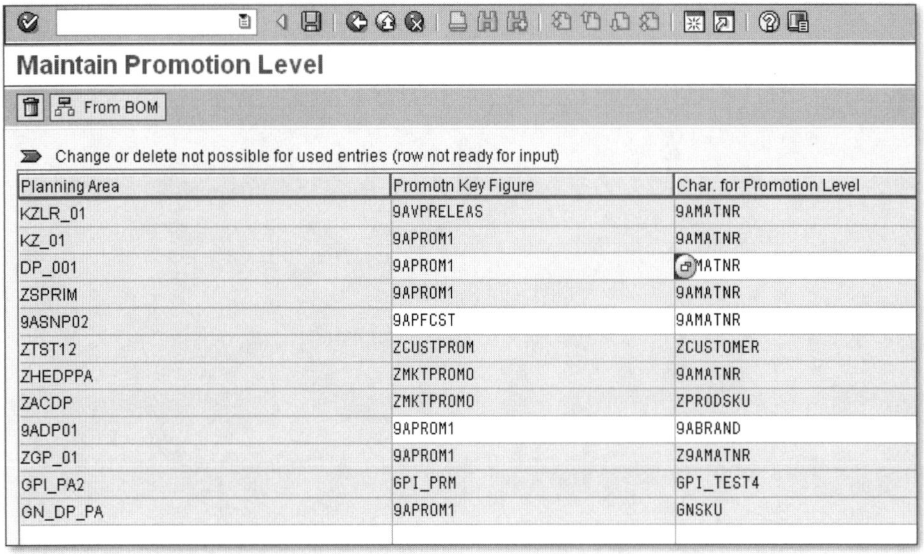

Figure 8.12 Maintain Promotion Level

The promotion attribute type, which groups together promotions with similar attributes, also needs to be defined. These promotion attribute types are used as a filter for selection and reporting purposes. Promotion attributes can be created in promotion planning by entering values for each of the promotion attribute types being defined. Figure 8.13 highlights the maintenance of promotion attribute types.

You can define promotion attribute types in the SAP APO Demand Planning system by following the menu path DEMAND PLANNING • PLANNING • PROMOTION • SETTINGS • MAINTAIN PROMOTION ATTRIBUTE TYPES. There is no restriction on the number of promotion attributes that can be created for a particular promotion attribute type.

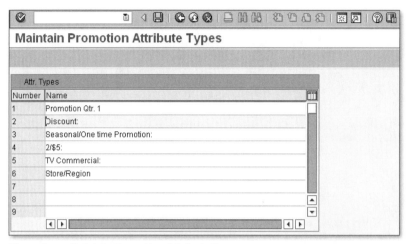

Figure 8.13 Maintain Promotion Attribute Types

If you're using interactive demand planning while you create the promotion, you should maintain parameters such as the name of the promotion, the promotion type, which denotes the absolute numbers or percentages of the baseline figures, a cannibalization group, a promotion base, the number of periods in the promotion, and the start or finish date in the interactive screen.

You access promotion planning in the interactive mode in the SAP APO Demand Planning system by following the menu path DEMAND PLANNING • PLANNING • INTERACTIVE DEMAND PLANNING.

In the demand planning book, promotions are created by clicking on the icon shown in Figure 8.14.

Figure 8.14 Promotions Planning Icon in Demand Planning Book

You can maintain promotion-related parameters interactively within the planning book as well, as shown in Figure 8.15.

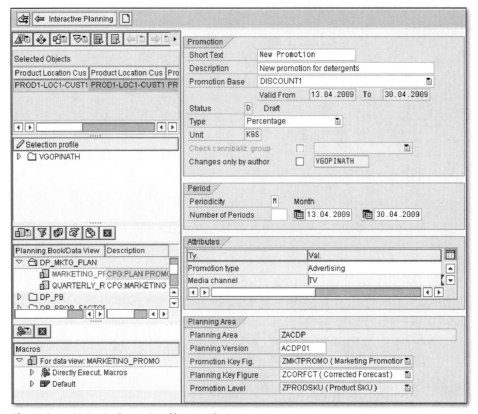

Figure 8.15 Maintain Promotion Planning Parameters

Enter the name and description of the promotion. The Promotion Base field is not mandatory. A promotion base consists of specific characteristics that can be assigned for the promotions. From here, take the following steps:

1. Define the type of promotion (Absolute or Percentage).

2. Optionally, make changes by the author only.

3. Select the periodicity for promotion maintenance.

4. Specify the promotion key figure, version, and planning key figure.

5. Save the promotion.

6. On the next screen, enter the promotion values. For % promotion, the system shows the value of the baseline forecast and based on the percentage, automatically calculates the promotion values.

7. On the next screen, select the characteristics you want to assign to the promotion and Click on Assign Objects.

8. Change the status of the promotion to Planned in Future, or Active in current periods. The promotion values will now be written to a live cache.

One way to use Promotion Planning in SAP APO is to create a baseline forecast in Demand Planning. This forecast can be reviewed and managed in interactive demand planning. Based on the settings and the parameters maintained, promotion plans are created. These promotion plans can be accessed through interactive demand planning. You can review the impact of promotions on total forecasted sales and make final adjustments to the total sales after taking into consideration the promotions during the consensus forecasting process.

8.3.5 Postpromotion Evaluation

SAP APO Demand Planning can reuse information from previously planned events. Postevaluation functionality modifies the actual data that is used as the basis for a forecast, taking into account the effects of a past promotion. The final forecast or the plan is comprised of two important components:

▶ Baseline forecast derived from statistical tools and techniques as well as changes from the demand planner using interactive demand planning

▶ Planned promotion for the short term

The actual sales data obtained after the promotional activities need to be "depromoted" to capture the accurate sales data without promotion. In SAP APO, the postpromotion key figure is used for this purpose. The system calculates this value as the difference between the actual sales data and the baseline forecast or plan. You make the settings in the univariate profile for forecasting. You can make the settings in SAP APO Demand Planning by following the menu path DEMAND PLANNING • ENVIRONMENT • MAINTAIN FORECAST PROFILE.

Select the relevant planning area and the master profile in the Master Profile tab and select the Univariate Profile tab as shown in Figure 8.16.

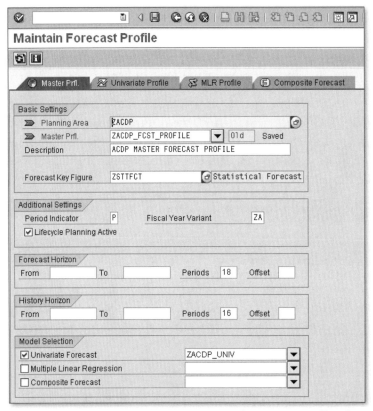

Figure 8.16 Select Planning Area and Master Profile in Master Profile Tab

The system corrects the key figures for producing the forecast in one of two ways:

1. If the Change values checkbox is selected, then the postpromotion values are subtracted from the actual key figure in the promotion period.

2. In the Univariate Profile tab, the promotion key figure is added, and you can select the Change Vals checkbox as shown in Figure 8.17.

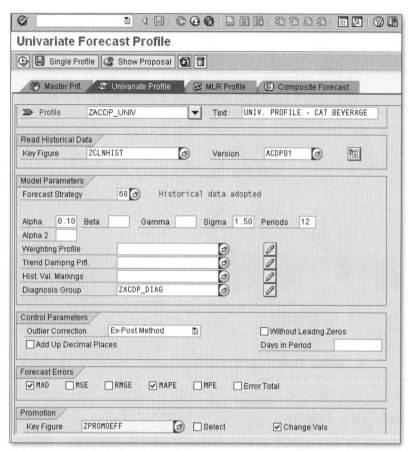

Figure 8.17 Select Change Value Checkbox and Include Promotion Key Figure

If the Select checkbox is selected, then the system selects all of the periods within the horizon of the promotion in the past and performs outlier correction for these periods. Any historical values that lie outside the tolerance lane are corrected. In this case you must also select the Outlier correction checkbox and make an entry in the Historical value markings field.

In the Univariate Profile tab, you add the historical value markings, set the outlier correction field, add the key figure for promotion, and select the checkbox for select indicator as shown in Figure 8.18.

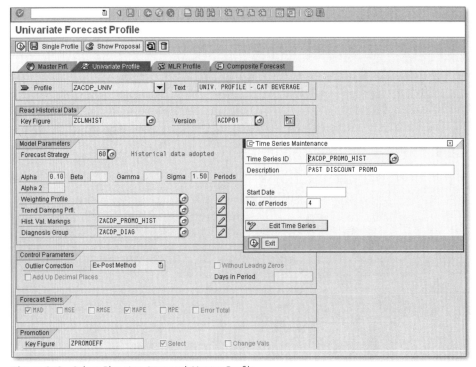

Figure 8.18 Select Planning Area and Master Profile

8.3.6 Promotion Reporting

This functionality allows you to report on promotions and other key figures in the planning area. The information is presented in table form and can include data from both detailed and aggregate levels. A promotions report contains one or more detailed reports. Promotion reporting can be done in conjunction with both promotions that are based on promotion bases and those to which no promotion base has been assigned. If you use promotion bases, then you can display the information on individual promotions. This is referred to as promotion analysis. In promotion reporting, you can also display promotion attributes. In addition, you can use standard macros to change the display of reports, such as changing the color of a key figure.

You can access settings for maintaining promotion reports (Figure 8.19) in the SAP APO Demand Planning system by following the menu path DEMAND PLANNING • PLANNING • PROMOTION • SETTINGS • MAINTAIN SETTINGS FOR REPORTING.

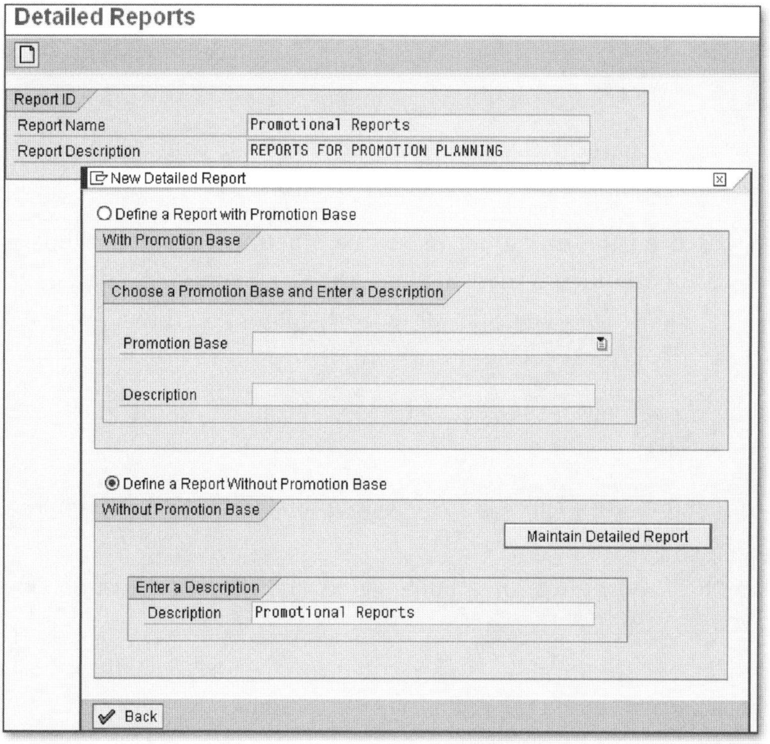

Figure 8.19 Maintain Settings for Detailed Reporting

The first step in creating the promotional report is to maintain settings related to planning area, version, and data view. Promotion reports are based on the data views in a planning area. The data view controls which key figures appear in a report and which time periods are displayed. Therefore, you should create a separate data view for reporting purposes where necessary key figures that are required for the reporting can be included. The next step is to create the general settings for the report, which includes the name and description of the report and the selection ID on which the report should run.

Once the report is named, you can define the settings for the detailed report. It can be based on a promotion base or exist without one. If the report is based on a promotion base, then you can select only the characteristics that are in the promotion base. If you select the Standard Settings option, the system copies all of the characteristics from the promotion base in the order in which they were defined, starting with the least detailed. If the report is not based on the promotion base, then the characteristics that are to be included in the report have to be selected individually. The order in which the characteristics are chosen determines the hierarchy of the characteristics in the report.

Select Display Object Values for characteristics for which the value is to be displayed. This checkbox is selected for at least one characteristic.

If the report is based on the promotion base case, then a second checkbox is available for the promotion-level characteristic: Display Promotion Analysis. If this checkbox is selected, then the values for individual promotions are displayed separately from those for the key figure in general.

After you've made the settings for the detailed reports, you can execute the report in three different modes:

1. Save, where the report is executed in the background, which can be scheduled, and the report can be viewed later.

2. Display, where the report is executed immediately and the data is lost on exiting the report.

3. Save and Display, where the report is executed immediately and the data is saved so that the report can be viewed again in the future.

8.4   Promotional Forecasting in Customer Collaboration

As discussed in Chapter 7, collaboration between trading partners can enable each party to get better insights into the market and lead to mutual success. Before planning promotions in a collaborative environment, trading partners must get on the same page. It is critical that they share information pertaining to promotional history, future promotions planned for different categories of products, and the vehicle for executing the promotional activities.

8.4.1   Promotion Planning in SAP SNC

Collaborative planning using SAP SNC was introduced in Chapter 7. The promotion planning function in SAP SNC allows partners to monitor the promotion results and plan and execute promotions in line with the dynamics of the market situation. The functionality in SAP SNC enables demand management analysts to display and change the planned promotion on the basis of collaborative inputs from customers. Both partners have the flexibility to move the planned promotions earlier or postpone them by changing the promotion dates. SAP SNC increases the visibility of the planned promotion because the trading partners can view the promotional data based on the location-product combinations and can analyze the effects of promotion in each of the specific areas.

The promotion planning functionality of SAP SNC can be accessed by following menu path SNC DEMAND • PROMOTION • PROMOTION PLANNING in the web UI. Demand, either through regular sales or promotions, is influenced by various factors based on the market conditions. Therefore, system-calculated promotions can and should be subjected to guidance from analysts at both partners to improve the quality of results. Taking this into consideration, SAP SNC offers the flexibility of manual override for promotional sales forecasts and order forecast quantities at the bucket level. Manual overrides are treated as final promotional quantities and have higher priority than the quantities calculated by the system. Manual changes are only possible for future time buckets. Planners can add the buckets for promotions at both the beginning and the end of promotion periods, and when the changes are made beyond the planned promotion period, the planned duration of the promotion is automatically extended. You can add the period for a promotion by clicking on the Change button as shown in Figure 8.20.

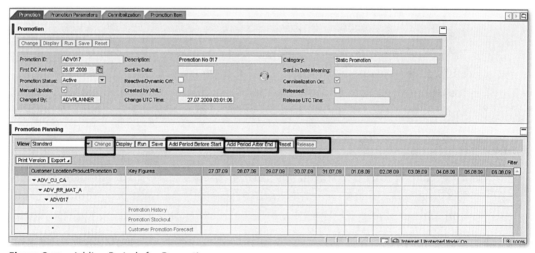

Figure 8.20 Adding Periods for Promotion

The planned promotion is then released to replenishment planning, and can be shared with the collaboration trade partner in the form of XML messages. On the SAP Easy Access screen, follow the menu path SUPPLY NETWORK COLLABORATION • TOOLS • SEND XML MESSAGES FOR TIME SERIES • SEND DEMANDINFLUENCINGEVENT-NOTIFICATIONS, as shown in Figure 8.21.

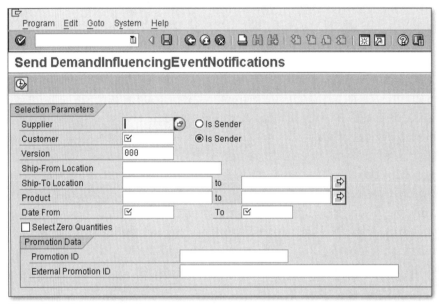

Figure 8.21 Event Notification

Before starting promotion collaboration, the customer and the supplier come to a basic agreement about the information that they'll exchange. For example, a customer can agree with a supplier that the customer will send only external promotion IDs by means of the XML message.

In the SAP SNC promotion collaboration process, a promotion is identified by a unique ID. The solution uses this information to determine the correct promotion ID from the promotion IDs that the customer sends in a Demand Influencing Event Notification XML message. This XML message can transmit both your internal ID and the customer's ID. If the XML message only contains the customer's promotion ID, the system checks if an existing promotion ID exists that already uses that buyer ID. If the system finds a match, it updates the promotion. If no promotion

ID exists for that customer promotion ID, the system creates a new promotion ID using the customer's promotion ID. The system can determine promotion IDs with your promotion ID only if the settings in Customizing are made appropriately. These settings define the content that is expected from the sender in a Demand Influencing Event Notification XML message. If the XML message does not transmit promotion IDs, SAP SNC can determine the promotion ID using the business add-in (BAdI) /SAPAPO/ICH_PROM_EXT.

The *promotion profile* is one of the promotion parameters assigned to a location or location-product combination. The promotion profile stores general promotion control parameters for the creation and handling of promotions. Promotion profiles are promotion independent.

The promotion profile functionality of SAP SNC can be configured by accessing the menu path SNC DEMAND • PROMOTION • PROMOTION PROFILE in the web UI.

As shown in Figure 8.22, to create a promotion profile, you must define a unique promotion profile name with the description and the promotion category.

Promotion Profile	
Promotion Profile	ADV_PROMOTION_PROFILE
Description	ADV_PROMOTION_PROFILE
Processing Type of Promotion	S
Promotion Pattern	
Sales Pattern	ADV_SALES_PATTERN
Distribution Pattern	ADV_DIST_RN_PATTERN
Dynamic Pattern	ADV_DYNAMIC_PATTERN
Post-Promotion Dip	
Settings for Reactive Promotion	
No. of Reactive Periods	
Threshold Value	
☐ Fix Total	
☑ Cannibalization for Promotion Product	
☑ Update Percentage Promotion	

Figure 8.22 Maintain a Promotion Profile

Processing Type of Promotion defines how the system tracks and responds to the actual promotion performance. Three possible categories exist:

1. **S (static promotion)**
   Promotions with fixed percentage distribution quantities per time period, which are applied to the total promotion quantity. The promotional quantities are not changed automatically during promotion execution. Manual changes are possible.

2. **D (dynamic promotion)**
   Promotions that are replenished with initial quantities, and then during the promotion execution replenishments are based on promotion sales. The only automated decision factor is the time of the replenishment, which should be determined based on reaching or exceeding thresholds (expressed as a percentage of total promotional quantity).

3. **R (reactive promotion)**
   Promotions based on initial distribution quantities that are then updated during promotion execution based on a comparison between expected sales pattern and actual sales The user can set the update to be either an adjustment of the total quantity or a redistribution of the remaining quantity.

If the appropriate patterns (sales, distribution, dynamic, and postpromotion dip) are already defined, then those patterns are included in the promotion profile.

There are two options for Promotion Profile Parameters:

▶ **Cannibalization for Promotion Product**
  This checkbox is used to turn the cannibalization on and off.

▶ **Update Percentage Promotion**
  The system reviews percentages and recalculates them by the current baseline forecast number.

A few settings for the reactive promotion are useful for you:

▶ **Threshold Value**
  Defines the threshold for the ratio between accumulated sales and accumulated expected sales (generated by applying a sales pattern to a promotion total). The promotion is adjusted only if the threshold is reached. The default value is 0.

▶ **Fix Total**
  If this checkbox is selected, the system does not adjust promotion totals accord-

ing to the ratio between accumulated sales and accumulated expected sales. For this option, the default is not checked. The number only applies to reactive promotions

8.4.2 Maintaining Promotion Patterns and Event Types

Patterns represent different behavioral sequences for a promotion. They specify critical promotional attributes that are required when a promotion is created. Because patterns are not date-specific, one pattern can be reused for many promotions.

The *event type* groups attributes of common promotion behaviors or types of promotions. Event types must exist before you create a promotion in the system because the system assigns promotion parameters to a location and product by event type.

Promotion Patterns

The promotion pattern functionality of SAP SNC can be configured by following the menu path SNC Demand • Promotion Parameters • Maintain Parameters in the web UI.

Various types of patterns can be maintained for promotions, namely, sales, distribution, dynamic, and postpromotion dip. *Sales promotion patterns* represent the promotion behavior, the daily (or more frequent) distribution of goods issued from the customer distribution center and, possibly, the goods received at the store level during the promotion. As shown in the Figure 8.23, sales patterns can be manually input or generated using report /SAPAPO/promotion_patterns_gen.

When the report is used for the generation of the sales pattern, the system retrieves historical data for a product-location–event type combination of past promotions and calculates the average value of all related promotions. Using this data, the system generates a sales pattern.

Dynamic promotion patterns incorporate the need to consume the available promotional inventory at the customer distribution center to a certain level before generating demand for the next replenishment run. The automated decision factor is the timing of the replenishment, which is determined based on reaching or exceeding sales thresholds expressed in percentages of total promotion quantity.

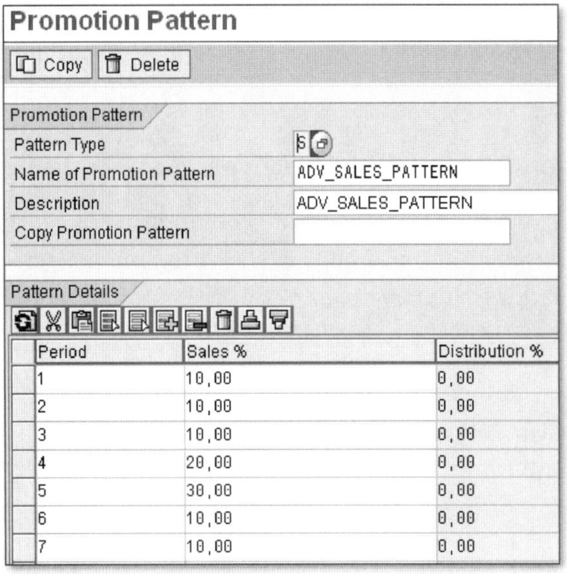

Promotion Pattern

| Copy | Delete |

Promotion Pattern

Pattern Type	S
Name of Promotion Pattern	ADV_SALES_PATTERN
Description	ADV_SALES_PATTERN
Copy Promotion Pattern	

Pattern Details

Period	Sales %	Distribution %
1	10,00	0,00
2	10,00	0,00
3	10,00	0,00
4	20,00	0,00
5	30,00	0,00
6	10,00	0,00
7	10,00	0,00

Figure 8.23 Maintain Sales Pattern

As shown in Figure 8.24, dynamic patterns are manually input and apply only to dynamic promotions. The percentage values for both Sales % and Distribution % are filled. The sum of all of the rows in the Distribution % column must equal 100%.

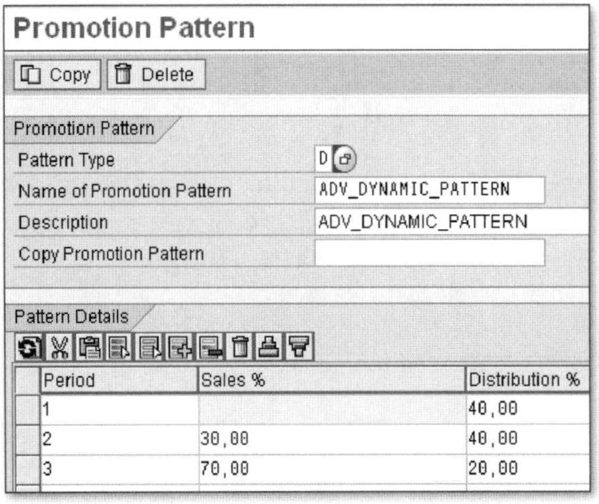

Promotion Pattern

| Copy | Delete |

Promotion Pattern

Pattern Type	D
Name of Promotion Pattern	ADV_DYNAMIC_PATTERN
Description	ADV_DYNAMIC_PATTERN
Copy Promotion Pattern	

Pattern Details

Period	Sales %	Distribution %
1		40,00
2	30,00	40,00
3	70,00	20,00

Figure 8.24 Maintain Dynamic Pattern

A *distribution pattern* defines what is necessary for efficient replenishment to occur during the promotion, for example, how the promotion goods are received at customer distribution centers (forward-buying to accumulate stock at distribution centers or agreements with customers to ensure a certain delivery cycle and quantity). The postpromotion dip pattern cannibalizes a product's baseline sale postpromotion, modeled using this pattern.

Event Types

The event type functionality of SAP SNC can be configured by accessing menu path SNC PROMOTIONS • PROMOTION PARAMETERS • MAINTAIN EVENT TYPES in the web UI.

As shown in Figure 8.25, a five-digit code is used for defining the event type, as well as the event type code.

Figure 8.25 Maintain Event Type

If the event type will be used in XML promotion messages, the event type code must be the same as the event type; otherwise, the event type code is optional.

8.4.3 Maintaining Offset Profile

The offset profile (Figure 8.26) is a summary containing a series of ten integers that correspond to ten typical events that occur during a promotion, such as the promotion start date or advertisement start date.

The ten events that comprise the offset profile are:

Offset for Internal Promotion Data:

▸ From First Arrival at DC Date to First Ship to Stores Date

▸ From Last Ship to Stores Date to Start of Post-Promotion Dip

Promotion Offset Profile

| Offset Profile | ADV_OFFSET_PROFILE | |
| Offset Profile Description | ADV_OFFSET_PROFILE | |

Offset for Internal Promotion Data

| From First Arrival at DC Date to First Ship to Stores Date | 3 |
| From Last Ship to Stores Date to Start of Post-Promotion Dip | |

Offset for External XML Data

1st Arr. at DC Date Based on Ship to Stores Date	
First Arrival Date Based on Purchase Order Date	
First Arrival at DC Date Based on First Ship to Stores Date	2

Figure 8.26 Maintain Offset Profile

Offset for External XML Data:

- First Arrival at DC Date Based on Ship to DC Date
- First Arrival Date Based on Purchase Order Date
- First Arrival at DC Date based on First Ship to Stores Date
- First Arrival at DC Date Based on Advertisement Date
- First Arrival at DC Date Based on Start Date in Store
- First Arrival Date Based on Last Arrival at DC Date
- First Arrival at DC Date Based on Last Ship to Stores Date
- First Arrival at DC Date Based on End Date in Stores

The offset profile can contain ten integers (offsets), each corresponding to one of the ten events above. These integers represent the number of periods for daily or subdaily promotion planning. The offsets 3–10 are used to convert the customer-entered promotion dates to First Arrival at DC Dates. It isn't necessary to maintain all of these offsets. Depending on what date the customer sends in, only the corresponding offsets are maintained. For example, if one customer always sends in the First Ship to Stores Date, you only maintain the offset number 5, first Arrival at DC Date Based on First Ship to Stores Date.

Once the system has the First Arrival at DC Date, it uses offset number 1 to calculate the First Ship to Stores Date Based on the First Arrival at DC Date. If no offset can be found for the date calculation, the system uses zero (0) as the offset.

8.4.4 Assigning Promotion Parameters

Promotion parameters can be assigned at two levels:

▶ Location-product

▶ Location

If the system cannot find a parameter at the location-product level, it automatically looks to the location level. Promotion parameters are not delivered with the standard system. They are created to fit the existing products and locations.

You can configure the assign promotion parameters functionality of SAP SNC by following the menu path SNC DEMAND • PROMOTIONS • SETTINGS• ASSIGN PROMOTION PARAMETERS in the web UI. As shown in Figure 8.27, the selection area is used to find the locations or location-products for which the promotions have to be planned. The selected location or location-product is displayed in the Select Master Data area. In the Promotion Parameters area, the event type, promotion profile, and offset profile specific to the location-product are given as input. Then the promotion parameters are assigned to either the selected location or the location products.

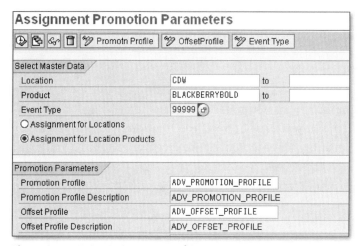

Figure 8.27 Maintain Assignment of Promotion Parameters

Manual changes, such as replacing promotion patterns or using another event type on an existing promotion, can be made. However, these changes are only possible for promotions that start in the future, not for ones that are currently running or have already run.

8.4.5 Create Promotional Planning in SAP SNC

The functionality of creating promotions in SAP SNC can create promotions for specific location-products. Multiple promotions can be created for one location-product, and one promotion can be created for multiple location-product combinations.

You can access the create promotion functionality of SAP SNC by following the menu path SNC DEMAND • PROMOTIONS • CREATE PROMOTIONS in the web UI. In the selection section of the screen, as shown in Figure 8.28, the details of the location-product are given as input for search criteria. You execute the search by clicking on the Go button. The system finds the appropriate location-products and displays them in the Selection List. You choose the item for which the promotion is to be carried out by selecting it.

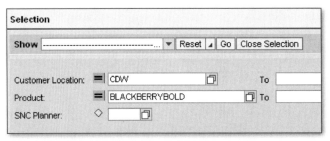

Figure 8.28 Selection for Promotion Creation

As shown in Figure 8.29, the system copies the items that you selected in the Selection List into Promotion Items. Optionally, you can manually add more location-products by using the Insert Line button. The total promotion quantity or percentage of baseline quantity for each item can be given as an input. If you enter both total and percentage, the percentage overrides the total. In the latter case, the system calculates the promotion total by multiplying the baseline forecast by the percentage that is entered.

As shown in Figure 8.30, the four dates — First DC Arrival, End DC Arrival, First Ship to Stores, and End Ship to Stores — define the dates on which the product is delivered to the customer's distribution center and the time period over which the product is delivered to the customer's stores. At least one of these dates needs to be specified. The other dates can be calculated using the offset profile assigned to the location-product.

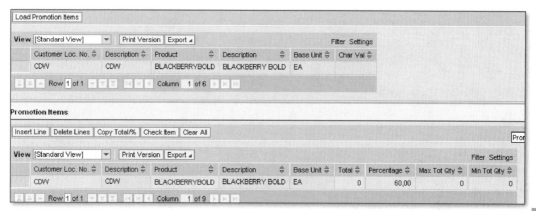

Figure 8.29 Promotion Items

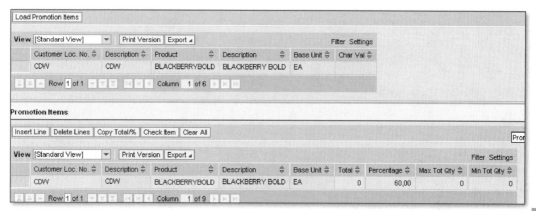

Figure 8.30 Promotion Data

Once you've filled in all of the requisite details for creating the promotion, you can create the promotion by clicking on the Create Promotion button.

As shown in Figure 8.31, after the promotion planning, you can track the promotion planning data. The dates for the End DC Arrival and other ship-to dates are calculated based on the First DC Arrival date.

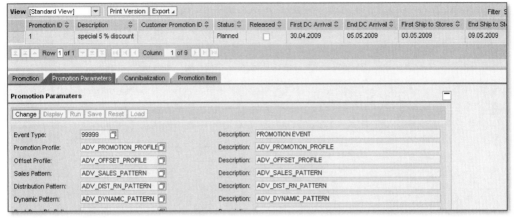

Figure 8.31 Promotion Planning Screen

8.5 Summary

In this chapter, we've seen that SAP APO acts as an enabler for the marketing function to carry out the promotion planning process. Using SAP APO Demand Planning, the promotion and other special events can be recorded independently and later merged with the consensus demand plan. The cannibalization effect of promotion on other products can also be taken into account. The postpromotion evaluation process allows the impact of promotions to be discounted from the actual sales while generating the statistical forecast. SAP SNC increases the visibility of the planned promotion and allows the partners to view the promotional data collaboratively.

Let's move on to Chapter 9, which covers how to impact demand through sales.

In this chapter, we'll discuss impacting demand through sales, and how SAP APO Demand Planning and Duet can help facilitate these processes.

9 Sales

A quick glance of the table of contents of this book would lead a reader to believe that only one chapter is devoted to sales. By the end of the book, or even by the end of the first chapter, you should recognize that sales is what the entire book is about. The demand in demand management is all about the sale or at least the potential sale.

If it were a game of baseball, then projecting demand would be all about bringing a sales executive through a pitch-black stadium, finding him a bat, getting him to home plate, and turning on the lights in time for him to swing at the pitch, which in this analogy would be the sales opportunity thrown by the customer. Impacting demand would be manipulating the pitcher to be more likely to throw a pitch when, where, and how your sales executive can hit it. Realizing demand, which comes a bit later, would be the moment when the pitcher throws the pitch and the sales executive swings, ideally knocking it out of the park.

Leaving behind the baseball metaphor, the sole reason for projecting demand is to prepare for the sale by getting the right amount of the right products to the right place at the right time and, if necessary, to drive more sales opportunities to achieve sales and profit targets. This chapter, however, focuses not on the process by which the sale is made, but rather on the feedback of the sales executive into the demand management process.

It's ironic that the one individual in the company with the broadest, deepest, and most detailed understanding of customers and their probable demand is the person with the least time to review and revise the projections of customers that will drive the rest of the organization. The secret to getting the crucial contribution of sales executives to the process, then, is to make their participation as intuitive and efficient as possible while offering insight, respecting that contribution, and delivering product to fill the orders they get.

9.1   Guidance, Incentives, and Information

Guidance, as you can see in Appendix A, is the expectations set by the company's executives with the financial analysts, shareholders, and potential buyers who make up the investment community. Whereas an organization's senior executives often seek guidance from sales executives and their managers, they know that the share price and frequently their continued employment depend less on accomplishing what their sales teams believe is possible and more on the financial market's expectations.

This top-line corporate revenue target is dissected by region, by business unit, by product contribution, and by about as many other ways as there are individuals who can be held responsible for influencing a customer's likelihood of buying. In the end, these targets lead to individual sales targets or quotas for individual sales executives.

Often the sales executive's compensation is structured around these quotas such that they are paid very little should they fail to reach their quotas and very generously when they exceed them. These financial incentives might be spread across groups or teams of individuals, and whereas it is possible that no financial incentives beyond positive reviews and potential promotions exist, it is very likely.

Historically it's unlikely that any sales executive having achieved a quota would be financially penalized or called to task for failing to close all of their projected sales volume. Put another way, financial incentives drive sales executives to predict any business that could possibly be closed in order to ensure that there will be inventory available to satisfy the order, but no penalties accompany the failure to close projected sales and the excess inventory and obsolescence that causes.

So although the sales executive is in the position to be the best arbiter of projected demand and the impacts of planned sales and marketing tactics on that demand, he is not always incentivized to clearly perform that task. That is not to say that anyone would act in a less than ethical manner, but to acknowledge the management adage, "You tend to get what you measure." For organizations that do not or cannot provide incentives that better balance revenue-and profit-margin-driving costs, Chapter 12 contains a section on identifying and compensating for biases in demand projections.

9.2   Configuring SAP APO Demand Planning for Sales Input

As mentioned in Chapter 2, demand planning is a process that falls within sales and operations planning and should not be done in isolation. The demand plan should be integrated with the business plan (see Appendix A) to meet both the corporate targets and the customer demand. The forecast obtained using the statistical methods can form a solid base for deducing the demand plan, but the real value comes from applying knowledge that systems cannot possibly have. Collaboration, both internal and external, needs to be deployed to obtain a realistic demand plan.

Imagine that someone with little to no knowledge about the customers and the pulse of the market decides alone on the demand plan. Such a situation would wreak havoc on an organization, resulting in low sales revenues, low customer satisfaction, and low profits. Sales officers and managers are the people in the organization who have a clear view of each customer account, including opportunities and problems within the account. Therefore, incorporating sales input into the demand plan is critical.

It is not necessary that the inputs from the sales and marketing teams be in complete agreement with the statistical forecasts. Here the demand planner plays a crucial role in consolidating their inputs and is responsible for developing a demand plan for review and consensus. If the input from the sales team were to come to a demand planner only as numbers, without supplemental information, then it would be difficult for the demand planner to make judgments on the proposed plan. However, if these numbers were backed by insights such as the market dynamics, economic situation, competitor's action, and so on, then it would enable the planners to understand the input, make judgment calls, and propose a consolidated plan.

Augmenting a demand plan with multiple inputs above and beyond statistical forecasts results in a more robust and reliable plan. The SAP APO Demand Planning component can incorporate sales input into the demand plan and contains advanced functionality to aggregate and disaggregate demand across different products and the organizational hierarchy.

9.2.1 Designing Planning Books and Layouts for Sales Input

As we saw in Chapter 4, in SAP APO Demand Planning, demand planners work with a planning book and then with certain data views within that book. The demand planning data can be viewed at different characteristic levels. In addition, the required key figures can be included in the planning book to view the forecasted and moderated quantity of the demand plan.

> **Note**
>
> The prerequisites for creating a planning book are that a planning area exists and a planning bucket profile has been created. The necessary key figures, such as the baseline forecast, which stores the value of the forecast generated by statistical models, and the sales input key figure, which stores the value of the input given by the sales, should already be defined in the system. The necessary characteristics for planning are defined and included in the planning object structure.

The path to access planning book design in SAP APO Demand Planning functionality is DEMAND PLANNING • ENVIRONMENT • CURRENT SETTINGS • DEFINE PLANNING BOOK.

In the planning book tab, the following details need to be specified:

1. The planning area on which the planning book is based.
2. A text (short description) for the planning book.
3. The applications and functions that should be accessible from this planning book.

As shown in Figure 9.1, the next step is to specify the key figures that are to be included in the planning book. In this case the Baseline Forecast and Sales Input key figures should be selected along with the other key figures.

> **Note**
>
> The key figures may be added to the planning book based on specific requirements. For a sales executive, the planning book may have the Baseline Forecast key figure for reference and the Sales Input key figure to input the sales forecast.

To add one key figure to the planning book, drag and drop it into the planning book icon on the left side of the screen. To add all key figures from the planning area in the planning book, click on the Select All icon at the bottom of the window.

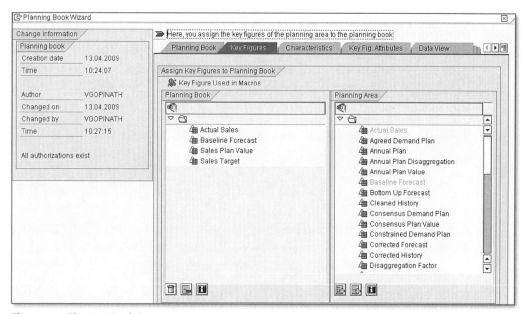

Figure 9.1   Planning Book Design

In the Characteristics tab, you can specify the characteristics that you need to include in the planning book. You can choose the characteristics from the list of characteristics that are already included in the master planning object structure on which the planning area is based. Examples of characteristics are region, product, and customer. To add one characteristic, drag and drop it into the planning book icon on the left side of the screen. To add all characteristics from the planning area to the planning book, click on the Select All icon at the bottom of the window.

In the Data View tab, you can create a data view for the planning book that is specific to the sales input. At least one data view should be present to use the planning book. Multiple data views can be defined for a single planning book. In the data view, the time bucket profiles for both the forecast period and the historical period are specified. This implies that time settings can be user-specific.

In the Key Figures tab for the selected data view, the specific key figure in the planning book, which will be used by the users of this data view, are included.

9.2.2 Assigning Users to a Data View

A sales team can have many personnel, and everyone can provide input into the demand plan. The data view for the sales team input is usually defined separately, with the specific key figures required for sales input included in the data view. The sales team is authorized to use only the planning book and the data view specific to the sales input. With regard to planning books and selections, the following authorization objects are particularly important:

- Planning Book: C_APO_PB
- Selections in Planning Books: C_APO_SEL3
- Functions in Supply Network Planning and Demand Planning (SDP): C_APO_FUN

A user accesses planning books from various transactions such as Interactive Demand Planning (/SAPAPO/SDP94) and Promotion Planning (/SAPAPO/MP34). For each of these transactions, a planning book and data view are assigned to a user.

A user can be restricted to a specified planning book or data view. To assign a user to a planning book follow the menu path DEMAND PLANNING • ENVIRONMENT • CURRENT SETTINGS • ASSIGN USERS TO PLANNING BOOK.

As shown in Figure 9.2, you click on the New Entries button to start with the assignment of a user to a specific planning book and data view.

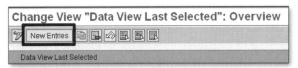

Figure 9.2 New Entries Button to Assign a User to a Specific Planning Book and Data View

Figure 9.3 illustrates how to add an entry to assign a user to a specific planning book and data view. To do this, enter the name of the user, the transaction code (i.e., /SAPAPO/SDP94), the planning book (i.e., DP_SALES_PLAN), and the data view (DP_STAT_FORECAST) and click on the Save button.

This way, you can limit a user's access to one data view in one particular planning book.

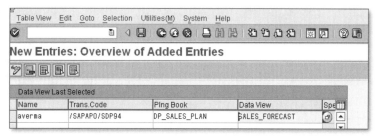

Figure 9.3 Addition of Entry to Assign a User to a Specific Planning Book and Data View

9.2.3 Creation of Consensus Demand Plan

The forecast developed using the statistical tools and techniques forms a "straw man," a working prototype from which the stakeholders of the organization can progress to a final consensus demand through debate and compromise. Demand Planning functionality supports both types of planning approaches:

▶ **Top down**
High-level planning that is disaggregated to the lowest levels. The rationale for the top-down approach is that the aggregated forecast is more accurate. The aggregated forecast can be derived across various groups such as product group and sales channel, and it can be disaggregated at the individual component level. The demand planner can generate the statistical forecast at a product group level and allow the statistical forecast numbers to disaggregate to individual products and accounts in proportion to their historic sales pattern.

▶ **Bottom up**
Planning is done at the lower level, and the demand is aggregated to the high level. The bottom-up forecast is provided by the sales executives for their own accounts. For instance, a sales person can enter a forecast to sell a specific product to a specific customer, say Dell, over the next six months. This forecast is at a product level and not at a higher level of aggregation. Once this information has been entered at the lower level, SAP APO enables its aggregation to higher levels, for example, forecast at the product group level for all customers.

Although the compilation and aggregation of disparate demand projections will be discussed in detail in Chapter 12, we'll provide a quick overview of how sales input is integrated into the consensus demand plan.

The sales team accesses the planning book to view the information that is required as an input to moderate the baseline forecast. The demand planning system then aggregates the demand at a higher level for the demand planner to review and arrive at the final consensus plan. The demand planner compares the multiperiod output of the statistically generated forecast to the collective sales forecast to analyze and understand exceptions. The alerting and the exception-based aspect of the demand planning functionality enable the demand planner to manage the forecast and incorporate the sales input into the final agreed plan.

To access planning book SAP APO Demand Planning functionality, follow the menu path DEMAND PLANNING • PLANNING • INTERACTIVE DEMAND PLANNING.

Figure 9.4 shows the planning book and the data view designed for the sales input. This is one of the many ways in which the planning book can be designed for the sales input and can be incorporated into the final demand plan.

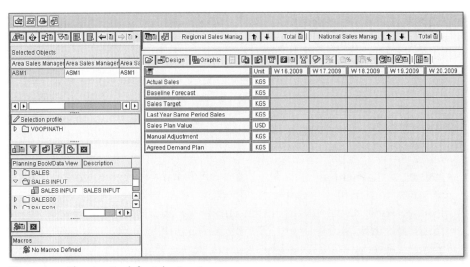

Figure 9.4 Planning Book for Sales Input

The key figures that are included in the sales input data view should provide the basic information to the sales team to enable them to modify the demand. A sample list of key figures is provided below:

▶ **Actual Sales**
Provides the history data over a period of time. The time frame for which the sales data is to be made visible depends on the user requirement.

▶ **Baseline Forecast**
Provides the forecast data that is derived through the statistical tools and techniques available in the demand planning.

▶ **Sales Target**
The sales team usually operates based on the target they have to achieve on a month-to-month basis. Providing information on the sales target in the planning book helps the sales team have visibility of their target over a period of time and is useful to them while moderating demand.

▶ **Last Year Same Period Sales**
Gives information to the sales team about the past sales for the same period for which they are providing input.

▶ **Manual Adjustment**
The sales team that is in close contact with the customer has the feel of the pulse of the market. They immediately detect any changes in the demand pattern in the market. The sales team incorporates these changes manually in the form of adjustments.

▶ **Agreed Demand Plan**
The total of the baseline forecast and the manually adjusted key figure.

As previously mentioned, the data view for the sales input can have different key figures from those mentioned in this list. The design of the data view for sales input is purely user and organization dependent. This is just one possible way of designing the data view. The Demand Planning functionality of SAP APO is flexible enough to cater to user-specific needs for creating the data view.

The process of developing a consensus demand starts with the sales team reviewing the current baseline forecast along with their sales target. The past year's historical input is available in the system and is used to enable the sales team to give their input.

The sales team then gives their sales input in the Manual Adjustment key figure, and final demand is arrived at by incorporating that input in the baseline forecast. The demand planner then aggregates both the sales input and the baseline forecast to a higher level and compares the sales input key figures and the system-generated forecast to arrive at a final consensus demand plan. In case of exceptions, when the deviations are too large, the demand planner gets information through the alerts functionality in Demand Planning. The demand planner can then discuss the exception with the appropriate stakeholder and resolve it.

9.3 Sales Input through Duet Demand Planning

One of the stipulations for sales executives to share their insights is that the process needs to be as intuitive and efficient as possible. Many would argue that whereas SAP APO Demand Planning offers power and flexibility to professionals familiar with and responsible for demand management, the multitude of capabilities can be intimidating to a more casual user, such as a sales executive. It's also likely that an online system requiring secure real-time connectivity to corporate servers is less than convenient for sales executives whose job is to be in the field with customers as much as possible.

Whereas the same web-based collaborative SAP APO screens that are available to customers can be made available to sales executives, these still require an online connection, and although leaner in terms of distracting capabilities, they are targeted at professional planners. The ultimate tool for gathering sales input and sharing statistical and marketing insights with sales executives would be as simple and accessible as a Microsoft Excel spreadsheet — which is exactly what Duet demand planning is.

Duet demand planning enables a sales executive to access and interact with the SAP APO Demand Planning system using Microsoft Office Outlook and Microsoft Excel. Sales input using Duet brings in a real-time, accurate, easy-to-use data provider, resulting in greater demand accuracy. With Duet, the sales executive can download the latest sales plan from SAP APO Demand Planning into a Microsoft Excel spreadsheet, review it offline offsite or during a meeting with the customer and then make changes to the sales plan. The updated plan can be uploaded whenever the executive is online. Thus, the uploaded plan is synchronized with SAP APO Demand Planning.

Executives can analyze data and do their own calculations in real time and even offline while using all of the functionality (standard functions and macros) of Microsoft Excel. In addition, graphs and charts can be displayed like any other standard Excel sheet.

9.3.1 Working with Duet to Input Sales Data

The sales team can update the forecast (i.e., on a monthly or quarterly basis) for rolling 12 months or more. However, the frequency of updates can change as required depending on factors such as market dynamics, economic situations, competitor's actions, and so on. Any ad hoc update of a forecast based on updated information still needs to be made in the system so that it is visible for improved decision making. As and when the updates are required based on the above factors, the sales executive can download the existing sales plan as a spreadsheet, incorporate the necessary changes to the spreadsheet, and upload this document back to the system.

In SAP systems, provisions are made to update the sales forecast at any given time using Duet. With Duet, the user gets a familiar and easy-to-use interface of Microsoft Office (Microsoft Excel) in the frontend, which is linked to the Demand Planning solution of SAP. The integration of Microsoft Office with SAP APO Demand Planning provides a simple interface and results in greater acceptability and usage of the tool for the planning process (see Figure 9.5 for the planning sheet that is the interface for planning.).

Duet enables the user to access and interact with the SAP system using Microsoft Office Outlook and Microsoft Excel.

9.3.2 Planning Sheets

With Duet, you can create customized planning sheets (Figure 9.5) to add, update, analyze, and manage the sales input data, either online to the SAP system or offline to be updated at a later stage into the SAP system.

You can preconfigure the planning sheets according to the requirements of specific users and provide them an effective work environment to suit their particular needs. Planning sheets include key figures and characteristics required for the specific planning scenario in the time period in question. Sales input is a key figure, which stores the value of the input given by the sales team. You can use the standard Microsoft Excel functionalities in the planning sheets.

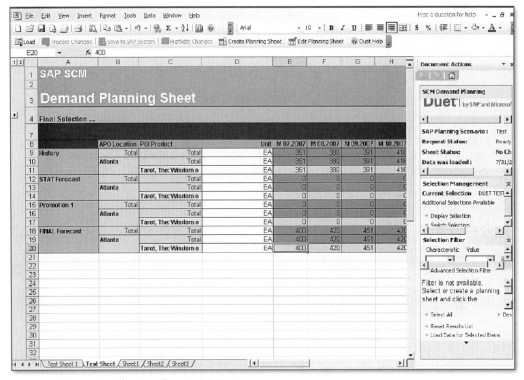

Figure 9.5 Planning Sheet in DP Duet

9.3.3 Designing Planning Sheets Using the Wizard

The administrator has the following options to create a planning sheet by using an interactive and easy-to-use Planning Sheet Wizard. Various options are available, based on individual user roles.

▶ **Based on an existing SAP planning scenario**
You can create a planning sheet based on an existing scenario in the planning system.

▶ **Based on an existing planning sheet**
The new planning sheet can have settings similar to the existing planning sheet.

▶ **Based on an existing SAP data view**
The macros available in the SAP data view can also be used in the planning sheet (Figure 9.6).

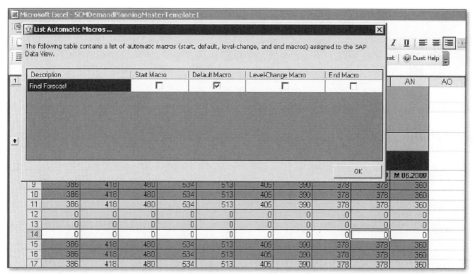

Figure 9.6 Planning Sheet Based on Existing SAP Data View in Duet

In the Planning Sheet Wizard, the administrator can perform the following steps while creating a customized planning sheet based on specific requirements:

▶ **Data view**
Select an SAP data view from the SAP system, and enter a new name for the planning sheet. Based on the specific requirements of the individual users, the data view may vary. A sales executive uses a data view to see the data at an aggregate account level and at a specific account level, whereas an account manager views data for his accounts only.

▶ **Select key figures**
Key figures are the values you plan (i.e., sales forecast) or values for information (i.e., historical values). The planner can assign the key figures for the planning sheets by selecting the required key figures. The planning sheet for sales executive has the key figure to enter a sales forecast. The key figure for baseline forecast and sales target is included for the sales team to refer to when they add the sales forecast information.

▶ **Define key figure sequence**
You can define the preferred sequence in which the key figure is to be viewed. The planning sheet can have the key figures in the following sequence, for example: baseline forecast, sales target, and sales forecast.

▶ **Select read-only key figures**
The key figures, which are used for reference only and cannot be changed, need to be assigned here. The sales executives can have view access to the baseline forecast, which is generated by the demand planning team.

▶ **Select characteristics**
Characteristics define the level at which the planning will be done, such as product or product group. The relevant characteristics can be assigned to the planning sheet.

▶ **Choose selection**
The management of data selection is a core function of demand planning with SAP APO and Duet. A selection includes all of the criteria you use to load data into the planning sheet. Selections available in SAP APO also exist in Duet for users with appropriate authorizations. An account manager handling specific accounts has a selection for those specific accounts only.

▶ **Define the planning horizon**
The administrator defines which periods of the planning horizon should be visible. The sales executive can have a planning sheet in which the planning horizon is one year in the future to enter the sales plan

9.3.4 Sales Input through Planning Sheets

The data for the specific user can be selected, downloaded, and viewed in the required format in the planning sheet. This can be done either online or offline, as explained as follows.

Sales Input Online

After the data is uploaded to the SAP system, the user can perform the following functions:

▶ **Update the sales forecast.**
The user can edit the data in the rows for which write access is available. In Figure 9.7, we can see the editable field. The user can make changes online to the editable field for entering sales forecast numbers on getting inputs from the customer.

▶ **Highlight the changes made to the sales forecast online.**
As you can see in Figure 9.8, you can click on Highlight Changes in the menu bar to highlight the changes made. This feature helps the reviewer quickly review the changes.

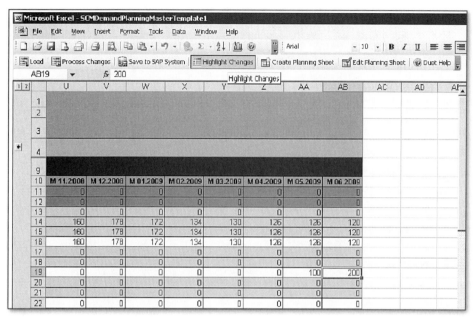

Figure 9.7 Updating the Sales Forecast

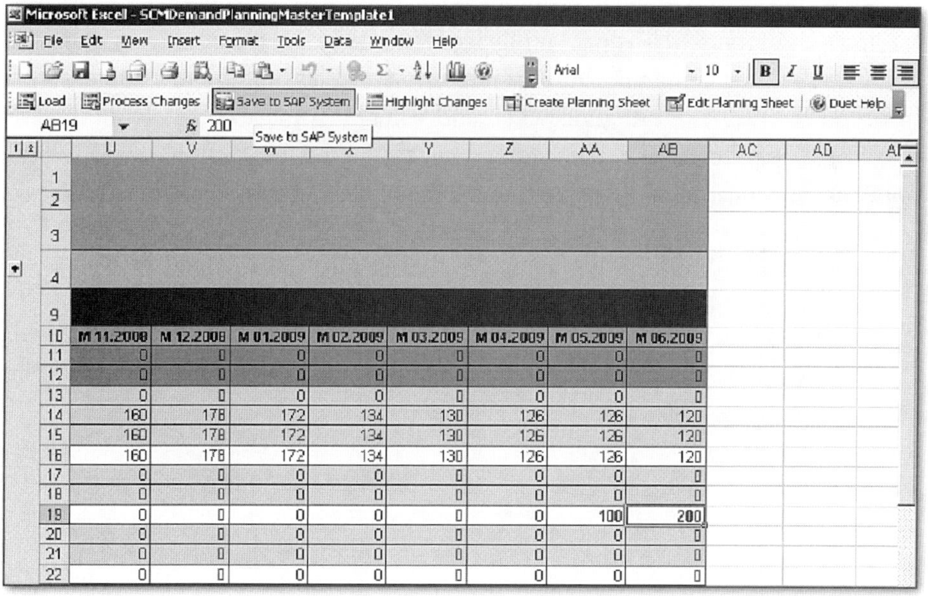

Figure 9.8 Highlighting Changes to the Forecast Before Uploading

▶ **Upload the changes made.**
The user can click on Save to SAP System in the menu bar to save the changes made.

Sales Input Offline

At the field level, with client for Duet installed, the sales team can easily capture accurate ground-level data on the Excel-based frontend of the Duet client without missing the granularity and minute details. Later, this granular-level data can be uploaded to the SAP system. The sales executive can download the latest sales plan from SAP APO into an Excel spreadsheet, review it offline, and make changes to the plan. The updated plan can be uploaded later and synchronized with SAP SCM.

9.4   Summary

The participation of the field sales force greatly increases the richness of the demand management process when the input can be gathered without negatively impacting their ability to sell. Whereas SAP APO Demand Planning can offer unparalleled insight to a sales executive by bringing together statistical analyses of history and leading indicators as well as marketing plans and executive commitments, it can be overkill. The Duet demand planning application enables online and offline gathering of account-level information when and where it is more convenient, in addition to making the entire organization's insights accessible during even a casual, opportunistic meeting with a customer.

This ends the section of the book devoted to impacting demand through sales and marketing strategies. The next chapter, Chapter 10, will focus on how all of the demand projections discussed so far can be brought together to form a single consensus demand plan around which the entire organization can rally and execute.

In this chapter, you'll learn to bring together the different demand projections, and you'll learn how you can use SAP solutions to transition from projecting and impacting demand to actually realizing demand.

10 Pulling It All Together

Chapter 2 introduced the concept of combining multiple demand signals into a single coherent projection of demand. Eight chapters later we have examined multiple strategies for interpreting, extrapolating, interpolating, and disassembling these demand signals into individual demand projections.

We're left now with a number of disparate, sometimes conflicting, demand projections that are each supported by proponents who believe strongly in the validity of the information and methodologies that led them to their conclusions. Without a disciplined, if not formal, process to bring together the best parts of these demand projections into a consistent whole, we're in danger of creating Sir Alec's camel at best and Dr. Frankenstein's monster at worst.

We hope this chapter on bringing together the different demand projections will itself bring together the chapters that came before it and pave the way for later discussions about how companies can and do use SAP solutions to move from projecting and impacting demand into the "rubber-meets-the-road" phase of realizing demand.

10.1 Map, Mirror, Headlight, and GPS

Forecasts are maps of future demand that we draw, like renaissance-era cartographers, based on information from a number of limited sources. Marketing executives, like ships' captains, can map the larger features from afar, but rely on sales executives as the intrepid adventurers who can provide insight into pockets of constantly changing local dynamics. The demand planning map-makers themselves can only interpret the diaries of them all and make basic assumptions. Rivers often appear between hills below higher mountains, and dips in demand almost always follow promotions aimed at customers but not consumers.

As the sum of the combined knowledge of all of those who have come before us, maps can very useful. As Sir Isaac Newton humbly claimed, "If I have seen farther than others it is because I have stood on the shoulders of giants." That said, maps are inherently snapshots of the past. Whereas no thinking corporation would paint the windshield of its trucks black and ask its operators to drive based on maps, most are fine with investing millions if not billions of dollars in inventories and promotions according to forecasts based on a snapshot of demand that could be over a month old.

It would be but a slight improvement for those same companies to suggest that their drivers use the maps in conjunction with rearview mirrors to guess which direction the road ahead will turn, making corrections when they come across the rumble strips on either side of the road telling them that they are about to crash. Out-of-stocks and excess or obsolescent inventory are the rumble strips of demand management and are the first warning signs for many billion-dollar companies that all is not well with their forecast.

Even integrated technology such as a global positioning system (GPS) device coupled with a map that can tell a driver exactly when and where to turn is not enough to navigate road hazards and traffic. For that, sometimes the driver needs to look out through the large windshield before him to see the road ahead.

Map, mirrors, headlights, and GPS need to work in conjunction, with each being respected for its strengths. Maps and GPS enable long-term planning and the monitoring of progress toward a target. Mirrors tell us where we have just been, and headlights illuminate the immediate future so we can respond to dynamic situations. Similarly, the rearward-looking univariate modeling, the forward-looking multiple linear regression modeling, the impacts of planned marketing activities, and the insights of sales executives reveal portions of the size and shape of the market to us.

10.2 Consensus Demand Planning

Within SAP APO Demand Planning, multiple demand projections can be stored and manipulated in individual key figures (as discussed in Chapter 5). This means planners can work with a univariate statistical forecast based on shipments to customers and a univariate statistical forecast based on original customer orders. Sales input, marketing promotional lifts, and causal forecasts generated with multiple linear regression can all be generated, maintained, and updated individually.

Like the map, mirror, headlights, and GPS, the individual demand projections must be brought together into a single *consensus demand plan.* The consensus plan is created after all of the inputs from various collaborative partners including customers, sales marketing, and demand planning teams are received and agreed upon. The result of a consensus demand plan is a single forecast number that can be released to supply planning and production.

SAP APO Demand Planning helps planners see all of the individual forecasts from collaborative partners in a single view, compare them, and raise alerts if the differences between them fall outside of a tolerance bandwidth. This enables planners to focus on exceptions rather than trying to look through their entire portfolio of characteristic value combinations. Notes entered by a sales or marketing executive in the individual cells can help planners understand why a forecast was increased or decreased. Consensus planning is an important process in the entire demand planning cycle.

The consensus planning process typically starts with the generation of a statistical forecast. Using this as a starting point, various team members can go into the system and change the forecast based on their insight. Each entry is kept separate, so that they don't overwrite each other's forecasts. Once the sales and marketing team has entered their version of the forecast, demand planners can look at statistical, marketing, and sales forecasts and either derive the consensus forecast based on predefined proportions or make manual changes based on their insight. Some organizations use parameters to decide which forecast should be selected for which period. An example of such a rule is to for the first three months, use the consensus forecast; for the rest of the months, use the sales forecast. All of these rules are supported by SAP APO Demand Planning and can be easily configured. Because the forecasts are stored in different key figures, they can be individually referred to in reporting forecast accuracy. Forecast accuracy can be calculated for each of the key figures based on the actual sales. This helps each team realize where they went wrong and improve future forecasts. Figure 10.1 shows the consensus planning book, with various forecasts such as market final or customer forecast. You can reach this screen by executing Transaction code /SAPAPO/SDP94 and selecting the consensus planning book.

	Unit	06/22/2009	06/29/2009	07/06/2009	07/13/2009	07/20/2009	07/27/2009	08/03/2009	08/10/2009	08/17/2009
Net Market Final Forecast(1)	EA	195,123	195,124	610,385	610,385	610,385	610,385	610,385	610,385	610,385
Net Customer Forecast (2)	EA	700,000	700,000	700,000	700,000	650,000	450,000	450,000	450,000	625,000
Net Commit Forecast (3)	EA									
Merge Parameter		2	2	2	2	2	2	2	2	2
Merged Forecast	EA	700,000	700,000	700,000	700,000	650,000	450,000	450,000	450,000	625,000
Net Intercompany Forecast	EA									
Persistent lock	EA									
Independent Forecast	EA									
Final Safety Stock	EA									
Build Plan Final	EA	700,000	700,000	700,000	700,000	650,000	450,000	450,000	450,000	625,000

Figure 10.1 Consensus Planning Book in SAP APO Demand Planning

The merge parameter controls which forecast should be used as the final forecast, which in this case is listed as the *merged forecast*. Notice that the merge parameter value for the 6/22/2009 time bucket is 2. This guides the planning book to accept the Net Customer Forecast (category 2) as the final forecast. So if the customer forecast was deemed the most accurate for the first three months of the demand horizon, then the merge parameter would be set to 2 for every time bucket within those three months,

The concept of leveraging different forecasts for different time periods for which they are each most accurate is worth following up on, which we'll do in the next section. First, though, we should consider that there may be value and insight coming from more than a single forecast in each time period. Customer forecasts or even some type of demand projection based on downstream demand may very accurately represent future demand except for the promotion being planned by the marketing group in three weeks.

A more sophisticated approach to consensus forecasting is to blend the individual demand projections, giving more weight to the individual components based on their more accurate periods or perhaps based on their historical forecast accuracy in general. In the example above, with three demand projections to choose from, you might let 50% of the consensus plan be driven by the customer forecast, with 30% going to the sales forecast and 20% to the marketing forecast. These rules are flexible and can be configured to suit your requirements using demand planning macros. The Transaction code for configuring the rules is /SAPAPO/ADVM. You can add key figures such as point of sale data, promotions, and so on if it helps in arriving at a consensus demand plan.

Once the basic configuration of creating a master planning object structure and planning area is completed, you can easily add new key figures to the consensus planning book. The steps in this process are:

1. Create a new key figure called Customer POS Forecast.

2. Add this key figure to the planning area.

3. Add this key figure to planning book and data view.

Let's look at each step in detail. To create a new key figure, use Transaction RSD1, select Type as key figure, enter the technical name of the Key, and click on Create. A pop-up appears (see Figure 10. 2), where you enter the description of and click to activate the key figure.

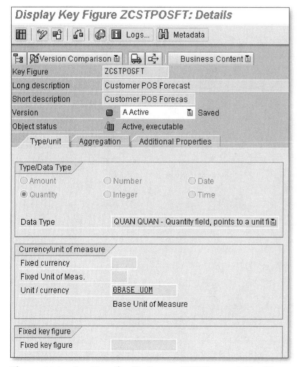

Figure 10.2 Creating the Customer POS Forecast Key Figure

Once this key figure is created, go to Transaction SAPAPO/MSDP_ADMIN and add the new key figure to the planning area as shown in Figure 10.3. Next, click on Save and then click on Activate.

Key Figure	Description	Accuracy	KeyFigType	Calculatn	Disagg. Key Figure	Time Dis.	Key Figure Time-Based Disaggregation
ZTAVCAP	Available Capacity	0	S	S		P	
ZTFINALLO	Final Allocation DC	0	S	S		P	
ZTHANDCAP	Handling Capacity at	0	S	S		P	
ZTINTRNST	In Transit at Channe	0	S	S		P	
ZTMANOVRD	Manual Allocation O	0	S	S		P	
ZTONHAND	On Hand at Channel	0	S	S		P	
ZTONORD	On Order at Channel	0	S	S		P	
ZTPO	PO at DC	0	S	P	ZTPROP	P	
ZTPROP	Proportion for Cust	0	S	S		P	
ZTSTOCK	Stock at DC	0	S	P	ZTPROP	P	
ZTSUMSUP	Sum of Supplies at D	0	S	S		P	
ZTSYSALLO	System Calculated Al	0	S	S		P	
ZTTOTINV	Total Inventory at C	0	S	S		P	
ZCSTPOSFT	Customer POS Forecas	0	S	S		P	

Figure 10.3 Adding the New Key Figure to the Planning Area

The final step is to add this key figure to the planning view, which is done by dragging the new key figure from the right side to the left, as shown in Figure 10.4.

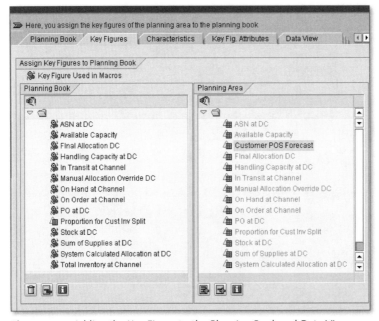

Figure 10.4 Adding the Key Figure to the Planning Book and Data View

With this complete, you can now see and manipulate the key figure in your planning book (Figure 10.5).

| | | Material type | ↑ | ↓ | | Total ▣ | | Plant | ↑ | ↓ | | Total ▣ | | APO Product | ↑ | ↓ | | Total ▣ | |

	Unit	16.06.2009	17.06.2009	18.06.2009	19.06.2009	20.06.2009	21.06.2009
Total Supplies	EA						
Manual Allocation Override	EA						
Final Allocation	EA						
Customer POS Forecast	EA						

Figure 10.5 The Customer POS Forecast Key Figure in the Consensus Planning Book

Once this key figure is available in the planning view and data is loaded, it can be compared against other demand projections, such as the sales forecast or marketing forecast. SAP APO enables this kind of comparison and exception management by using macros and alerts. Macros are simply custom-defined logic implemented to carry out calculations. You don't need to know any kind of programming language to write macros; it they can be written using the drag-and-drop capabilities within SAP APO Demand Planning. By adding two key figures or writing IF, ELSE statements are all carried out in the macro builder within Demand Planning. Figure 10.6 shows a very simple macro in which the consensus demand plan is a total of the agreed demand plan, special events, and trade promotions. To create the macros, use Transaction code /SAPAPO/ADVM.

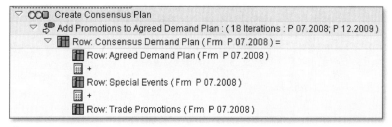

Figure 10.6 Simple Macro to Sum Three Demand Projections

The macro can be made slightly more sophisticated by applying proportions, or *weights*, to the component demand projections, as we discussed earlier. In this case, the consensus plan will be made up of 60% of the agreed demand plan, 20% of the special events, and 20% of the trade promotions. The macro to accomplish this would look like Figure 10.7.

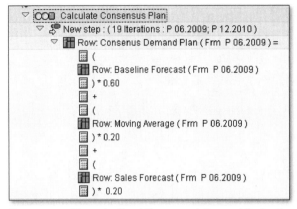

Figure 10.7 Macro to Blend Component Demand Projections into a Consensus

Beyond simply adding and subtracting rows of numbers, macros can also be used to generate exception notifications. For example, if the new consensus plan were to differ from the annual plan (which might be a key figure representing management revenue targets) by more than 20%, then alert notifications could be posted in those cells on the planning book. The macro to accomplish this would look something like Figure 10.8.

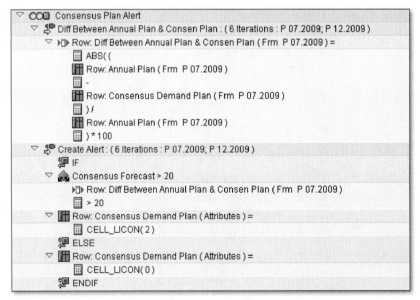

Figure 10.8 Macro to Post Alert if Key Figures Differ by More than 20%

Once these alerts are in place, they can be generated in real time whenever changes are made to the data. Figure 10.9 shows alerts generated in periods 10.2009, 11.2009, and 12.2009 on the Consensus Demand Plan line. You can access the consensus planning view can be accessed using Transaction code /SAPAPO/SDP94.

	Unit	P 07.2009	P 08.2009	P 09.2009	P 10.2009	P 11.2009	P 12.2009
Annual Plan	EA	12,500	12,500	12,500	12,500	12,500	12,500
Annual Plan Value	USD	125,000.00	125,000.00	125,000.00	125,000.00	125,000.00	125,000.00
Quarterly Operation Plan	EA						
Actual Sales	EA						
Last Year Same Period	EA						
Baseline Forecast	EA	29,602	23,118	42,680	50,920	57,800	55,909
Bottom Up Forecast	EA	13,455	12,445	11,245			
Agreed Demand Plan	EA	12,344	11,245	11,100	12,345	11,267	12,134
Special Events	EA						
Trade Promotions	EA				14,000	18,000	22,000
Free Samples	EA						
Consensus Demand P...	EA	12,344	11,245	11,100	26,345	29,267	34,134
Consensus Plan Value	USD	172,816.00	157,430.00	155,400.00	342,485.00	380,471.00	409,608.00
Unconstrained Deman...	EA	12,344	11,245	11,100	26,345	29,267	34,134

Figure 10.9 Consensus Demand Planning Book with Alerts

10.3   Demand Combination in SAP APO

Multiple types of demand parameters such as forecasts, shipments, sales orders, promotions, inventory, and so on can be neatly organized and sliced and diced for reporting in SAP NetWeaver Business Warehouse (BW).

Before starting the technical configuration of demand combination, only relevant key figures should be highlighted. If a large number of key figures are selected, the process to extract data becomes resource intensive.

Before we go into detail, let's familiarize ourselves with the relevant terminology. Data in SAP NetWeaver BW is stored in *InfoProviders*. This is a generic term used to describe objects in which data is stored and retrieved for reporting. Two basic types of InfoProviders are InfoCubes and DataStore objects. An *InfoCube* is an object that stores transactional data within SAP NetWeaver BW and is made up of a set of tables that are normalized and interlinked according to the star schema. It has all of the key figures in a central table called a fact table. All characteristics, or dimensions, are linked to this fact table, as shown in Figure 10.10.

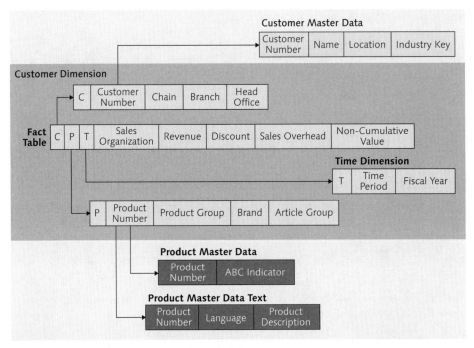

Figure 10.10 Star Schema Structure of an InfoCube

A DataStore object (DSO), another common term, is also an object in which data is stored in SAP NetWeaver BW and can be used for reporting. Unlike InfoCubes, a DSO is like a flat table structure. No fact or dimension tables are associated with a DSO.

InfoCubes and DSOs can be created using Transaction RSA1, and then by selecting required characteristics such as products, customer, location, and so on and key figures such as sales orders, statistical forecast, promotions, and demand planners forecast (Figure 10.11).

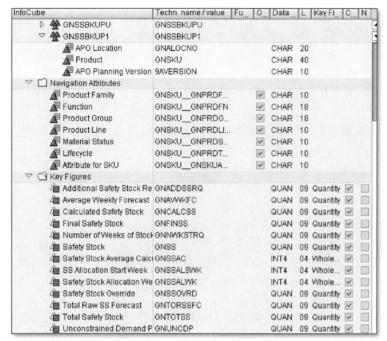

Figure 10.11 Characteristics and Key Figures in an InfoCube

Once this InfoProvider is ready, it needs to be linked to the data source. SAP provides predefined data sources for master and transactional data in SAP ERP and SAP APO. To extract demand planning data to SAP NetWeaver BW for a specific planning area, a data source needs to be generated on the SAP APO side. Use Transaction /SAPAPO/MSDP_ADMIN. In the menu go to tab EXTRAS • GENERATE DATA SOURCE and a screen will pop up (see Figure 10.12). On that screen enter the required data source name and execute. You can hide or choose only the required fields for data analysis and save the data source. Before linking it to an InfoProvider on the SAP NetWeaver BW side, you need to replicate this data source. This can be done by going to Transaction RSA1. Right-click on the source system (in this case it will be the SAP APO source system) and select Replicate Data Sources. The data source is now ready and can be linked to the InfoCube or DSO built on the SAP NetWeaver BW side.

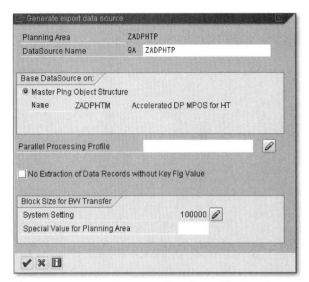

Figure 10.12 Create DataSource Based on a Planning Area

To link the data source to an InfoProvider (InfoCubes and DSOs), right-click on the InfoProvider and select Create Transformations. As shown in Figure 10.13, required fields of the data source and the InfoProvider can be linked together. Certain rules, constants, calculations, or data conversions can also be carried out here.

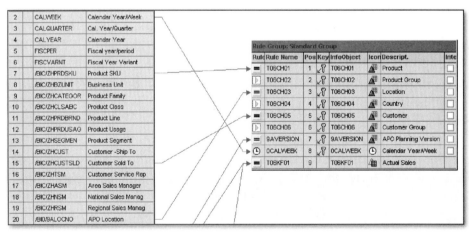

Figure 10.13 Mapping of DataSource Fields to InfoCube Fields

The next step is to create data transfer processes and an infopackage. An infopackage enables users to define what data needs to be extracted from the planning area. If forecast data is extracted for only a year, filter dates can be entered, as shown in Figure 10.14. If data is extracted based on other relevant filters for products or customers, they can be handled in the infopackage. The infopackage also helps schedule extraction from SAP APO to SAP NetWeaver BW. You can set up the scheduling so that extraction is triggered after the planning run is completed or data is released to SNP or to R/3 for the MRP run. You can execute scheduling using process chains via Transaction RSPC.

InfoPackage	IP for DP Planning Area(ZPAK_D61EW8JBHQ6NZW3D7PVY2YIPW)
DataSource	ZADPHTP / ZADPHTM(9AZADPHTPS2)
Data Type	Transaction Dat
Source System	SCM 5.0 Client 001 STORM(SC5CLNT100)
Last Changed By	Date	Time	00:00:00

| Data Selection | Extraction | Processing | Data Targets | Update | Schedule |

Load transaction data from the source system

Enter Selections (Optional):

InfoObject	Technical	Description	From Value	To Value	Ty	D	Type (Varia	R	Data	Field	Conv
	CALMONTH	Calendar Year/Mor							NUMC	8	PERI
	CALWEEK	Calendar Year/Wee							NUMC	8	PERI
	CALQUARTER	Calendar Year/Qua							NUMC	7	PERI
	CALYEAR	Calendar Year							NUMC	4	
	FISCPER	Fiscal year / period							NUMC	9	PERI
	FISCVARNT	Fiscal year variant							CHAR	2	
	/BIC/ZHPRDS	Product SKU							CHAR	42	PROD
	/BIC/ZHBZUN	Business Unit							CHAR	28	ALPH
	/BIC/ZHCATE	Product Family							CHAR	28	ALPH
	/BIC/ZHCLSA	Product Class							CHAR	5	ALPH

Figure 10.14 Screen to Set Filters for Data Extraction from Planning Areas

Once data is extracted to an InfoProvider, various key figures such as Customer Forecast, Merged Forecast, and Sales Orders can be seen, as shown in Figure 10.15. You can use Transaction code listcube to check data.

Similarly, you can extract data from other sources to SAP NetWeaver BW. Once all of the data is present in one or many InfoProviders, it can be joined using infosets or MultiProviders. You can write queries to report data from these InfoProviders and display it to users in required formats.

OCALWEEK	9ALOCNO	9AVERSION	Material/Product	Build Plan	Commit Forecast	Customer Forecast	Merged Forecast	Net Boards Forecast	Sales Orders- Open	ZQSHIP
201101	7000	000	L2A1157-033	0	0	0	0	0	0	0
201036	7000	000	L2A1157-033	0	0	0	2,880	0	0	0
201038	7000	000	L2A1157-033	0	0	0	2,880	0	0	0
201040	7000	000	L2A1157-033	0	0	0	2,880	0	0	0
201043	7000	000	L2A1157-033	0	0	0	2,880	0	0	0
201015	7000	000	L2A1157-033	0	0	0	2,880	0	0	0
201016	7000	000	L2A1157-033	0	0	0	2,880	0	0	0
201017	7000	000	L2A1157-033	0	0	0	2,880	0	0	0
201025	7000	000	L2A1157-033	0	0	0	0	0	60,270	0
201026	7000	000	L2A1157-033	0	0	0	0	0	60,260	0
201005	7000	000	L2A1157-033	0	0	0	2,660	0	0	0
201013	7000	000	L2A1157-033	0	0	0	2,880	0	0	0
200921	7000	000	L5B9728-002	0	0	0	0	0	6,750	18,000
200923	7000	000	L5B9728-002	0	0	0	0	0	0	2,250
200926	7000	000	L5B9728-002	0	0	0	0	0	0	5,625
200927	7000	000	L5B9728-002	0	0	0	0	0	0	68,625
200929	7000	000	L5B9728-002	0	0	0	0	0	7,200	0

Figure 10.15 InfoProvider with Multiple Key Figures

10.4 Summary

Projections of demand, as we have seen in earlier chapters, can come from many different parts of the organization. It is rare to find anyone who does not have an opinion of what the future might be. We've had insight into these demand projections, and the more efficiently a company's processes are at collecting and assimilating these disparate projections, the more insight can be gained.

In this chapter we've discussed the different demand projections, and you should hopefully have a broad understanding of projections and how they can work for you. In the next chapter, the value of this insight will become more obvious as we examine the decisions that companies make based on the demand plan. These decisions commit resources such as inventories, production lines, trucks, rail cars, employees, and the capital that pays for them.

This chapter introduces you to realizing demand. We'll look at the three time horizons — strategic, operational, and tactical — and learn about how SAP can help organizations take advantage of visibility into downstream demand.

11   Realize Demand

In Chapter 1, our ill-fated hot dog cart owner projected demand enough to decide where to put his cart and even did some advertising to impact demand by talking to the construction foreman. What he failed to do was act in advance by, in his case, buying materials and building inventory. Managing demand takes a significant amount of time and attention from a number of individuals with many other critical responsibilities within an organization. This investment can only pay off for companies willing to align their actions with their plans.

This chapter will look at the decisions companies make, specifically those that can benefit from improved visibility into future demand. We begin with revisiting the balance sheet and income statement from Chapters 1 and 3, because they're what these decisions will attempt to impact. From there we'll divide the decisions into three time horizons: strategic (long-term) decisions, operational (medium-term) decisions, and tactical (short-term) decisions. Finally, we'll end this chapter on realizing demand by looking at how organizations can invest to take advantage of visibility into downstream demand.

11.1   The Balance Sheet and the Income Statement

Chapter 1 introduced the balance sheet and income statement, and Chapter 3 explained at a high planning level the impact of demand management on them both. With a better understanding of the methods by which organizations project and impact demand, we can now revisit the balance sheet and income statement to understand in more detail how they are affected by decisions that can be improved with knowledge gleaned from better demand management.

The balance sheet lists what the company owns and what it owes. As the name suggests, for public companies the assets and liabilities are always in balance. A healthy balance sheet is also balanced in that it shows enough capital available to invest in opportunities or compensate for unexpected expenses without holding so much money in reserve that shareholders question if the senior management team is investing to maximize the return on their investments. The investments that the management teams make also show up in the balance sheet either as inventory; physical assets such as plants, trucks and warehouses; or more intangible assets such as brand or new product pipelines.

Dividing the amount of money that a company makes by the value of its assets gives investors a metric called return on assets. This measure enables them to compare how efficiently any number of companies across different industries are currently using their money. This means that over the medium and long term, senior management teams would like to keep their assets low in comparison to their revenues.

As an example asset, inventories are one of the larger items on companies' balance sheets for many industries. Money that has been spent on building products is an expense that has been paid either to suppliers for materials, to employees for their time, or for any number of contributions. This expense exists whether the products are sold or are still sitting in the warehouse, which makes it part of the income statement rather than the balance sheet. The fact that a certain amount of money is tied up in inventory, though, makes the inventory and the sunk capital that it represents an asset.

An organization's demand management practices have the potential to affect its assets by offering visibility to future demand that can be used to better leverage assets ahead of time. Sections 11.2 to 11.5 will go into detail for each of these effects. To introduce them now, though, demand management can impact a company's balance sheet through the following list seen in Figure 11.1.

▶ Reduced safety stock buffers

▶ Less obsolete inventory

▶ Fewer production schedule interruptions

▶ Increase in orders shipped from default source

▶ Smarter capital investments

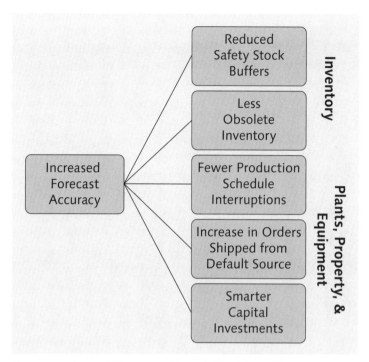

Figure 11.1 Demand Management Impacts the Balance Sheet

As opposed to considering what a company owns and owes, the income statement helps investors understand how much a company makes and spends. As we said above, whereas the money tied up in existing inventory sitting in warehouses waiting to be sold is an asset (as are the warehouses themselves), the money spent on materials, salaries, and warehouse rent and insurance is an expense because it has already been paid out. When that inventory is eventually sold, the money received becomes revenue. The difference between the expense to buy, make, move, store, and sell the product and the sales price is profit.

As with the balance sheet, a company's demand management practices can affect the income statement as well. Figure 11.2 illustrates how this might happen through:

- Increased in-stock %
- Performance-based price premiums
- Accelerated visibility to new product success
- Reduced inventory
- Increased yield on marketing spending

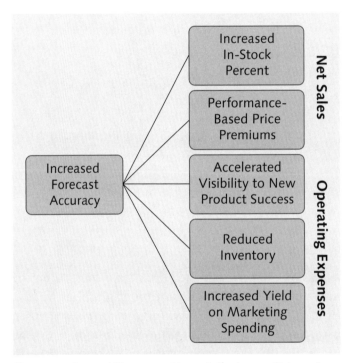

Figure 11.2 Demand Management Impacts the Income Statement

11.2 Strategic (Long-Term) Decisions

You may be saving money for retirement or for your children's college fund. You may be considering buying a slightly larger house than you currently need in anticipation of starting a family sometime in the future. These are strategic decisions that we make based on a rough idea of long-term goals. Not all strategic decisions are long-term; for instance, you could switch jobs in a short period of time.

Any large decision you make can be strategic — not necessarily just the ones made well in advance. The reason that "strategic" and "long-term" go together so well is that strategic decisions are the only ones worth making so far in advance because they require so much time to work toward. Why isn't it worth deciding right now what you're going to have for dinner a month from now? Because things change over time, and there isn't much you can do right now to make that dinner more economical or enjoyable that you can't wait and do a day or two beforehand. In fact, your favorite vegetables might go on sale or you might be in the mood for Thai food between now and then.

In short, you postpone your decision until you get to the best balance of efficiency and visibility of demand (and supply). If you want a tiramisu for dessert, then you need to make it a day ahead (because it has to sit for eight hours or more). If you postpone that decision until the afternoon of the day on which you want to eat your tiramisu, then you'll need to go out to a restaurant to eat because you won't have time to make it. Clearly, it would have been more economical to make the decision the day before.

Companies also face lead times on their decisions. If they want to enter a potential growth market for their products in Russia, for example, they can decide early to begin to build up a presence, cultivate a supply base, and train a local sales force. Alternatively, they can postpone the decision until the market has already begun to grow and be forced to buy a local company at a greater expense to gain these things.

Visibility of probable future demand can be critical to long-term decisions, which are often the most expensive decisions a company makes. If in January you have a forecast for an item's March sales, and you don't plan to make any decisions that affect March production or distribution based on that forecast until the next time you develop a forecast in February, then the exercise is completely academic. We'll discuss how organizations can decide which future periods' demand plans are most relevant to track performance against in a future chapter. As we discuss decisions that commit resources, though, it's a good time to introduce the concept that the accuracy of a demand plan is only important when someone is committing resources against it. Figure 11.3 lists examples of investment decisions that companies might make based on demand projections quarters and years in the future.

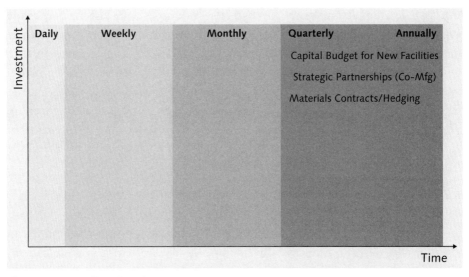

Figure 11.3   Long-Term Decisions

11.3   Operational (Medium-Term) Decisions

Companies hold inventory for a number of reasons, as we've discussed in previous chapters. The best of reasons is to balance against the productivity of their production and distribution assets. If it takes five hours to clean equipment and change over some of the tools to go from one product to another, then it probably doesn't make much sense to schedule a run for two hours worth of production every time somebody orders an item. It's often worthwhile to run production somewhat longer and move the excess product into inventory to fill future orders. Balancing the costs of holding inventory and utilizing assets is part of the sales and operations planning process that leads to a production schedule. This is good example of an operational, medium-term, decision.

Other similar decisions concerning inventory might include how much excess or safety stock to make to buffer against uncertainty in customer demand and where to position it across the network of plants and warehouses. The production schedule and the inventory plan both lead to a procurement plan that ensures that the organization has enough raw materials.

Again, these are all operational decisions that need to be made in advance for many companies. Some companies have invested in technology and training that enables them to postpone these decisions and respond with production or distribution when they get a better picture of what demand looks like. Figure 11.4 adds medium-term decisions to our continuum.

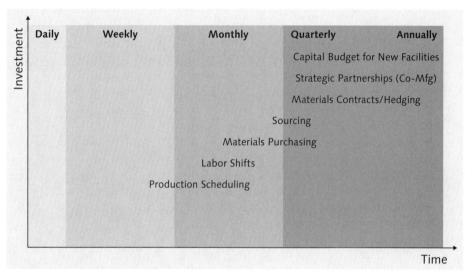

Figure 11.4 Medium-Term Decisions

Operational decisions may appear to be less important because they impact a smaller amount of expense or revenue than longer-term strategic decisions. However, what they may lack in individual size they make up for in volume. The decision to run a production line for five extra hours and store the inventory seems small compared with the expense of building a new plant, but the amount of inventory held by most companies for all products over the course of a year dwarfs the cost of any single new plant. Operational decisions are as important as longer-term decisions and are potentially more complex because of the number of decisions that need to be made.

Note, though, that the decision to hedge against the costs of oil as a component in making plastics, for example, only requires knowing how much oil will be used in all plants over the course of a year. This is a much different demand plan than estimating how many red pencil cases will need to be produced in a plant in Cleveland in July. Forecasts errors tend to cancel each other out as categories get broader. Fewer red pencil cases may be sold because students preferred green, but the total number of pencil cases the company expected to be sold was about right.

We can call this continuum of breadth versus detail *granularity*, enabling us to say that forecast accuracy decreases as granularity increases. We add granularity to the picture in Figure 11.5.

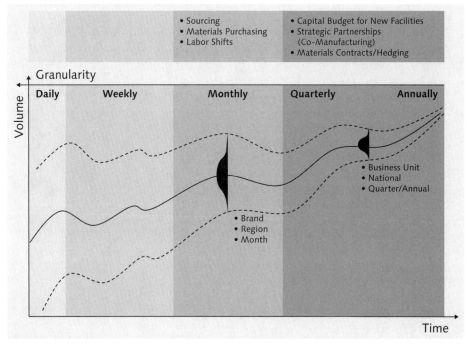

Figure 11.5   Forecast Accuracy Decreases as Granularity Increases

Granularity and Time

Granularity is not the same thing as time at all, yet we are able to plot them on an axis together because in planning it is generally permissible to decide on a rough course of action further out and then add more specific details as the time comes closer. When planning a vacation, for example, you might decide six months ahead to go to the ocean rather than going to the mountains. This allows you to investigate ocean resort towns and buy swimsuits. Four months before your vacation you may have selected a specific town and booked a plane or train ticket. Three months ahead, you may have decided on a specific hotel or vacation home. As the time for you to go on vacation gets nearer, you continue to make more detailed (granular) decisions about what you'll do. Companies do the same thing when choosing how much of which products to make and where to store them.

The inverse relationship between granularity and accuracy is true at least for statistically based demand projections. Some causes of variability that impact the accuracy of a demand projection are depicted in Figure 11.6. Note that supply variability is included as well. Whether sales fall short of projections because customers didn't want or need the product or because your warehouses were out of stock, the fact remains that they still fell short.

Supply Variability
- Price Change
- Unexpected Promotion
- Competitor's Promotion
- Statistical Forecast Error

- Raw Materials Shortage
- Unexpected Machine Downtime
- Backup on Shared Resource
- Materials Quality Issue
- Shortage of Qualified Operators
- Natural Disaster
- Sub-Contractor Issues

Demand Variability
- Competitor's New Product Hits
- Partner's New Product Hits
- Your New Product Hits

Figure 11.6 Causes of Demand and Supply Variability

Variability and the Bell Curve

A projection of demand, stripped of all pretension, is the amount that will be sold within a specific time period. That number can either be exactly right, higher than the actual result, or lower than the actual result. It is extremely unlikely that the actual result is exactly what was projected. The bell curve is an example of a distribution that describes how likely it is that the actual demand will be greater than or less than a specific number.

The forecasted number is directly in the middle of the bell curve, with half the curve to its left and half the curve to its right (or below and above if the curve is on its side as in Figure 11.6). Because it is in the middle, with 50% of the area of the curve to the left, there is a 50% chance that because of variability the actual demand will be less than the projected demand. Similarly, because 50% of the area of the curve is to the right, there is a 50% chance that the actual demand will be higher than the projected demand. Variability is why actual demand might be higher or lower than the projection, and the bell curve is an example of a probability distribution that describes the likelihood of actual demand based on the demand projection.

These probabilities become very relevant when organizations ask questions like "How much inventory would we need to carry to meet 99% of the possible actual demand?" Drastically oversimplifying it, the company in question could find the sales volume at the far right of the curve, at which 99% of the curve's volume is to the left.

11.4 Tactical (Short-Term) Decisions

Short-term decisions tend to be smaller scale and more tactical in nature, but thanks to granularity, the sheer number of them more than make up for this. Deciding where to store inventory coming off a truck or a production line has less overall impact on a business than deciding where to build a new production facility, but deciding where all of the company's inventory gets stored every day rapidly becomes a very big deal.

Tactical decisions are subject to much greater impact from variability (like those in Figure 11.6) than medium- and longer-term decisions because more of these decisions are made more frequently and at a greater granularity. Figure 11.7 illustrates these larger forecast error curves.

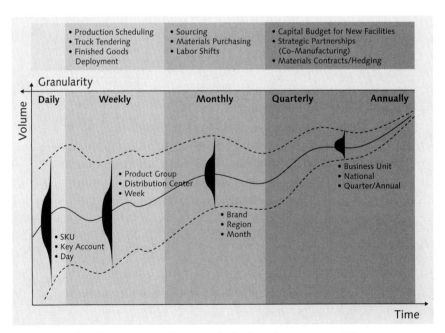

Figure 11.7 Short-Term, Granular Decisions Suffer from Greater Forecast Error

Figure 11.7 has a number of concepts in operation simultaneously, and grasping their interconnectivity is critical to understanding how, why, and when forecasting impacts a company's income statement and balance sheet. At the top are the decisions that need to be made for the company to have product to sell to its customers. The decisions become less general (more granular) as we get closer to today's date (moving from right to left in the figure).

It is intuitive that we know less about what will happen a year from now than about will happen in 10 minutes. The irony inherent in statistical demand projection is that organizations know more accurately the total volume of sales they will make globally in the next year than they know how much of one product a single customer will order tomorrow. Because long-term decisions tend to be more general and short-term decisions very precise, statistical forecasting becomes less and less useful as we come closer to the moment of truth when a customer places an order.

Fortunately, as discussed in Chapter 8, in the short term it's possible for organizations to take advantage not only of demand projections based on statistical algorithms, but also on visibility of downstream demand.

11.5   Impact of Downstream Events on Demand Management

Whereas the nature of statistics makes aggregate forecasts based on a larger base of data more accurate, downstream demand (the demand for your products by your customers' customers) is inherently granular. A few key customers may share shipments from the warehouses. A syndicated data provider may track sales figures for certain products in certain regions. Downstream data is very relevant over the short term, but it can't take into account plans for new products, planned changes in prices, or upcoming promotional events. Also, because downstream demand data is often only available for isolated segments of the market, it becomes less accurate at aggregate levels where demand for more and more products, regions, or customers without this data available must be extrapolated. As Figure 11.8 suggests, the accuracy of downstream demand declines over time and as granularity decreases. The newly added curve represents projections based on downstream demand data, which, unlike statistical projections based on historical orders, is more accurate in the short term and grows less accurate over time.

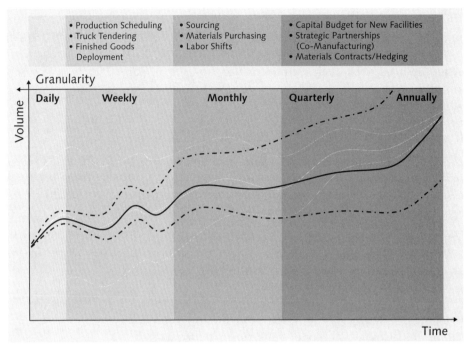

Figure 11.8 Downstream Demand Data Loses Relevance over Time and at Aggregate Levels

Therefore, as we have learned from Chapter 10, it is best to combine the two methods of demand projection (statistical demand projection and downstream demand projection), as shown in Figure 11.9. This improves the demand projections at the correct levels to support short-term, tactical decisions while maintaining the superior forecast over the long term at the aggregate levels required for long-term, strategic decisions.

Looking at the error bands around the demand projections in the short- and medium-term time horizons in Figure 11.9, it is apparent that by leveraging visibility of downstream demand, organizations can have a much better estimate of the right amounts of the right products in the right places at the right times to satisfy customers. This means that when committing resources, decisions made with the benefit of downstream demand will be more effective.

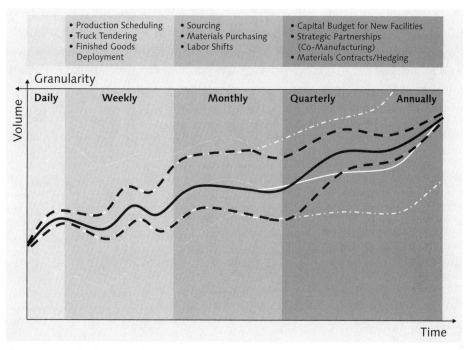

Figure 11.9 Hybrid Statistical-Downstream Demand Projection Improves Decision Support for Decisions Across All Time Horizons

Unfortunately, for many manufacturers and distributors the first view of downstream demand comes with the customer's order. More often than not, this leaves just enough time to run the order through a credit check, source it to a warehouse with the products in stock, pick, pack, and ship it to the customer (Figure 11.10).

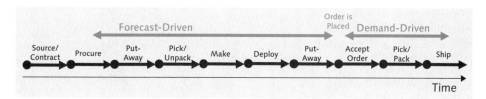

Figure 11.10 Visibility of Downstream Demand from Customer Orders

All of the decisions leading up to having the product ready in time to service the customer order take place when statistical forecasts and intelligence gleaned from sales and marketing executives are the main inputs to demand projections. With these types of projections being less accurate in the short term at the granularity necessary to satisfy a customer order, companies need to build buffers of inventory and/or production capacity to compensate for the higher variabilities. Figure 11.11 illustrates the ensuing costs of excess inventories and production and distribution that hit both the balance sheet and the income statement.

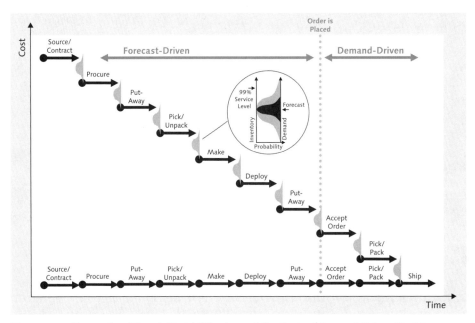

Figure 11.11 Demand and Supply Variabilities Impact the Costs of Forecast-Driven Decisions

To narrate the image, before a customer's order for a pallet of breakfast cereal or a drum of solvent can be filled, that product had to be put away in a warehouse somewhere. Someone had to decide how much of which product to put where in the warehouse based in part on a demand projection that was generated from historical shipments. Why use shipments that could have happened three months ago to guide where to put a pallet today? Because it's the best information available to that decision maker at that time.

Before the decision was made to put away the pallet, somebody else had to decide how many pallets should be sent to which warehouses. Prior to that, somebody decided how many pallets would be made in which production facilities. For every piece of inventory waiting to fill a customer's order, there is a chain of decisions that each were based in part on the best demand projections available at the time.

The timing of how far in advance products are built is the result of a decision that balances the number of and flexibility of production lines, storage tanks, packaging machines, forklifts, and other physical assets with the amount of inventory (cycle stock and safety stock) to be carried. This decision is predicated on the assumption that up until the order is placed, demand projections do not improve in quality.

Put more simply, until the customer orders, the best indicator of demand is the demand projection based on what they have ordered in the past. Because visibility of future demand doesn't improve until the moment that the customer orders, there is no benefit to delaying decisions on how much to make or where to make and store it.

However, organizations that improve their visibility of downstream demand by finding out what their customers are selling or consuming (Chapter 8) and integrate it into their overall demand plan (Chapter 12) are set up to receive a great benefit for those operations that fall within their enhanced downstream demand visibility window.

Without downstream demand data, it makes no sense for our cereal manufacturer to wait to package product. However, when downstream demand data is available, it makes the demand projection more accurate. This could enable the cereal maker to buy an extra packaging machine to package the same amount of cereal in half the time if it brought the decision of how much of which cereal to package within the "window" of downstream demand data. This is shown in the circular call-outs in Figure 11.12.

To go back to that pallet of cereal or solvent, if a manufacturer sells three different sizes of the product and can receive information about how much their customers are actually reselling or consuming, then it might make sense to invest in storing the product in bulk and having additional capacity to package it into any of the three sizes later when the demand picture becomes clearer. The extra cost is more than compensated for by the reduced amount of safety stock cost and higher revenue resulting from fewer lost sales resulting from waiting until the demand projection is more accurate.

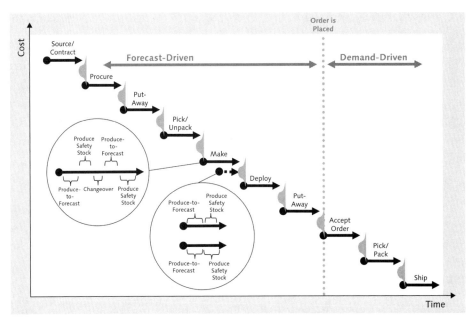

Figure 11.12 Investing in More or Better Production Lines To Postpone Committing to Building a Product Doesn't Work without Better Visibility

Figure 11.13 is another complex image that distills much of what you'll take away from this chapter and the preceding chapters. The message is twofold:

1. The cost of additional production or storage capacity (like redundant process steps that enable organizations to postpone decisions until a later time when better demand information is available) can be more than compensated for by savings in waste and fewer lost sales.

2. The further downstream in their customers' and customers' customers' supply chains that organizations can see, the further in advance they can better predict granular demand and the more decisions they can make based on this more accurate demand data.

Many companies believe that this demand-driven approach is the only answer to the growing product proliferation and accelerated product lifecycles that increasingly typify the markets for their products. Without it they face the dilemma of increasing inventory, which impacts balance sheet assets and income statement expenses, reducing customer service levels or making them unable to increase their portfolio of products.

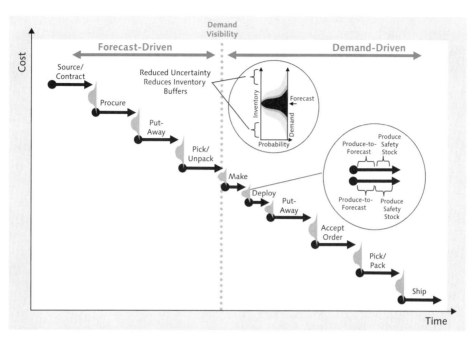

Figure 11.13 Extending Visibility to Downstream Demand and Investing in Faster, More Flexible Assets and Processes Yields Results

In Figure 11.14, the inner circle describes how much of each conflicting objective the company can achieve. It may be possible for them to increase the number of products and channels, but doing it requires more production lines or vehicles and/or more out-of-stocks.

By becoming more demand-driven, customers increase their ability to better achieve all of these objectives at the same time. In some cases these companies do need to increase the number or size of physical assets on their balance sheet to initially become more responsive (faster and more flexible), but they make up for it in inventory savings and higher revenues from a reduced number of lost sales due to out-of-stocks and perhaps even price premiums for higher customer service levels and shorter order lead times. Figure 11.15 illustrates the company's ability to realize these benefits by leveraging improved demand projections resulting from integrating different demand signals (downstream demand, etc.).

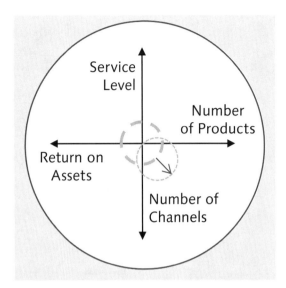

Figure 11.14 Choosing Between More New Products, Better Service Levels, or Less Inventory

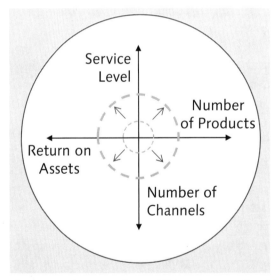

Figure 11.15 Becoming Demand-Driven Increases Capabilities Across the Board

A lot of companies have looked to lean manufacturing and even lean enterprise concepts to try to reduce waste throughout their supply chains. Whereas many of these eschew the need for planning, preferring demand-driven techniques, remember that the accuracy of downstream demand visibility diminishes over time and at aggregate levels where companies make some of their most critical strategic decisions. A mix of forecast and demand-driven decision-making results in the best possible result for the balance sheet and the income statement.

Fortunately, the supply planning tools in SAP APO support this hybrid approach. Other books from SAP PRESS, such as *Sales and Inventory Planning with SAP APO*, go into more detail on this topic. The remaining section in this chapter will be limited to passing the demand plan from SAP APO Demand Planning into the SAP APO Supply Network Planning (SNP) component.

11.6   Operationalizing the Demand Plan

Once the demand plan is agreed upon and confirmed, it can be released to SAP APO (SNP or MRP) or used by SAP APO Global Available-to-Promise for allocations. We'll explore these options in this section.

11.6.1   Supply Network Planning (SNP)

The primary function of SNP is to develop a supply plan while considering manufacturing and distribution resources to meet demand at the right time, at the right place, and in the right quantity, while considering all of the constraints. To accomplish this, it uses various engines such as Heuristics, Capable to Match (CTM), and Optimizer.

The best way to define the solvers is through an analogy. Let's assume that one had to attend a meeting in San Francisco and had to come from Tokyo to attend it. If there were no constraints on how to get to the meeting and at what cost (even flying first class), and you could even get there in the available time, the situation is best reflective of the results produced by the Heuristic solver. Going a step further, if some constraints had to be considered, and you couldn't be late for the meeting, such as needing to develop a feasible, though not an optimal plan, this would be reflective of a CTM engine. Finally, if you were given a travel budget to work with for the entire trip, which covered hotel, cab, flight, and food, and you had to optimize across all of the variables, that would be equivalent to the Optimizer solver. Figure 11.16 illustrates the SAP SNP trade-offs.

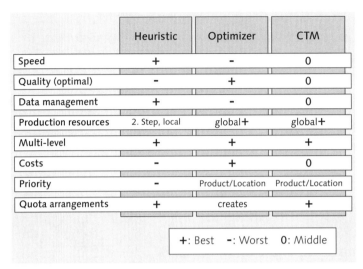

	Heuristic	Optimizer	CTM
Speed	+	-	0
Quality (optimal)	-	+	0
Data management	+	-	0
Production resources	2. Step, local	global+	global+
Multi-level	+	+	+
Costs	-	+	0
Priority	-	Product/Location	Product/Location
Quota arrangements	+	creates	+

+: Best   **-**: Worst   **0**: Middle

Figure 11.16 SNP Solver Trade Offs

SNP Heuristics

The Heuristic solver plans in two steps. In the first step, it creates the supply plan considering infinite production capacities, and in the second, it adjusts the plan for any capacity constraints. The planning run processes each planning location sequentially and determines sourcing requirements and valid sources of supply and corresponding quantity based on predefined percentages for each source of supply (quota arrangements) or procurement priorities for transportation lanes and production process models (PPMs) or production data structures (PDS). The dependent demands are then passed through the next levels of the supply chain to calculate a plan. However, this plan is not necessarily feasible. The planner can then use capacity leveling to adjust the plan and formulate a feasible plan.

The heuristic planning sequence is governed by low-level codes of the location products. The low-level code specifies the bill of materials (BOM) level and supply chain location at which a location product is situated. The SNP heuristic needs this information to be able to determine the correct planning sequence for the location products, thus ensuring that demands are fulfilled correctly. The heuristic run considers all demand for a given product-location combination within one period as one demand.

As you can see in Figure 11.17, the heuristics considers all of the demands within a specified period (e.g., week, month, etc.) as one demand and plans level by level if multilevel heuristics is chosen. In single-level heuristics, planning is carried out only at one level.

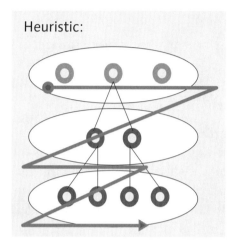

Figure 11.17 Heuristics Considers All of the Demands within a Specified Period

SNP Optimizer

As the name suggests, the SNP Optimizer offers cost-based planning. The engine searches through all feasible plans in an attempt to find the most cost-effective (in terms of total cost) plan. The total cost includes:

▸ Production, procurement, storage, and transportation costs

▸ Costs for increasing the production capacity, storage capacity, transportation capacity, and handling capacity

▸ Costs for violating (falling below) the safety stock level

▸ Costs for late delivery

▸ Stockout costs

Through the cost profiles, weights can be assigned to various costs to fine tune their relative importance. During optimization-based planning, soft constraints such as due date or safety stock can be violated in order to come out with the most cost-effective plan. The optimizer considers entire available capacities such as production, transportation, handling, and storage. The optimizer makes the following decisions within cost-optimization-based planning:

▶ Which products are to be produced, transported, procured, stored, and delivered and in which quantities (product mix)

▶ Which resources and which production process models (PPMs) or production data structures (PDSs) to use (technology mix)

▶ The dates and times for production, transportation, procurement, storage, and delivery

▶ The locations for production, procurement, storage, and delivery and the source and destination locations for transportation

As illustrated in Figure 11.18, the optimizer plans all distribution demands for all locations in the distribution network before exploding the BOM and processing dependent demand at the production locations. Unlike heuristics, optimizer considers costs at various levels of the supply chain to come out with the optimal plan. Similar to heuristics, the optimizer considers various demands within a specified period as one demand.

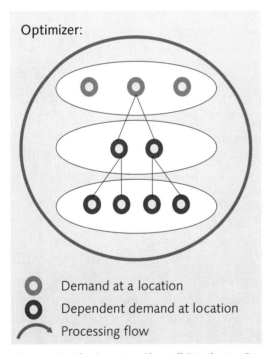

Figure 11.18 The Optimizer Plans All Distribution Demands

Capable to Match

CTM planning is intended for mid- to long-term planning, and unlike the SNP optimizer, CTM does not optimize the cost. Instead, uses order-based priorities to influence the sequence of demands and the selection of the procurement alternatives. CTM planning does not consider the individual production and distribution levels one after the other, such as the classic MRP run, but considers them at the same time. This guarantees that CTM planning generates a plan that can be executed on schedule.

As mentioned earlier, CTM planning works on an order basis and allows you to determine and trace the relevant receipts and supplies for each demand in the entire supply chain, after the CTM planning run.

CTM planning creates procurement proposals for the source of supply for in-house production and transportation lanes. In the process, CTM considers resource and material capacities across all levels of the supply chain. If the production capacity of one resource is not sufficient to cover the total demand, CTM evaluates another procurement alternative for the remaining quantity.

As you can see in Figure 11.19, CTM selects orders based on defined priorities and plans all the way through. It considers capacities simultaneously.

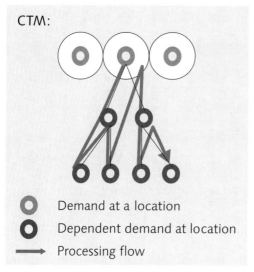

Figure 11.19 Capable to Match

Demand Planning provides Transaction /SAPAPO/MC90 - Release Demand Planning to Supply Network Planning. In this transaction various parameters can be adjusted, as shown in Figure 11.20, to release required demand. The screen is divided into various sections such as source of data, the target where the data is to be released, and the parameters. These parameters include the horizon of data to be released, product, location filters or selections, and product location characteristics name.

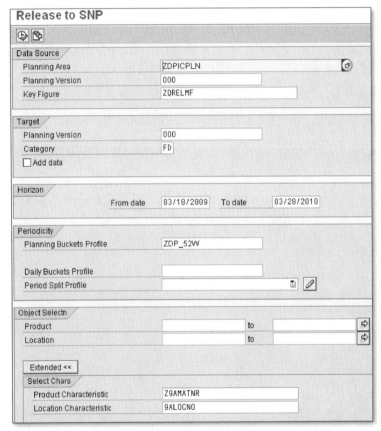

Figure 11.20 Releasing the Demand Plan from SAP APO Demand Planning to SNP

In the following sections, we'll go into more detail about these specific parameters.

DataSource

▶ **Planning Area**

The planning area on which demand planning is operationalized.

▶ **Planning Version**

The active version on which demand planning is carried out.

▶ **Key Figure**

The source key figure that needs to be released to SNP. Usually this is the consensus or final plan key figure. Multiple key figures can be released to SNP to different categories.

Target

▶ **Planning Version**

The active version in SNP to which the demand plan is released to.

▶ **Category**

A forecast such as final forecast or customer forecast can be released to the required category (FA, FC) in SNP. Priorities can be assigned to these categories (FA, FC) to facilitate the prioritization of different forecast types in SNP to help organizations give more priority to the customer forecast versus the internal forecast.

Horizon

SNP may require a smaller-duration forecast released for their daily run versus a larger-duration of forecast released during a weekly run. The horizon controls how much data is released from Demand Planning to SNP. The start and end dates can be made to roll as we move into the future by giving the current date as the starting date and using a +/– offset for the end date. This data can be saved in a variant. For example, if demand planning is executed for three years, and only a year's data needs to be released for SNP, then this can be controlled by using the horizon. The settings for such a scenario will be From date: current date and To date: current date + 365.

Periodicity

Demand plans can be created in weekly buckets or periodicities, but SNP might plan at the daily bucket level. Sometimes demand needs to be split from Demand Planning to SNP based on certain proportions. These requirements can be supported using the split profile. Split proportions can be specified, and when data is released from Demand Planning to SNP, the forecast in SNP will appear as per these splits. You can maintain period split profiles using Transaction code /

SAPAPO/SDP split. These splits are used when a certain type of disaggregation needs to be executed from higher time buckets to lower-level time buckets, for example, from months to weeks and from weeks to days.

Object Selection

If there is a sudden surge or decline of demand, then the forecast of certain products or locations can be adjusted and released to SNP, without releasing the demand for all of the products. If only certain materials need to be released to SNP or for a certain locations, values can be specified here. If the values are left blank, all of the materials will be released to SNP.

Select Chars

In Demand Planning, if the standard objects 9AMATNR and 9ALOCNO are not used owing to customizing, then the InfoObjects that are used for material and location are to be specified here.

If release to SNP is based on filters besides the material and location, such as active or inactive status, sales areas, or product groups, you should use background jobs with a release profile. The transaction code is /SAPAPO/MC8S – Maintain Release Profiles. Once this release profile is created, it is added to an activity, /SAPAPO/MC8T – Define Activities for Mass Processing, and this activity is added to a background job, /SAPAPO/MC8D – Create Demand Planning in the Background. In the background job, we can use selection profiles that have more filtering capability than just material and location.

11.6.2 Materials Requirement Planning (MRP)

A demand plan can be transferred directly to SAP ERP as Planned Independent Requirements, so its MRP engine can create a supply plan for this demand. There are two mechanisms through which a demand plan can be released.

1. Background job (transfer profile)
2. Release from an InfoProvider

Background Job

In the Transfer Profile (Figure 11.21) we'll talk about various parameters used to release demand to SAP ERP.

APO (Source)

▶ **Planning Area**

This is the source planning area in which the demand plan is developed.

▶ **Key Figure**

Key figures such as Forecast, Marketing Forecast, and Customer Forecast need to be released from Demand Planning.

▶ **Planning Version**

This is the source planning version.

▶ **Period Split**

You can also split the forecast when transferring the demand plan; that is, you can go from weekly to daily split, monthly to weekly or daily split, and so on. Transaction code /SAPAPO/MC8U – Maintain Transfer Profiles is used to create the transfer forecast profile. Once this release profile is created, it is added to an activity using Transaction code /SAPAPO/MC8T – Define Activities for Mass Processing, and this activity is added to a background job using Transaction code /SAPAPO/MC8D – Create Demand Planning in the Background.

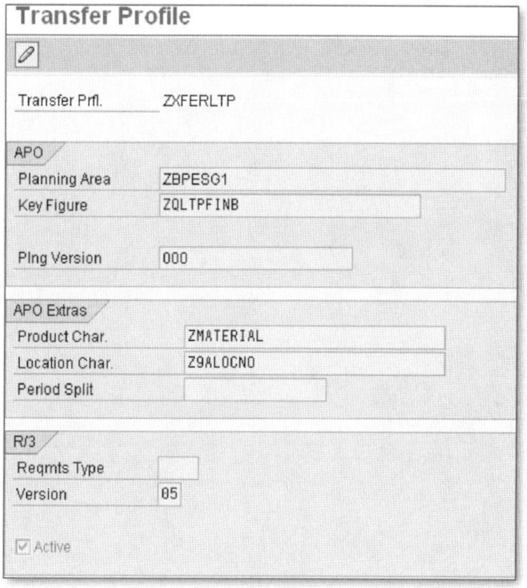

Figure 11.21 Transfer Profile to Send Demand Plan to SAP ERP

You enter the key figure to be released into the Transfer Profile screen. Use the APO Extras section if the standard 9AMATNR and 9ALOCNO characteristics are not used.

ERP

▶ **Requirements type**
Strategy for planning, for example, planning with final assembly, made to stock.

▶ **Version**
The target version in ERP 00.

▶ **Active**
If this checkbox is selected, then the active version is considered in the MRP run.

Release via an InfoProvider

Another method of releasing data from Demand Planning to MRP is the use of Transaction /SAPAPO/REL_TO_OLTP – Release from InfoProvider to ERP System, which is shown in Figure 11.22. There is an additional step in which data needs to be extracted from the planning area to the InfoProvider. Once data is stored in the InfoProvider, it can be released.

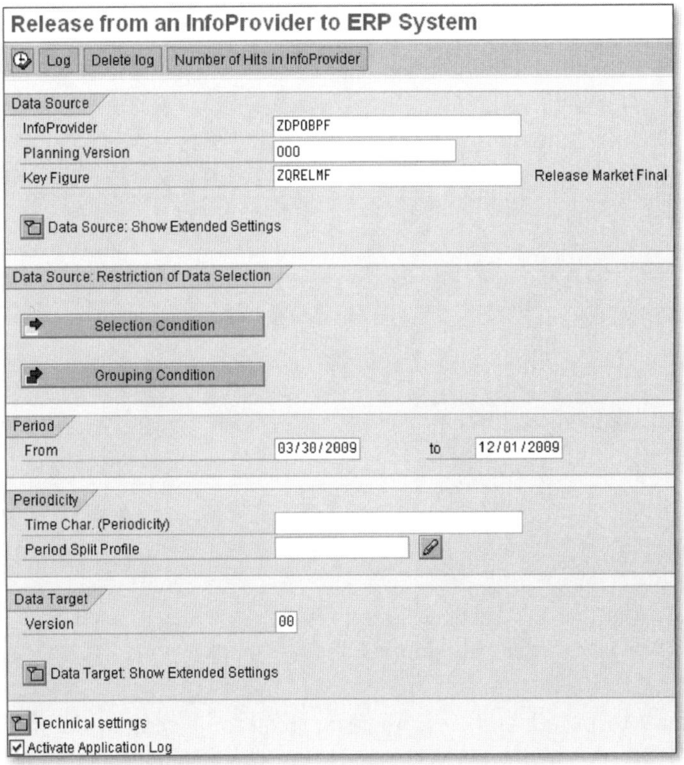

Figure 11.22 Releasing Through an InfoProvider

Various parameters on the screen control what data is released, which we'll discuss in the following sections.

Data Source

This is the InfoProvider where data is stored after extraction from the planning area. You enter the key figure that needs to be released here.

Data Source: Restriction of Data Selection

If you need to send only selective data, you can use selections to filter only required data.

Period

SAP ERP may require a smaller duration of forecast released for a daily MRP run versus a larger duration of forecast released during a weekly MRP run. This horizon will control how much data is released from Demand Planning to SNP. The start and end dates can be made to roll as you move into the future by giving the current date as starting date and using a +/– offset for the end date. This can be saved in a variant.

Periodicity

Demand planning can be done in weekly buckets, but MRP might plan at the daily bucket level, or perhaps demand needs to be split from Demand Planning based on certain weightings. These requirements can be supported using the split profile. Various proportions can be specified, and when data is released, it will be split accordingly.

Data Target

Data Target is usually 00, which means it's an active version that is being transferred.

11.6.3 SAP APO Global Available-to-Promise (GATP)

GATP is a component in SAP APO that authorizes order commitments based on available inventory in the supply chain network. Orders that are entered in SAP ERP are seamlessly checked to ensure that sufficient inventory exists to fill them based on rules predefined by the organization. GATP check results in a commit date for the order items.

When the supply for a given product is constrained, planners will ration or place limits on stock for certain customers. These rations are known as allocations. Instead of using the reservation process in SAP ERP, allocations can be enforced with GATP and Demand Planning. In such a scenario, allocations allow planners to restrict the quantity or supply that will be available for each customer. Demand planners adjust the demand based on various parameters in Demand Planning such as customer forecast, customer orders, marketing forecast, and past sales. In a constrained supply situation, planners can allocate certain stock to customers based on customers' past sales, priority, and so on. The numbers can be entered or derived in the Demand Planning books, which can then be used in the GATP component. So when a sales order is entered before committing to all of the available stock to the customer, GATP looks at the allocated quantity in Demand Planning and commits stock only up to the allocated quantity.

The configuration for creating planning books is the same as the configuration of the Demand Planning planning area, with some exceptions. Besides 9AMATNR and 9ACUST_NO we need to add InfoObjects 9AKONOB and 9AVKORG to the master planning object structure in Demand Planning. The configuration of master planning object structures and planning books is explained in detail in Chapter 9. These objects are mapped to objects on GATP, and the connection to the planning area is maintained via customizing settings SPRO. You can use macros to calculate the allocated quantity or manually enter them in the planning book. Figure 11.23 demonstrates allocations in GATP.

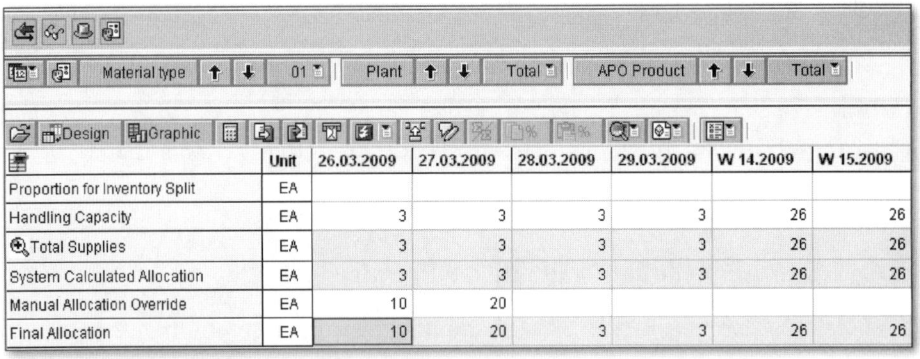

	Unit	26.03.2009	27.03.2009	28.03.2009	29.03.2009	W 14.2009	W 15.2009
Proportion for Inventory Split	EA						
Handling Capacity	EA	3	3	3	3	26	26
Total Supplies	EA	3	3	3	3	26	26
System Calculated Allocation	EA	3	3	3	3	26	26
Manual Allocation Override	EA	10	20				
Final Allocation	EA	10	20	3	3	26	26

Figure 11.23 GATP Allocations

These allocations are based on total supplies, handling capacity, and manual override as entered by planners. If an order comes in for the period 26.03.2009 for 25 units, GATP will look at the final allocation quantity of 10 units and will confirm only 10 units.

11.7   Summary

Engaging in demand management without applying it to support decisions to commit resources is an academic exercise at best. The time, talent, and resources consumed by a demand planning process should yield improvements to the balance sheet and income statement like any other investment an organization makes. However, far from being merely a transactional input, the availability of more accurate demand plans at different levels in different time periods can actually justify changes in traditional planning and operations cycles.

Having driven operations planning and hopefully ended up with having the right amount of the right products in the right places at the right times, it's time to complete the cycle with performance measurement and continuous improvement. After the sale is made, the accuracy of the demand plan, or more precisely, of multiple iterations of the demand plan, can be assessed. This is what we'll focus on in the next chapter.

In this chapter, you'll learn about how you can capture your sales figures and use them efficiently in order to develop your perspective on the sources of demand.

12 Process and Performance Management

The trouble with continuous improvement of continuous processes is that it's like taking apart a jet engine and looking inside while the plane is still in the air. Of course, this is a terrible overstatement of the true situation, but it helps us to remember that just because last week's or last month's demand plan is over, that doesn't mean everyone involved isn't working just as hard on the next month's plan.

With all of the asset- and income-impacting decisions in the previous chapter being heavily influenced by the demand plan, it really isn't an option to ignore the accuracy of the resulting demand plan and its key inputs. In this chapter, we'll look at how organizations can capture their sales figures and use them to reduce the effects of systematic biases and gain insights into the more credible sources of demand insight in your organization.

12.1 Identify and Confront Bias

Bias is a consistent tendency to provide projections that are overly high or overly low. It can result from incomplete data sets, inadequately maintained smoothing constants, or even systematic bias that is built into reward plans. Figure 12.1 shows an example of a forecast that, like an eternal optimist, shows a positive bias. The dashed line of the forecast is continuously higher than the dotted line showing actual demand.

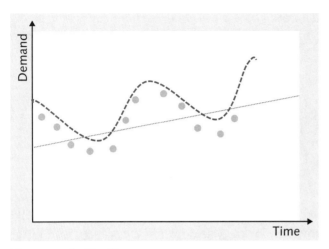

Figure 12.1 Positive Bias

In contrast, it is also possible for demand projections to develop a consistent negative bias, as shown in Figure 12.2. Again, the dashed line represents the forecast, which is, this time, continuously below the dotted actual demand.

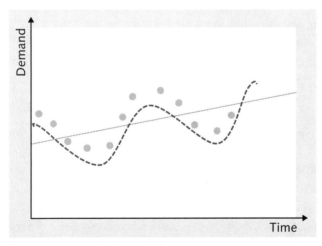

Figure 12.2 Negative Forecast Bias

One cause of bias, as we mentioned, is systematic. In some cases, individuals responsible for demand projection are incentivized to add buffers. Any sales executive who has ever failed to sell enough to make his quota (and hence receive a bonus or promotion) because the company was temporarily out of a product that a customer wanted to buy would be very tempted to artificially increase future demand projections to ensure that products are in stock.

This bias is by no means intentionally dishonest, because most sales executives would see the loss of a sale to a customer as damaging to the company itself, not only in terms of revenue but also in terms of relationship with the customer. Most sales organizations also do not own responsibility for excess or obsolete inventories, which means they would not likely even recognize that their forecast bias is costing more money than it's saving.

12.2 Assigning Responsibility for Accuracy

Production and inventory managers might have different biases from sales executives, depending on how their success is measured. With goals of plant efficiency or inventory reductions, they might conclude that a few lost sales are worth the savings to the company. Again, the individuals may not even knowingly engage in a bias, but simply choose to be consistently optimistic or pessimistic about demand for a product, region, channel, customer, and so on.

Organizations that are serious about demand management and believe that when done well it can impact the balance sheet and income statement as much as a productive manufacturing line, efficient warehouse, or engaging sales force need to consider assigning responsibility to individuals for their contributions to the process. It's ridiculous to suggest that a sales executive be punished for bringing in an unexpected windfall order at the end of a fiscal quarter, assuming that there's inventory or capacity to fill that order. However, every individual who contributes to projecting or impacting demand should receive feedback on how accurate that contribution was and some incentive to maintain or improve their accuracy.

12.3 Absolute and Weighted Metrics

That there are three kinds of lies — lies, damned lies, and statistics — is a remark that Mark Twain attributed to 19th century British Prime Minister Benjamin Disraeli. Forecast accuracies are such statistics and can sometimes insidiously lie to us while telling the truth. Figure 12.3 shows an example.

Forecast Error

	January	February	March	April	May	June
National Forecast	2,600	2,800	2,600	2,800	2,700	2,400
National Sales	2,600	2,700	2,700	2,700	2,600	2,500
National Forecast Error	0	-100	100	-100	-100	100
Eastern Forecast	1,200	1,400	1,000	1,000	1,200	1,200
Eastern Sales	1,000	1,000	800	800	900	1,100
Eastern Forecast Error	-200	-400	-200	-200	-300	-100
Western Forecast	1,400	1,400	1,600	1,800	1,500	1,200
Western Sales	1,600	1,700	1,900	1,900	1,700	1,400
Western Forecast Error	200	300	300	100	200	200

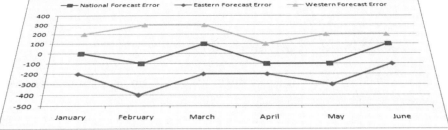

Figure 12.3 Errors in Eastern and Western Forecasts Cancel Out

A cursory glance at the national forecast would show no particular biases and indicate good demand plans. A more careful look at the eastern and western forecasts would expose a strong negative bias in the east and a strong positive bias in the west. It's likely that many customers who traditionally received product from the closer western distribution centers were serviced more than once from the east either because the west didn't have enough inventory or because the inventory in the east was building up and threatening to go bad.

Regardless of whether they are percentages or straight volume-based error measures, negative and positive errors can hide each other at higher levels. To ensure that two wrongs don't make a right, organizations believing that lost sales and excess inventories (Figure 12.4) are important calculate absolute error measurements. Where the dashed forecast exceeds the dotted actuals, too much product was made or stored (excess inventory). Where the dotted actuals exceed the forecast, not enough product was made or stored, and it needs to be expensively shipped from afar or customer orders will be lost.

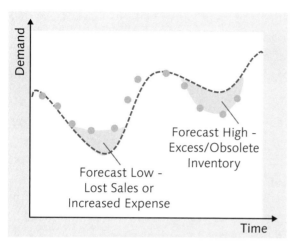

Figure 12.4 High and Low Forecast Errors Can Be Equally Expensive

Figure 12.5 shows the national forecast as measured in absolute terms (as a percentage).

	January	February	March	April	May	June
Forecast Error						
National Forecast	2,600	2,800	2,600	2,800	2,700	2,400
National Sales	2,600	2,700	2,700	2,700	2,600	2,500
National Forecast Error	15%	25%	19%	13%	19%	13%
Eastern Forecast	1,200	1,400	1,000	1,000	1,200	1,200
Eastern Sales	1,000	1,000	800	800	900	1,100
Eastern Forecast Error	17%	29%	20%	20%	25%	8%
Western Forecast	1,400	1,400	1,600	1,800	1,500	1,200
Western Sales	1,600	1,700	1,900	1,900	1,700	1,400
Western Forecast Error	14%	21%	19%	6%	13%	17%

Figure 12.5 Absolute Forecast Error Treats High and Low Errors Equally

311

Note that regardless of whether the sales were higher (west) or lower (east) than the forecast, the difference is still considered forecast error. Also notice that it is no longer possible to calculate aggregate error (the national forecast error) by simply using the national forecast and national sales figures. The forecast error must be calculated at the detailed level and then aggregated up as well.

In this example, the component forecast errors (east and west) were simply averaged. This can become an issue, though, when there is significant difference between the regions. Even in our example, the western region's forecasts were higher, which means that 1% of error in the west costs more than 1% or error in the east. For example, in January 1% of the western forecast is 14 and 1% of the eastern forecast is only 12. In Figure 12.6 the errors are *weighted,* or multiplied by their respective forecasts before being averaged together.

Forecast Error

	January	February	March	April	May	June
National Forecast	2,600	2,800	2,600	2,800	2,700	2,400
National Sales	2,600	2,700	2,700	2,700	2,600	2,500
National Forecast Error	15%	25%	19%	11%	19%	13%
Eastern Forecast	1,200	1,400	1,000	1,000	1,200	1,200
Eastern Sales	1,000	1,000	800	800	900	1,100
Eastern Forecast Error	17%	29%	20%	20%	25%	8%
Western Forecast	1,400	1,400	1,600	1,800	1,500	1,200
Western Sales	1,600	1,700	1,900	1,900	1,700	1,400
Western Forecast Error	14%	21%	19%	6%	13%	17%

Figure 12.6 Weighted Forecast Error Percentages Take into Account Relative Size Differences

In April, the aggregate (national) forecast error has improved by 2% because the larger western forecast had a lower error than the smaller eastern forecast. When forecast errors are aggregated across products as well as regions, weightings can sometimes include average selling price or profit margins to differentiate from building an excess 1,000 $2 screwdrivers and an excess 1,000 $200 drills.

12.4 Lagged Accuracy

Chapter 11 claimed that like a tree falling in the woods with no one around to hear, a forecast for a product, region, customer, and so on in a time period when no decisions need be made makes no sound. Projections of demand can only impact the balance sheet and the income statement if they are driving decisions to commit resources. At the end of the week or month when all sales have been made, not a lot of operational decisions are left to make. This, then, is probably the wrong version of the forecast to test for accuracy.

If raw materials are generally purchased by production facilities one month prior to the finished goods being sold, then the amount and type of materials purchased was based on the forecast as it existed one month ago. This is the *one-month lagged forecast* against which the error should be measured. Figure 12.7 shows the calculation of a one-month lagged forecast.

Forecast Error						
	January	February	March	April	May	June
Eastern Forecast	1,200	1,400	1,000	1,000	1,200	1,200
1 Month Lagged Eastern Forecast	1,200	1,200	1,200	1,200	1,200	1,200
Eastern Sales	1,000	1,000	800	800	900	1,100
Eastern Forecast Error	17%	29%	20%	20a%	25%	8%
Eastern Forecast Error (1 Month Lag)	17%	17%	33%	33%	25%	8%

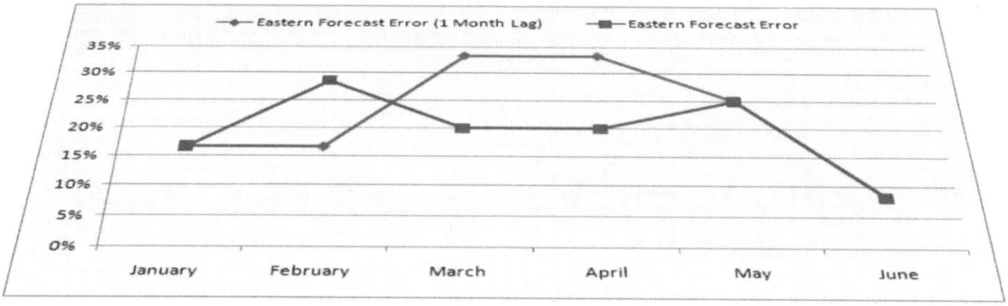

Figure 12.7 Lagged Forecast Accuracy

As Figure 12.7 shows, in the 1 Month Lagged Eastern Forecast row for February, one month prior to February, when materials were being ordered, the forecast for February was 1,200 units. It was later changed to 1,400 (as is shown in the Eastern

Forecast row and the February column), maybe as a sales promotion was finalized, but not in time to affect the raw materials purchase. The result is that whereas the absolute percentage error for February looks like 17%, the lagged forecast error on which material purchases were committed was actually 29%. March and April both show a similar story as well.

Companies sometimes track multiple lags at different levels of aggregation. If contract rates are agreed upon nationally with suppliers five months in advance, then the five-month lagged forecast error should also be tracked at the national level as a companion to the one-month lagged regional forecast. The five-month lagged forecast error is measured at a national level because the contract with the supplier is for a single, national amount that will be purchased. Because nobody really cares where the materials will be shipped five months out, the regional forecasts are immaterial.

Again, aggregates are not limited to regions, but could be any combination of characteristics, as we discussed in Chapter 5. In our example above, the company could choose to group the forecasts for all of the products that were made from the raw materials in question at a national level.

This process may seem overly complex, and indeed some very large and successful organizations today choose not to invest in tracking lagged forecast accuracies. However, most people agree that what gets measured gets done, and we have proven that the ability to impact assets, costs, and product availability is based on having more accurate demand projections at the times that decisions are being made. For companies intent on improving their top and/or bottom lines with demand management, there are clearly benefits in lagged forecast accuracy measurement.

12.5 Reporting Forecast Accuracy with SAP APO and SAP NetWeaver BW

SAP APO comes with a business warehouse (BW) component that is contained within and completely integrated with standard SAP APO delivered systems. The BW infrastructure has features to extract the planning data and run reports for this data in the SAP Business Explorer. This is illustrated in Figure 12.8.

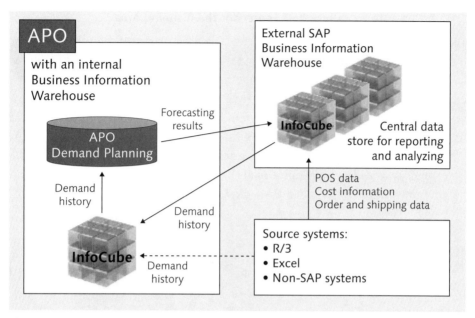

Figure 12.8 Integration of SAP APO and SAP NetWeaver BW

Historical data can be transferred to SAP APO from SAP ERP, SAP NetWeaver BW, Excel, and legacy systems and saved in InfoCubes. InfoCubes are used in SAP NetWeaver BW and Demand Planning as central data containers to store historical data and archive planning data. The historical data is the basis for forecasting within Demand Planning. The demand plan is created as a result of the forecast. Within SAP APO Demand Planning, you can use macros to calculate and monitor forecast accuracy and generate alerts for errors as triggers to fine-tune your forecast in line with market demand. However, for key performance indicator (KPI) reporting such as forecast accuracy, the usual practice is to extract the planning data from SAP APO Demand Planning and archive it in InfoCubes for reporting. You can then use the SAP Business Explorer frontend to run reports on the data stored in the InfoCubes.

12.5.1 Steps for Extracting Planning Data

In this section we'll review the steps you need to take extract your planning data.

Step 1: Generate an Export DataSource for the Planning Area

The first step of the procedure to extract the data from the planning area and store the planning data in an InfoCube is the creation of an export DataSource. Follow menu path ADVANCED PLANNING AND OPTIMIZATION • DEMAND PLANNING • ENVIRONMENT • ADMINISTRATION OF DEMAND PLANNING AND SUPPLY NETWORK PLANNING. Right-click on the planning area and in the context menu select Change. In the planning area screen menu, select EXTRAS • DATA EXTRACTION TOOLS to bring up the DP/SNP Data Extraction screen shown in Figure 12.9. Click on the Generate DataSource button. The DataSource name begins with 9A because that's the default naming convention. Enter a name for the DataSource and click on Continue.

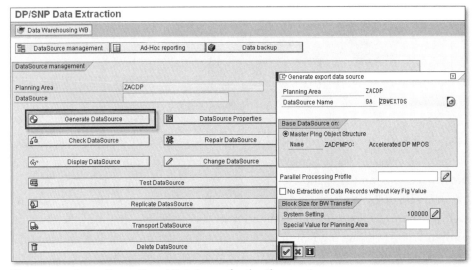

Figure 12.9 Generating an Export DataSource for the Planning Area

In the DataSource, the Customer version Edit screen that appears, and you can specify which fields you want the system to use as filters, while extracting data, by checking the selection box (Figure 12.10).

Select Hide field for the fields (InfoObjects) that you do not want to export or extract. The number of fields you transfer directly affects performance. Therefore, you should only transfer fields that you require for reporting purposes. After you edit the DataSource, select DATASOURCE • GENERATE to generate the export DataSource.

DataSource: Customer version Edit

Header Data

DataSource	9AZBWEXTDS	Package
Description	ZACDP / ZADPMPOS	

Extraction

ExtractStruct.	/1APO/EXT_STRU001000178
Direct Access	X
Delta Update	☐ DataSource for Reconciliation ☐

Field Name	Short text	Selection	Hide field	Inversion	Field
/BIC/ZCATEGORY	Category	☑	☐	☐	[
/BIC/ZCLSABC	Product Class	☑	☐	☐	[
/BIC/ZPRDBRAND	Product Brand	☑	☐	☐	[
/BIC/ZSEGMENT	Product Segment	☑	☐	☐	[
/BIC/ZASM	Area Sales Manager	☑	☐	☐	[
/BIC/ZNSM	National Sales Manager	☑	☐	☐	[
/BIC/ZRSM	Regional Sales Manager	☑	☐	☐	[
/BIC/ZCUST	Customer	☑	☐	☐	[
/BIC/ZTSM	Teritory Sales Manager	☑	☐	☐	[
/BI0/9ALOCNO	APO Location	☑	☐	☐	[
/BIC/ZBZUNIT	Business Unit	☑	☐	☐	[
/BIC/ZCHANNEL	Sales Channel	☑	☐	☐	[
/BI0/9AVERSION	APO Planning Version	☑	☐	☐	[
/BI0/9ADPDANT	Proportional Factor	☐	☑	☐	[
/BI0/9ADPDANTF	Fixed Proportional Factor	☐	☑	☐	[
/BIC/ZACTSAL	Actual Sales	☐	☐	☐	[
/BIC/ZAGGDP	Agreed Demand Plan	☐	☐	☐	[
/BIC/ZANPLDIS	Annual Plan Disaggregation	☐	☐	☐	[
/BIC/ZANUPLAN	Annual Plan	☐	☐	☐	[
/BIC/ZANUPLVAL	Annual Plan Value	☐	☐	☐	[

Figure 12.10   Selecting and Hiding Fields in the Export DataSource

Step 2. Replicate the DataSource

After generating the export DataSource, you must replicate it to create a replica for data extraction and make it available in the Data Warehousing Workbench for further use. To do so, right-click on the source system in the modeling area of the workbench (Transaction RSA1) and click on Replicate DataSources, as shown in Figure 12.11. This replicates the DataSource in the logical system of the SAP SCM client source system under the DataSources section of the workbench (Figure 12.12). Note that in this case the system in which you are operating is Demand Planning. The technical name of the source system is based on the client. For example, if you're planning in system SC5 client 100, the technical name of the source system is SC5CLNT100.

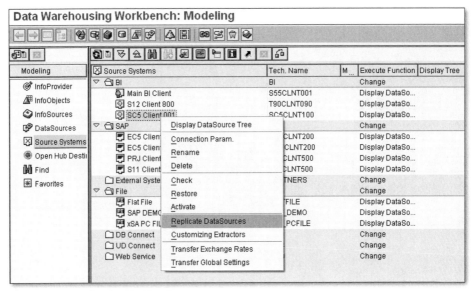

Figure 12.11 Replicating the DataSource

When the system messages cease at the bottom of the screen, the system triggers a background job that finishes the replication process by creating the necessary changes in the system for data transfer from the DataSource to the logical SAP SCM client. Check in the job overview (Transaction SM37) that this job has finished before proceeding to the next step.

Step 3: Create an InfoCube to Store the Planning Data

To create an InfoCube for storing archived planning data, create a basic InfoCube by running program /SAPAPO/TS_PAREA_TO_ICUBE. Follow the menu path TOOLS • ABAP WORKBENCH • ADMINISTRATOR DEVELOPMENT • ABAP EDITOR. Enter Program name "/SAPAPO/TS_PAREA_TO_ICUBE" and click on Execute as shown in Figure 12.12.

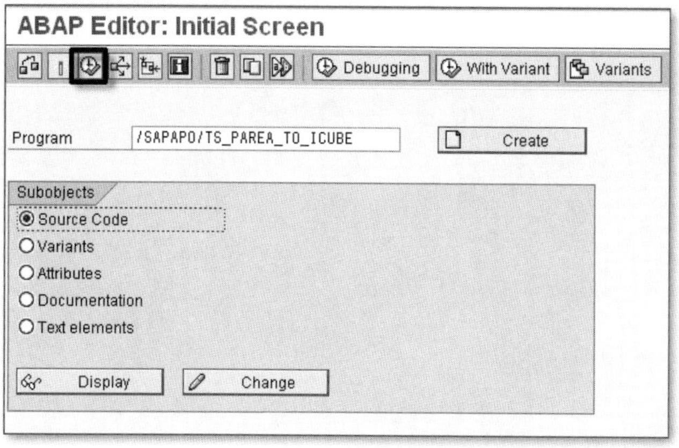

Figure 12.12 Generating an InfoCube to Store Demand Planning Data

In the screen that opens up, as illustrated in Figure 12.13, enter the name of the Demand Planning area whose planning data you need to store, the name of the InfoCube in which the data needs to be stored, and the InfoArea where the Info-Cube needs to be created and click on Execute. InfoAreas are used to organize the objects in the SAP NetWeaver BW: Each InfoProvider or InfoCube is assigned to an InfoArea. This hierarchy can be displayed in the Data Warehousing Workbench.

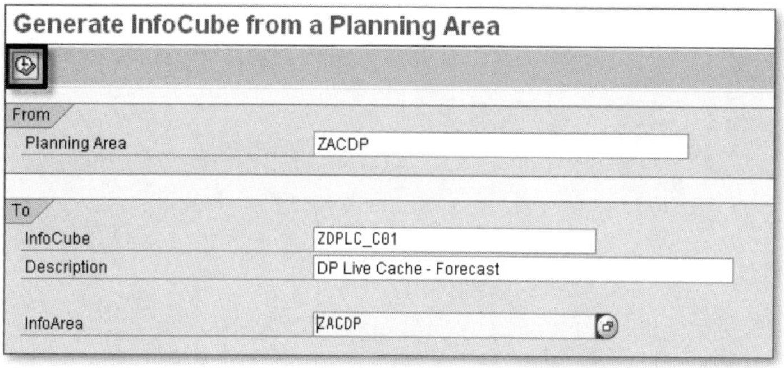

Figure 12.13 Generating an InfoCube from a Planning Area

Based on the parameters entered, the system creates an InfoCube with all of the characteristics and key figures applicable for the planning area, as shown in Figure 12.14.

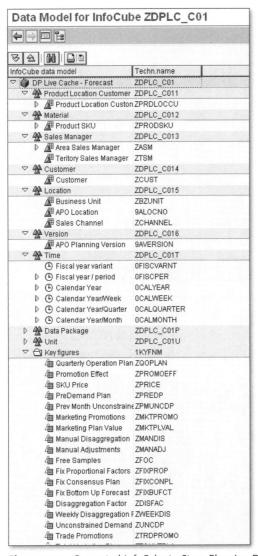

Figure 12.14 Generated InfoCube to Store Planning Data

Step 4: Create Transformation

The transformation process allows you to consolidate, cleanse, and integrate data. When you load data from one SAP NetWeaver BW object such as a DataSource into another SAP NetWeaver BW object such as an InfoCube, the data is passed through a transformation. A transformation converts the fields of the source into the format of the target.

To create the transformation, select Create Transformation in the context menu of the InfoProvider created in step 3 in the InfoProvider section of the Data Warehousing Workbench, as illustrated in Figure 12.15.

Figure 12.15 Creating Transformation

In the screen that opens up, as illustrated in Figure 12.16, select a source for your transformation and select Continue.

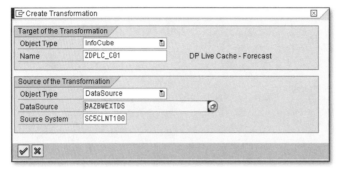

Figure 12.16 Create Transformation Screen

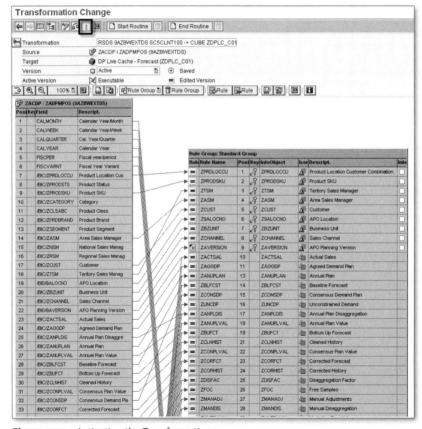

Figure 12.17 Activating the Transformation

The system proposes a transformation, as shown in Figure 12.17, and maps the source fields from the DataSource to the target fields in the InfoCube. You can use this transformation as it is or modify it to suit your requirements. A transformation consists of rules that define how the data content of a target field is determined. Various types of rules are available to the user such as direct transfer, currency translation, unit of measure conversion, routine, and read from master data. Activate the transformation after you're done making changes to the transformation.

Step 5: Create Data Transfer Process

You use the data transfer process (DTP) to transfer data within SAP NetWeaver BW from a persistent object to another object in accordance with certain transformations and filters. To create a DTP, select Create Data Transfer Process in the context menu of the InfoProvider created in step 3 in the InfoProvider section of the Data Warehousing Workbench, as illustrated in Figure 12.18.

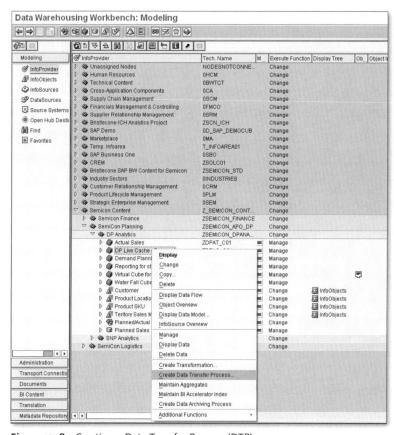

Figure 12.18 Creating a Data Transfer Process (DTP)

In the screen that opens up, Select a source for your DTP and select Continue, as illustrated in Figure 12.19.

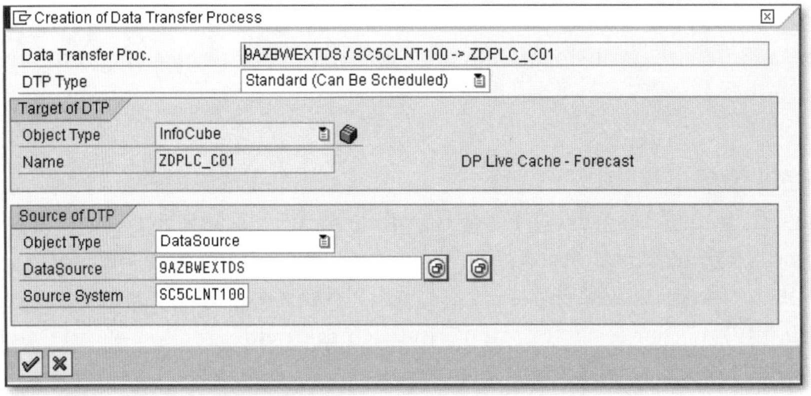

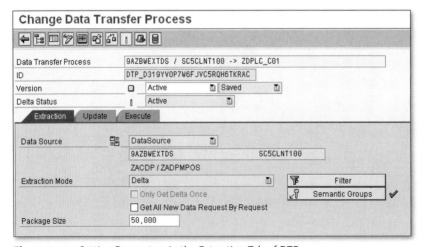

Figure 12.19 Creation of Data Transfer Process

The extraction mode of a DTP is either Full or Delta, as shown in Figure 12.20. You use this property to control the dataset read upon extraction. The Full mode enables extraction of all requested data whereas, the Delta mode enables extraction of data that is new (since the last extract). The package size describes the number of data records that are contained in one individual data package that is read by the extractor. The number specified here has a direct impact on memory consumption during extraction.

Figure 12.20 Setting Parameters in the Extraction Tab of DTP

To filter the data, click on the Filter button. In the screen that opens, as shown in Figure 12.21, you can set filter criteria to allow only data that meet filter criteria to transfer the data from the DataSource to the InfoCube.

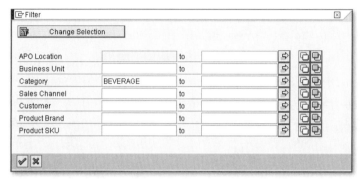

Figure 12.21 Setting a Filter in the DTP

The data transfer process can be scheduled in the process chain to run at scheduled intervals. Figure 12.22 shows an example where the data extraction is scheduled weekly at 1900 Hrs.

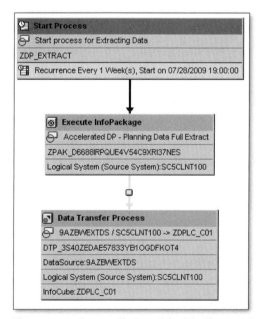

Figure 12.22 Process Chain to Schedule Planning Data Extraction

Planning data is extracted periodically at scheduled intervals. These extractions provide a snapshot of demand at different points in time. These snapshots provide the basis for lagged accuracy reporting. The reports can be configured to pick the forecast data from each of these snapshots to represent the one-month lagged forecast or other multiple lags and use these numbers to compare with the actual demand data to calculate the forecast error and forecast accuracy.

SAP Business Explorer can be used to develop reports for displaying the planning data. The report is based on the InfoCube that stores the planning data extraction. The query can be published as a web query, and the use can access it in an Internet browser by clicking on the link. The link can also be stored as a favorite in the browser. The system prompts the user to enter the login information and displays the query selection criteria, as illustrated in Figure 12.23. Based on the selection criteria entered, the system runs the SAP Business Explorer report and displays the data.

Figure 12.23 Running the Business Explorer Query

Figure 12.24 shows the forecast accuracy report output. The report displays the forecast accuracy using the previous month's forecast (one-month lag forecast). The reports can be run for a range of time periods to monitor the forecast accuracy and analyze for trends.

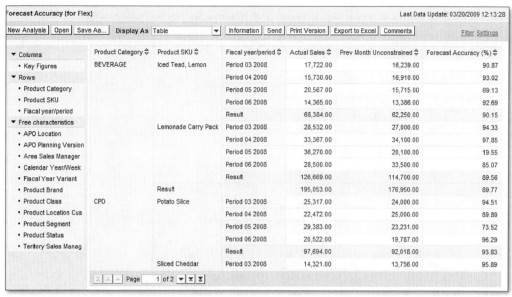

Figure 12.24 Forecast Accuracy Report Using SAP Business Explorer

Similarly, forecast accuracy can be generated for the various forecast streams coming from internal and external teams in a company following a consensus and collaborative planning process to determine which forecast streams are more accurate vis-à-vis others and allow comparison.

For extensive reporting, it's a good idea to implement an independent SAP NetWeaver BW server and only transfer the data that is relevant for planning to the SAP APO system, and extract the planning data back to the independent SAP NetWeaver BW server. This independent system then becomes a central data store for reporting and analysis, containing both transaction data and planning data from different systems. This allows for other KPI reporting such as perfect order fulfillment that would not normally be available within Demand Planning.

The forecast accuracy and other demand-planning-relevant metrics can also be reported using SAP BusinessObjects, which has capabilities for dashboard reporting and rich interactive data visualization capabilities. Figure 12.25 shows an example of demand planning metrics reporting in SAP BusinessObjects.

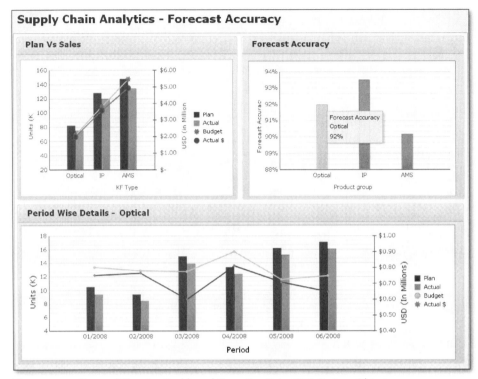

Figure 12.25 Demand Planning Dashboard Reporting Using SAP BusinessObjects

The dashboard can be developed using the Xcelsius component of Business Objects. SAP BusinessObjects also has capabilities to interface with SAP NetWeaver BW to get the stored data and display the information in dashboards.

12.6 Summary

Investors and stakeholders today have a lot of options for investing their money. Similarly, customers have many options among vendors selling closely related products. In such an environment, continuous improvement is not an option; it's a mandate. Measuring the contributions of individual departments and executives to the demand management process and assessing them for accuracy at the time and place where the organization's resources are committed is the first step in continuous improvement.

SAP offers packaged metrics from the Supply Chain Council's Supply Chain Operations Reference Model (SCOR) within the SAP NetWeaver BW application. Customers can begin with these packaged analytics and expand out to develop visibility of the effectiveness of and opportunities within their demand management processes.

The next step in continuous improvement is planning and managing changes to the process, technology, and organization. Chapter 13 will focus on this from the perspective of selecting and implementing a demand management organization, process, and solution, but many of the insights apply equally to incremental changes to existing demand management processes, organizations, and solutions.

This chapter covers how to plan for and start the process to implement demand management, with an eye for success.

13 Managing a Change Process

In the previous chapters, we talked about how SAP APO Demand Planning can help implement demand management. This chapter identifies how an organization can set upon the journey to implement demand management and ensure success. A detailed discussion about how to select an implementation partner follows, including coverage of project governance methodology and managing scope to ensure a successful project delivery. Subsequent sections focus on identifying various components to be considered while defining the success of the project and mechanisms necessary to track the benefits of the change.

13.1 Selecting a Team or Partner

There's more to a successful supply chain implementation project than simply selecting the best enabling technology for the job. The choice of an implementation partner is perhaps the most important decision that the organization will make after it selects a product.

13.1.1 Different Types of Implementation Partners

Organizations invest tremendous time and resources into undertaking a thorough analysis to identify and select the right software vendor for their supply chain solution. Unfortunately, the same due diligence is frequently missing when an implementation partner is selected, even though (or perhaps because) implementation costs typically exceed licensing fees. Too often, a software choice is made, and only then does an implementation partner get involved. This tendency adds unnecessary risk to supply chain projects. Even with the ideal software technology, many things can and will go wrong during the implementation, and an organization's ability to overcome those obstacles depends on the quality of its relationship with its implementation partner. If more care is given to selecting the right implementation partner with the right experience and skills, chances of hiccups in the project can be minimized.

At a broad level, implementation partners can be divided into five categories, each of which we'll discuss in the following sections.

Management Consults

Management consultancies vary in size from global consulting firms to small, but generally focus on executive-level management consulting. These companies begin with a strategic analysis of the situation. This can be useful for companies that are working on defining or redefining their supply chain strategy. Typically, the consult's understanding of information technology (IT) is weaker than their grasp of other important topics such as strategy, operations, and marketing. More often than not, these firms do not participate in the implementation of software and other technology that supports the changes they recommend. In some cases, though, they may partner with another firm or contingent contractors.

System Integrators (SIs)

SIs also vary greatly in size, but they all focus on the development, deployment, and integration of business processes and enabling technology. A trusted SI partner ideally already knows and possibly has implemented other IT systems in the organization, and should understand the overall technical architecture and IT strategy of the organization. However, their understanding of supply chains may not be their strong suite. In cases like these, they too may, like general practitioners in medicine, outsource to a practice with more specialized skills after making the initial diagnosis.

Boutiques

Boutiques are small to midsized firms and focused consulting shops. Some are neutral on the subject of software vendors, but through natural talent development, many have focused skills on a specific set of supply chain applications. These firms can assist a client with selecting a supply chain solution vendor. In addition, if the application selection has already been done, these firms can bring in supply chain best practices expertise in certain industries, and very deep product knowledge of the selected solution. As an analogy, if the generic systems integrator is a general practitioner, then the boutiques are the surgeons and cardiologists.

Vendor Professional Services Organizations (PSOs)

Many software vendors offer their own professional services expertise through consulting engagements. Consultants from software vendors usually know their product well, but they are also usually more expensive and in short supply. Although some good supply chain experts can be found, most vendor PSO consultants tend to be technical experts in their company's product, and lack knowledge of business and/or industry best practices.

In-House Information Technology Organization

The internal IT team is almost always a part of the implementation team. Whereas they understand their processes and issues very well, they may lack SAP knowledge and specific expertise. On the other hand, where IT knows the business very well, they can facilitate the supply chain implementation and become a collaborator between business and external consultants. When working with internal IT teams, it is essential not only that they receive proper training, but also that these resources are dedicated to the project and not subject to other internal assignments.

13.1.2   What to Look for in an Implementation Partner

With the wide range of consulting organizations, it can be difficult to identify the right partner for your supply chain implementation. To select one or more partners, you should use well-balanced evaluation criteria, similar to the vendor selection process. As a project team, before you start on the selection journey you should identify these key selection criteria and their order of priority. You'll be surprised at what you come up with! Whereas the criteria may be the same, the prioritization may be completely different, based on supply chain and/or IT maturity. The typical criteria are:

▶ Process and industry knowledge

▶ Solution expertise

▶ Past experience and references

▶ Price

When the engagement is driven by the business rather than IT, where the company has developed a business case, the priority would be in the order listed above. When the engagement is IT driven, price is usually the driving factor. The essential question that should be answered is what the cost to the business is if the initiative is unsuccessful, partially successful, or successful.

The following sections provide a short list of topics that should initiate the thought process. The relevance of the questions in these sections depends on your internal business and IT structure and direction.

Company Focus

Evaluate the partner's focus. Are they a specialist in supply chain management, or is this one of their multiple practice areas? How long have they been working with the SAP SCM technology? How many people do they have with the skills required for the project? Is the partner large enough and skilled enough to support a project of your scope?

Scope of Service Offerings

Evaluate the scope of their offerings. Do they have experience in handling projects of your size and complexity? Do they primarily offer supply chain consulting, SAP SCM consulting, or both? Have they done such projects before? Can they assist you with change management? Can they offer help with setting up the help desk, so you can provide end-user support after you're live with the product? Alternatively, do they offer a managed service for end-user support? Does the consulting partner offer upgrade services? Do they have expertise in integrating with other systems, especially the types you have in your game plan? Do they understand the big picture of your technical architecture? If you want the solution hosted off-site, do they have previous experience in hosting the similar solution, and if so, what service level agreements can they sign up to?

References

Does the implementation partner have references in the same industry, or a similar industry, as yours? Do they have experience with companies of similar size and complexity? Do they have reference stories or case studies? Do they understand best practices for implementing supply chain solutions? Take the time to conduct reference calls and customer visits. What is the industry analyst's perspective on their capabilities?

Process Expertise

Does the implementation partner have specific expertise in your business processes? In addition to references, do they have a best practices process template, based on the SAP SCM solutions, for the business processes in your industry? Such content is often the difference between the consultants who are just aware of the best practices (those that have theoretical knowledge) and those who have implemented them.

Solution Expertise

Does the implementation partner have the specific product expertise? Is your supply chain partner a certified partner of SAP? To qualify for SAP Services partnership, a firm must fulfill rigorous criteria, which include demonstrating a proven track record with SAP and having a verified support and project delivery model. However, certification is just a starting point to understanding the implementation partner's solution expertise. Beyond this, you need to consider if the implementation partner understands the relevant best practices in your industry, Do they have accelerators and enablers, for example, blueprint and training material for your industry segment? Can they showcase that capability? Such expertise is the difference between a consultant who has only attended product training and a consultant who brings significant value to the engagement to lower your risk and accelerate your implementations. Finally, do they have a close partnership with SAP, which is important because it gives the consulting firm a clear view into where the SAP SCM solution is heading, and they can use the information to address your requirements such that future migrations will be easier.

Engagement Model

What is the consulting firm's engagement model — fixed price, time, and material, a combination of the two (hybrid), or a value-based pricing model? If it's a hybrid model, what component of the fee is fixed? If it's a time and material model, is there a "not to exceed" clause? Are there any holdbacks on a fixed fee model? If you have risk sharing based on a value pricing model, such as percentage of their fees being tied to results and variable, what percentage of the fee is fixed, and what are the terms on it? How flexible is the firm in combining various approaches to fit your needs?

Methodology

How does implementation partner's project methodology map to your principles for project governance? Is there a balance between governance and execution, or it is so overbearing that it can drown the project? Is it flexible enough to meet your specific needs?

Geographical Coverage

Does your partner have the geographical coverage and scale to support a project of your scope and in various geographies? Do you want a partner with offices around the world, an internationally renowned partner, or a regional or local partner? Are you a big fish or a small fish to them?

Chemistry

Supply chain projects take time, create change, and can cause frustration at times — both small and large. At the end of the day, people are the most important factor. Does the partner complement your company and your staff? Can you work effectively with the implementation team? How do you know? Have you met them?

Trust

Have you worked with the implementation company before? How well do they know your business objectives and cultural and organizational quirks? Does the partner complement your company and your staff? Can they show you a roadmap to success?

13.1.3 Importance of Implementation Methodology

Your implementation partner can claim to have a depth of SAP implementation experience and can even offer cherry-picked references. A review of the implementation methodology, however, can also reveal a lot about the delivery capability of the various players under consideration.

A disciplined, methodical approach to SAP implementation isn't optional. It's a requirement for success in the complex world of supply chains and is on par with the firm's status as an accredited SAP services partner. When evaluating the firms proposing proprietary SAP implementation methodologies, a good reality check is to assess how closely a particular methodology maps to the AcceleratedSAP (ASAP) methodology. The ASAP methodology is intelligently conceived, well constructed, and battle proven. Having said that, an absolute reliance on ASAP might reveal a firm's limitation. Whereas ASAP should form the core of any SAP implementation methodology, it's important to note that in the real world, there's no one-size-fits-all methodology, and strict adherence to any rigid, cookie-cutter methodology can have disastrous consequences.

A firm that has successfully done SAP SCM implementations should be able to draw upon a suite of proven implementation methodology based on ASAP and ValueSAP that enables them to select the precise methodology components best suited to address the unique requirements and industry-specific challenges of your specific supply chain implementation.

13.2   Governance Model

The role of project governance is to balance the risk of the organization's investment against the opportunities and benefits that the outcomes will provide the business. It addresses the risks to ensure that the implementation provides value to the organization and the risks are properly mitigated.

For IT projects, project governance is about monitoring the project status and controlling the risk of the project not delivering the business value the company requires, within the time and budget available. Project governance is about understanding the business opportunities that the project can deliver, but also appreciating the consequences of failure and putting in place strategies to minimize the risk and optimize the investment so that the business goals are achieved.

Project governance can be seen as consisting of nine key roles:

1. Establish the basis for project governance, approval, and measurement — including defining roles and accountabilities, policies and standards, and associated processes.

2. Evaluate project proposals to select those that are the best investment of funds and scarce resources and are within the firm's capability and capacity to deliver.

3. Enable, through resourcing of projects with staff and consultants, harnessing and managing of business support and the provision of the governance resources.

4. Define the preferred business outcomes (end states), benefits, and value — the business measures of success and overall value proposition.

5. Control the scope, contingency funds, overall project value, and so on.

6. Monitor the project's progress, the stakeholder's commitment, the results achieved, and the leading indicators of failure.

7. Measure the outputs, outcomes, benefits, and value — against both the plan and measurable expectations.

8. Act to steer the project into the organization, remove obstacles, manage the critical success factors, and remediate project or benefit-realization shortfalls.

9. Develop the organization's project delivery capability — continually building and enhancing its ability to deliver more complex and challenging projects in less time and for less cost while generating the maximum value.

Project governance outlines the relationships between all internal and external groups involved in the project and ensures that required approvals and direction for the project are obtained at each appropriate stage of the project. A good project governance framework defines a clear flow of information regarding the project to all of the stakeholders and ensures appropriate review of issues encountered within each project. The important specific elements of good project governance include:

▸ A compelling business case stating the objects of the project and specifying the in-scope and out-of-scope aspects.

▸ A mechanism to assess the compliance of the completed project to its original objectives.

▶ Identification of all stakeholders with an interest in the project.

▶ A well-defined method of communication to all of the stakeholders during the project execution phase.

▶ A project charter identifying a set of business-level requirements as agreed by all stakeholders and agreed specifications for the project deliverables.

▶ Clear assignment of project roles and responsibilities.

▶ A current, published project plan that spans all project stages from project initiation through development to the transition to operations.

▶ A system of accurate upward status- and progress-reporting including time records.

▶ A central document repository for the project.

▶ A centrally held glossary of project terms.

▶ A process for the management and resolution of issues that arise during the project.

▶ A process for the recording and communication of risk identified during the project.

▶ A standard for quality review of the key governance documents and of the project deliverables.

13.2.1 Project Governance Framework

The success of any demand management implementation can only come about through a well-thought-out and well-executed deployment governance framework. A governance framework enables an organization to more rapidly implement positive change by establishing team structure, focusing on knowledge transfer, and enabling people. The governance framework for an implementation must be supported by a structure starting with a leadership commitment and ending with project-based activities that support — from the top down and bottom up, respectively — the transformation of the business processes.

The example governance structure shown in Figure 13.1 creates the context for executing the project by enabling scope management, change management, and issue resolution.

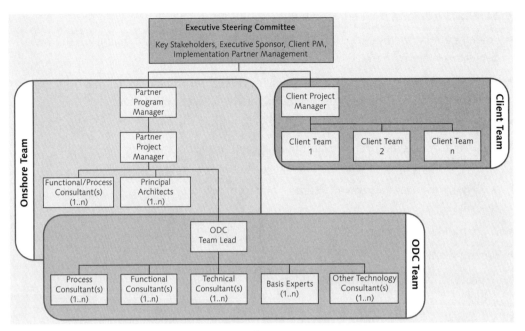

Figure 13.1 Project Governance Framework

The following is a list of the main roles in project governance:

▶ **Executive steering committee**
The executive steering group establishes strategic initiatives and provides oversight and concurrence.

▶ **Program steering group**
The program steering group provides direction for the program and serves as a point of escalation.

▶ **Program sponsor**
The program sponsor takes ultimate responsibility for the success of the program through active participation and oversight.

▶ **Program manager**
The program manager directs the planning and delivery of a program of streams and projects as defined in the program charter.

▶ **Project manager**
The project manager is responsible for the planning, monitoring, control, and delivery of the project.

▸ **Solution architect**

The solution architect is responsible for the solution design, implementation, and transition.

With the involvement of multiple people from the organization, and the implementation partner, it becomes essential to identify the key players and their responsibilities to keep the project running smoothly. Always remember that a group responsibility is no one person's responsibility. A powerful tool used by a number of organizations is the RACI model. It is a useful tool in identifying key players and their responsibilities during the project lifecycle.

The RACI (responsible, accountable, consulted, and informed) model is an analytical tool used in business process management that helps understand and identify the individuals involved in the execution of a certain business process. The first step in creating an RACI chart is developing a two-dimensional matrix in which the horizontal axis has the names of the people or functional roles, and the vertical axis has the deliverables, relevant processes, or activities (Figure 13.2).

	CEO	CFO	Business Executive	CIO	Business Process Owner	Head Operations	Chief Architect	Head Development	Head IT Administration	PMO	Compliance, Audit, Risk, and Security	Service Manager
Create a framework for defining IT services			C	A	C	C	I	C	C	I	C	R
Build an IT services catalog			I	A	C	C	I	C	C	I	I	R
Define SLAs for critical IT services	I	I	C	C	R	I	R	R	C		C	A/R
Define OLAs for meeting SLAs			I	C	R	I	R	R	C		C	A/R
Monitor and report end-to-end service level performance			I	I	R		I	I			I	A/R
Review SLAs and UCs	I		I	C	R		R	R			C	A/R
Review and update IT service catalog			I	A	C	C	I	C	C	I	I	R
Create service improvement plan			I	A	I	R	I	R	C	C	I	R

Figure 13.2 RACI Chart

The following is a breakdown of the RACI acronym and what it means:

▶ **Responsible (R)**
The individual who performs the work.

▶ **Accountable (A)**
One individual for each task to whom R is accountable. If it comes to it, this individual has the power to modify the business process.

▶ **Consulted (C)**
The individual who needs to be consulted because he has information and capability necessary to complete the work.

▶ **Informed (I)**
The individual who needs to be informed about the outcome of the process but need not be consulted while completing the task

Creation of a RACI chart requires a careful approach of identifying all of the activities and roles involved during the project lifecycle and establishing the relationship between the activities and roles. The process described below can act as a good guideline for a RACI chart creation process:

▶ Identify all of the processes and activities involved and list them on the left-hand side of the chart.

▶ Identify all of the roles and list them along the top of the chart.

▶ Complete the cells of the chart by identifying who has the R, A, C, and I roles for each process.

▶ Every process should have one and only one R as a general principle. A gap occurs when multiple roles exist that have an R for a given process.

▶ Resolve overlaps. Every process in a role responsibility map should contain only one R to indicate a unique process owner. In the case of multiple Rs, you need to further detail the subprocesses to separate the individual responsibilities.

▶ Resolve gaps. Where no role has been identified that has the R for a process, the individual with the authority of role definition must determine which existing or new role is responsible. Update the RACI map and clarify the role with the individual who assumes the role.

13.2.2 Key Elements of Successful Project Governance

You need to be aware of a few key elements to have a successful project governance.

Building Team Structure

The composition of the transformation team is one of the most critical factors in transforming the way an organization manages demand. Membership on the project team is dependent on the scope of the project, but should not be defined solely by subject matter expertise. The differing viewpoints of management, process participants, and the customer also should be considered. Involving key resources from the wider organization and outside the process brings objectivity.

At this point, leadership engagement and accountability across the company and on the project team is critical. Project measurements can determine if the project is on track internally, but only measurement of cross-company accountability (success metrics) can determine the organizational impact of the effort.

From the beginning, the team needs to execute all of the traditional vehicles for project success and governance around work plans, issues lists, budget, and so on. Additionally, a comprehensive communication plan that includes all stakeholders, associates, and customers should be created and used.

Managing Risk

Risk is inherent in all projects and comes from all aspects of the projects, people, process, and technology. A critical role of the governance structure is to understand the nature of risk and to develop the appropriate strategies to mitigate against it. Need for risk management grows as the three contributors of risk — people, process, and technology — grow in reach and diversity. For instance, the risk factors would be relatively low if the demand planning solution was limited to a small and well-contained division of a company, which is has mature demand planning processes and does not include any new technology or technology dependence on trading partners. On the other hand, risk management requirements would be very high if the same solution was being deployed for a large multinational origination, spanning a number of geographies, with varying degrees of process maturity and technology dependence on a number of trading partners.

Focus on Knowledge Transfer

A good implementation should provide two types of knowledge transfer. One is specific job training, often delivered in a classroom setting with supportive, on-the-job coaching. The second type of knowledge transfer is less weighted toward classroom training and more toward shadowing and on-the-job coaching. In either case, knowledge transfer is a way of supporting the organization through a culture shift to a new work environment. A proper governance framework requires both types of training. A training program should cover following topics:

- Job designs, including job descriptions and skill-set required
- Individual assessments to identify the effectiveness of training imparted and readiness to execute the solution
- Organizational assessments to identify resource gaps and training needs
- Training content development and delivery (train the trainer approach)
- Ongoing performance evaluation and training program

Emphasis on Change Management

A change management program may include the following:

- Implementation of a targeted and integrated communication program
- Design and implementation of a highly visible, organization-wide program and process
- Design and delivery of training
- Revised performance management program that integrates key performance indicators in the job description
- Design and development of ongoing communication vehicles to celebrate successes

Supporting People

A project owner acts as a relationship manager, who specifically focuses on the people issues related to the process and technology changes. The project owner partners with executive management and line managers to develop the plans for employee transition. A key component of that plan is knowledge transfer.

The project owner is best positioned to support future adjustments and changes because of his initial involvement.

Deliver Without Fail

A successful implementation project is often dependent on factors beyond the scope of the project work itself. The project owner must work within the organization to identify and leverage management practices, reward systems, policies, and so on to ensure the project alignment with the organizational vision.

The governance framework allows the organization to identify upfront the success criteria for critical deliverables and then deliver — without fail.

13.3 Sequencing and Scope of Solutions Implementation

One of the most critical aspects of project scope and sequencing is ensuring that various components are sequenced in the order to drive maximum impact, while respecting change management and internal resource availability issues. Whereas a number of factors can influence sequencing, a few criteria are the essential focus. We'll discuss these criteria in the following sections.

13.3.1 Quick Benefit Realization

Companies should focus on initiatives that provide the quickest return on investment (ROI) (Figure 13.3). Most of these initiatives don't have major dependencies on other systems. Implementation of a Demand Planning solution is one of those examples.

Often it can be implemented in a stand-alone mode and subsequently integrated into the overall systems landscape. Depending on the size of the project, a Demand Planning implementation may be phased and sequenced by:

- Geographic scope
- Solution scope
- Customer and product scope

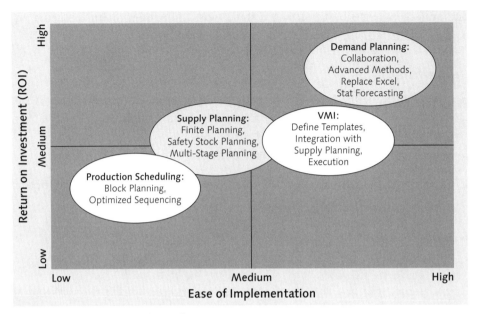

Figure 13.3 Identifying Quick Benefits

13.3.2 Minimizing Change Management

Change management is the biggest challenge in most implementations. While considering project sequencing, it is important to minimize interim business solutions that will be replaced in a short period of time (e.g., three to six months). This may work well for the IT team, but for the business user team it means unlearning and relearning, that is, added change management complexities.

13.3.3 Minimizing Rework

An essential component of every engagement is the development of *a global blueprint, also known as a global design*. The purpose of a global blueprint is to design the ideal end-state solution and then implement it in short phases, similar to connecting Lego® blocks. Doing a phased implementation without a global design is not recommended. This would be analogous to building a house without a blueprint.

13.3.4 Staffing Constraint

Staffing is the other important factor that will dictate how project components are sequenced and phased. Whereas consulting firms can be engaged to help with project execution, internal business acumen can rarely be replaced. More projects are sequenced and resequenced and/or phased because of staffing issues than any other issue.

None of the sequencing and phasing factors mentioned in this section are mutually exclusive. They coexist, and the weighting of each one of the factor defines the final project phasing and sequencing. The sequencing approaches in Figure 13.4 are very similar. The difference is in the sequencing of the SNP project, impacted by staffing issues.

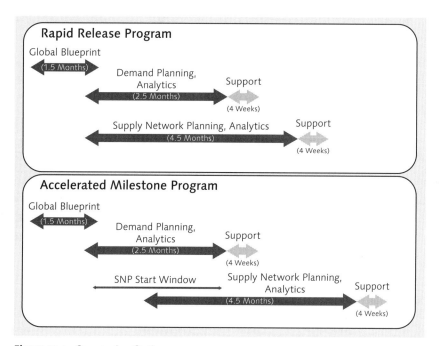

Figure 13.4 Sequencing Options

The rapid release program would allow the organization to start the Demand Planning and SNP implementation initiatives simultaneously and complete the project before the end of the year, whereas in the accelerated milestone program, the SNP project start would be delayed by a few weeks to ensure proper phasing of key client resources and change management requirements, and the go-live would be pushed to next fiscal year.

The consulting partner should be willing to provide such options, but with the various interdependent subprojects still scheduled tightly. Many firms shy away from such tight scheduling because of their lack of confidence about being able to hit the deadlines for individual subprojects that have tightly coupled dependencies.

13.4 Project Management Methodology

When starting a project, an organization is faced with a multitude of questions, such as:

▶ How do we best use the selected solution's capabilities?

▶ How and when does the project start?

▶ How can costs be kept low?

▶ How do we manage both the project and business risk?

▶ How do we build internal expertise?

▶ How and when do we handle change management?

SAP offers a knowledge-intensive methodology for solution implementation named AcceleratedSAP (ASAP) (see Figure 13.5). It leverages the insights that SAP and its partners have gained through years of hands-on experience on projects in many different customer environments and industries. ASAP provides content, tools, and expertise based on thousands of successful implementations. It helps in reducing project time, cost, and risk.

Figure 13.5 AcceleratedSAP (ASAP) Methodology

Aligned with formal project management standards and procedures (including the Project Management Institute), ASAP provides project management expertise that is specific to SAP software and critical to a successful implementation. By using the ASAP methodology and tools during an implementation project, a typical project team can simplify and streamline efforts in the following ways:

- Faster implementations with significant time savings
- More reliable projects thanks to proven tools and best practices
- Lower risk
- More-efficient use of resources
- Reduced costs
- More effective project management based on tools and templates aligned with best practices from the PMI

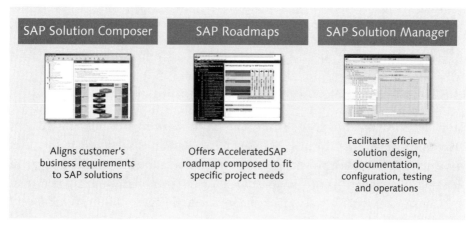

Figure 13.6 ASAP Toolset

13.4.1 ASAP Toolset

ASAP employs three core tools to deliver the solution, as shown in Figure 13.6.

- **Solution Composer**
  This tool helps the user develop an initial understanding of the business requirements. It provides an overview of the industry value chain and a mechanism for articulating key opportunities and aligning them to the SAP application via business maps and engagement tools for SAP software. Solution Composer

helps modify standard business maps quickly and easily to target customers' challenges and core processes with relevant solutions.

- ► **ASAP Roadmap**

    The ASAP Roadmaps outline the activities involved in implementing, upgrading, or enhancing SAP software. They contain a set of deliverables, accelerators, role descriptions, and additional guides. The roadmaps can be tailored to the customer's specific project requirements. ASAP Roadmaps cover aspects of project management, business process requirements, configuration, testing, and technical solution management. They are accompanied by accelerators, samples, and best practices information.

- ► **Solution Manager**

    The Solution Manager is a platform that provides integrated content, tools, and methodologies that are needed to implement, support, operate, and monitor SAP enterprise applications. It helps to manage the solution design, documentation, configuration, testing and operations phase. It supports both SAP and non-SAP software, helping in reducing the total cost of ownership for the current investments

13.5 Global Engagement Delivery Model (GEDM)

Based on ASAP methodology, Bristlecone has developed a Global Engagement Delivery Model (GEDM) to enable rapid implementation of supply chain solutions to clients by leveraging a proven execution framework with built-in risk mitigation plans that guarantees successful and timely delivery of engagements to customers. Unlike traditional project management methodologies, this proven delivery model is designed specifically for delivering high-impact supply chain applications in a significantly faster time frame, while also reducing risk. In some cases the implementation duration is reduced to as little as 60 working days, for a complete Demand Planning solution implementation, including reporting and analytics.

Used in countless successful SAP supply chain implementations, this delivery methodology is most relevant to the following core needs of the clients:

- ► Project ROI
- ► Accelerated time frames for implementation
- ► Phased realization of business benefits

- Optimized onsite and offsite offshore staffing model
- Risk and reward commitment
- Postlaunch optimization and business process enablement

GEDM is designed to optimize the following groups of resources needed for implementation:

- Onsite client-facing resources
- Offsite resources within the same geography as the client
- Offshore resources from the global delivery centers

The typical onsite to offsite resource ratio varies based on the project needs and is tailored to ensure that project success, timeline, and costs are optimized.

GEDM is broken into multiple phases: assessment and discovery, blueprint, realization, go-live preparation, go-live, and support. We'll discuss each of these phases in more detail in the sections below.

13.5.1 GEDM: Assessment and Discovery Engagement

The first phase in our client engagement model is the assessment engagement. Global organizations today are challenged to maximize the efficiency and effectiveness of their supply chains. A smoothly working supply chain can deteriorate over time as the organization adds more products, suppliers, plants, or distribution centers, evolves its customer mix or product mix, implements new postponement or replenishment strategies, or simply scales organically or inorganically over time. Localized fixes to specific problems might be effective workarounds, but eventually will suboptimize the supply chains. As time passes, key metrics such as on-time delivery, forecast accuracy, lead time, supply chain response time, inventory turns (inverse of days of supply), and cash-to-cash cycle time begin to degrade below that of well-heeled competitors. This typically means it is time to assess the supply chain to identify key issues and opportunities for optimization.

Therefore, this phase is appropriate for clients to understand their current supply chain challenges and to identify opportunities to maximize the strategic value of their supply chains. The purpose of the assessment engagement is to:

- Evaluate the effectiveness of the client's supply chain
- Identify the opportunities for improvement or optimization

▸ Estimate the value of realization of these opportunities

▸ Recommend a realistic roadmap for achieving the optimized results

The assessment framework, which is part of the delivery model, is a comprehensive framework developed for assessing the supply chain processes and their performance to discover issues and challenges and identify improvement opportunities for our clients. This proven framework allows us to deliver an extremely rich and actionable assessment of the client's supply chain process in a short amount of time. As a reminder for Chapter 3, Figure 13.7 illustrates the process at a high level and the deliverables.

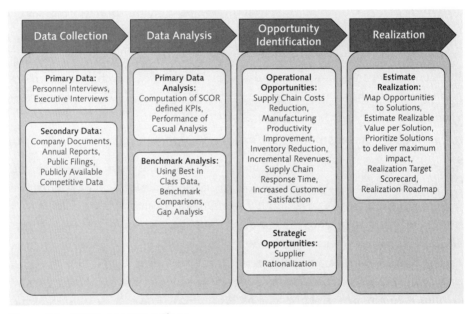

Figure 13.7   GEDM Assessment Phase

13.5.2   GEDM: Blueprint

The second phase in the engagement delivery model is the blueprint engagement. This is an important phase that is a critical to ensuring the success of the SAP Demand Planning implementations from the perspective of time, budget, technology, change management, business impact, and so on. The blueprint phase not only focuses on defining the detailed requirements and scope of the proposed implementation, but it also addresses another key element of success: global design.

The Bristlecone global business blueprint provides an end-to-end view of the proposed business solution, helping to:

- Define the detailed requirements of all of the key business processes in scope
- Ensure that information on all of the peripheral processes is captured to the extent required to determine a global design
- Determine how the SAP product set can be leveraged to its maximum potential
- Identify where business process changes are useful and feasible and will have direct business impact
- Confirm the gaps between what the product offers and the solution needs and determine appropriate approaches to satisfy the needs
- Determine where additional third-party applications or custom development may be required
- Finalize business process and technical architectures
- Enable detailed planning of multiple releases of realization, go-live, and post-launch support
- Understand and highlight the magnitude of potential organizational and business process changes and adjust the scope of approach accordingly as well as recommend appropriate change management needs

The approach involves studying the current system, organization, and business processes, defining to-be process, organization structures and procedures, optimizing the processes to map to the best practices, defining business scenarios, determining integration and reporting requirements, and defining an end-user training plan and a change management plan.

This blueprint, which is part of the delivery model, is a comprehensive framework developed to define, in detail, the supply chain processes and the solution definition to ensure that the proposed implementation meets all of the business requirements and highlights the gaps and challenges that need to be addressed to deliver the solution.

Figure 13.8 illustrates the process at a high level and the deliverables.

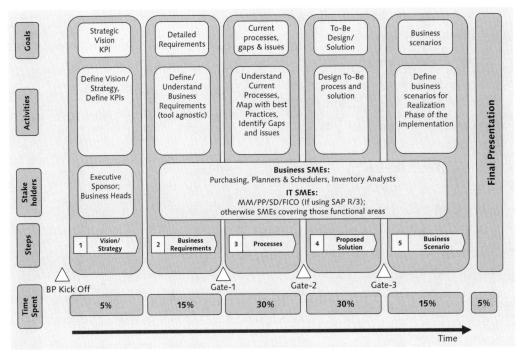

Figure 13.8 GEDM Blueprint Phase

13.5.3 GEDM: Realization

The third phase of the Bristlecone GEDM model is the realization phase. During this phase, the system is configured according to the solution design finalized during the blueprint phase, iterative prototyping and validation of the solution occurs, extensive unit testing is completed, and knowledge transfer takes place.

The following activities occur during this phase:

▸ Define scenarios

▸ Build prototypes

▸ Create test environments

▸ Define and test security

▸ Define, create, and test interfaces

▸ Define and test data conversion and migration requirements

▸ Create enhancements and extensions

- ▸ Define reports and forms

- ▸ Complete unit testing and user acceptance testing

- ▸ Execute knowledge transfer to business users and IT

- ▸ Develop training content and complete the train the trainer activity

Figure 13.9 explains the details behind the processes in the realization phase.

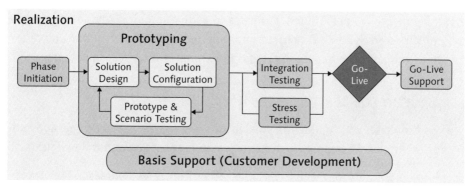

Figure 13.9 GEDM Realization Phase

The realization phase kick-off begins with organizing logistics for the team to design and deploy the solution. Each high-level task defined during the blueprint phase has a subset of activities that are discussed further. A key focus is on ensuring adherence to time lines, especially during the solution configuration and integration testing activities. Solution design and configuration follow an iterative approach, each activity revising and reinforcing the other.

In some instances where the solution calls for untested functionality or unique processes, prototyping precedes solution configuration, in effect making design-prototype-configure the critical loop in realization.

Solution design is the foundation on which all processes are built. Key deliverables at this stage are design documentation replete with schematics depicting the activities the planner needs to perform during the planning cycle, also known as a day in the life of a planner. This activity also focuses on design of master data, interfaces between various processes, integration of different modules, and a complete schedule of background jobs. The deliverable will be validated and revised iteratively.

Prototyping and configuration follows a good design. At this stage, any gaps and unanticipated issues should be identified, and appropriate workarounds are adopted. If no plausible workaround is possible, it's back to the drawing board for solution design. Scenario testing is the main form of testing the solution design and leveraging iterative prototyping.

At the completion of design and configuration, the solution traverses according to standard procedures (development system to test system to production environment) before go-live preparation, go-live, and go-live support activities. Again, the roll-out varies on a case to case basis, with big-bang deployment at one end of the spectrum and a phased geographical and functional approach at the other.

13.5.4 GEDM: Go-Live Preparation

During this phase, you conduct the final integration testing, stress testing, and conversion testing of the supply chain management application and train all users.

The following is a list of the activities that occur during this phase:

▶ Scheduled training and delivered it to end users
▶ Conduct any change management training
▶ Complete final integration and user acceptance testing, including customizations, extensions, and end-to-end interfaces
▶ Test reports and forms
▶ Complete stress testing
▶ Enable production system

13.5.5 GEDM: Go-Live and Support

During this phase, data is converted and/or migrated from existing systems, the new system is activated, and post-go-live support is active.

The following is a list of the activities that occur during this phase:

▶ Convert master data and verification and signoff
▶ Cut over to production system and final set of data
▶ Schedule system jobs
▶ Begin post-go-live support

This methodology and associated accelerators are an example of a framework that enables quick implementation while mitigating risks that delay the project or affect its success.

13.6 Defining Project Success Criteria

There are two dimensions to measuring project success: performance against forecasted operational and financial metrics and performance against project management plans. For a project to be successful, it should meet both criteria. If at the end, the project meets its operational and financial target metrics bit significantly misses its budget, schedule, and specification targets, then the project may have been completed by brute force, and the organization's ability to repeatedly implement such complex projects may be in question. If the reverse is true — it met its project management criteria but missed its operational and financial targets significantly — then the project is definitely not a success.

The traditional project management models to measure project success focus on the development process and dimensions of *within time*, *within budget*, and *according to requirements* (quality and functional specifications) of a project (Figure 13.10).

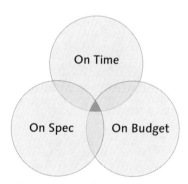

Figure 13.10 Traditional Measures of Project Success

However, compliance with time, budget, and specifications is not sufficient to measure dimensions such as the quality of the solution delivered and the satisfaction of the project stakeholders' expectations. Incorporating these dimensions into the project success measurement model is an important step to defining project success.

During the project lifecycle, everything about the project is viewed as being of the utmost importance. This viewpoint, however, is not realistic, and generally places the project at a higher risk of failure. Certain requirements might be deemed more important by one stakeholder than another. Therefore, it is important to consider all of the perspectives, especially about a complex — and usually changing — project. There needs to be a deeper understanding of the various factors determining project success to help show why it is not always important to strive for success equally on all fronts.

In the following sections, we'll discuss the factors you need to consider when defining the success of a project. The relative importance of these factors can change over the course of the project.

Quantitative ROI	Initial	Year 1	Year 2	Year 3
Gross Benefit	16.03	3.12	3.14	3.16
Reduced Inventory	16.03	-	-	-
Reduced Transportation Costs	-	-	-	-
Reduced Inventory Carrying Costs	-	1.12	1.12	1.12
Reduction in SCM Costs	-	-	-	-
Increased Capacity Utilization	-	2.00	2.02	2.04
Gross Investment	(1.25)	(0.50)	(0.50)	(0.50)
Software	-	(0.25)	(0.25)	(0.25)
Hardware	(0.25)	-	-	-
Consulting Services	(1.00)	(0.25)	(0.25)	(0.25)
Net Cash Flow (NCF)	14.78	2.62	2.64	2.66
Discounted Cash Flow (DCF)	13.43	2.16	1.98	1.82
Net Present Value (NPV)	19.40			

- All numbers in $ millions
- Supply Chain benefits estimated in Div A, B and C
- Inventory benefits include FG, WIP and RM categories
- Some Gross Investment assumptions have changed with time

Figure 13.11 ROI Model

13.6.1 Financial and Operational Metrics

To get funded, almost every project forecasts an ROI, which is driven by improvements in operational metrics. At Bristlecone, we go through a very structured but quick process to identify and quantify opportunities for improvement. Figure 13.11 is an example of such a business case that was developed for deploying a demand planning solution for a Fortune 1000 company. This project is deemed to be a success when the project meets or exceeds its targets for inventory and capacity utilization and for net present value.

13.6.2 Stakeholder Satisfaction

Every project needs to yield the results to satisfy its stakeholders. However, having said that, there might also be numerous qualitative requirements coming from various stakeholders during the course of the project. Examples of such requirements may be a targeted go-live based on internal and external commitments. Some stakeholders may have critical needs and are impacted directly, whereas for others the effects are less obvious, or they may even be adversely affected. All these requirements should be documented with their impact on the project budget and timelines, and the project owner and executive sponsors should make decisions about prioritizing these requirements or considering them as the future initiatives. It may not be possible to accommodate all of the requirements from various stakeholders, but keeping them in view and mitigating risk from such requirements having an adverse impact may help achieve higher stakeholder satisfaction at the end of the project.

13.6.3 Meeting Project Objectives and Requirements

Tracking the project objectives and deliverables specified in the project charter helps bring perspective to the degree to which the requirements must be met by the project. Is it important to put all of the requirements into the application under development, or can the wish-list items and lower-priority items be excluded from the end result?

More often than people realize, the originally specified project results may have little impact on solving the most important problem in your organization. This occurs because, during the blueprinting stage, all parties may identify a more important problem to address that was not considered while defining the project. At that time, subject to the agreement of the customer and partner, the project charter should be changed to identify the new objectives, how they will be achieved, and the impact of these changes on the budget and timelines.

13.6.4 Within Budget

This measurement helps measure the importance of the budget to the project. If there's a fixed budget that cannot be adjusted, then it plays a major role in defining the project success and needs to be closely monitored during the lifecycle of the project. If there is some flexibility in terms of budget, or the focus is not solely on the budget, then it may not be the most important factor in the project success.

13.6.5 Within Timelines

This is an important criterion to consider because any delay in the implementation means delay in the benefits realization, which has a direct impact on the bottom line for the project and the organization. However, there may be situations where a change in the scope or an organizational change may require the timelines to be changed. When there's a set time frame for when a project must be completed (e.g., to meet regulatory requirements), this measurement needs to be closely monitored, because delivering the functionality late may not result in the estimated benefits. In all such cases, this measurement becomes one of the most important factors in defining project success. However, in other cases, where there might be flexibility, this measurement can have relatively less importance based on the stakeholder requirements.

13.6.6 Value Added to the Organization

The value added by a project is very important measure to define project success. The higher the value-added a project provides to the organization, the more successful a project is considered. If the project involves just technology replacement due to retirement of vendor support, the value-added to the organization is minimal and this factor has low importance in defining the project success. Whereas in another case, if the purpose of the project is to change the business process to create an improved planning process and better external and internal collaboration, the project can drive an immediate ROI. In such a scenario, value-added would play a very important role in defining project success.

13.6.7 Quality Requirements

The level of quality is often affected by the amount of time spent testing and validating the project results. If the result is an integrated planning environment or a customer-facing application, the quality factor would play an important role in defining the project's success, because it requires a clean release with close to zero or no defects. If this were a simple data integration and analysis application with sufficient resources to address any short-term issues, then this factor would play a relatively smaller role in defining project success.

13.6.8 Team Satisfaction

The culture of an organization has a lot of influence on identifying team satisfaction and its role in defining project success. This factor addresses the team and how far the stakeholders are willing to push to reach their project objectives.

13.6.9 Relationship with the Consulting Partner

The quality of relationship between the partner and the client is often directly associated with what the client perceives to be the quality of the project. In a highly collaborative approach to consulting, you want your relationship with your client to be as open, honest, and trusting as possible. The nature of the relationship supports your client's strong, ongoing commitment and participation in the project itself, which in turn, helps ensure that the project effectively addresses problems in their organization.

13.6.10 Ability to Sustain the Implementation Successfully

This outcome should be one of the major goals for any consultant. However, the exact nature of the problem may never arise in the client's organization again, so it is often difficult to assess if the client has learned to solve that problem. Also, few consultants are willing to scope a project to the time required to assess whether a client really can solve the same type of problem in the future.

13.6.11 Ability to Be a Customer Reference

One of the most powerful outcomes that define the success of the project is that both partners are willing to work with each other again. One of the ethical considerations for any consultant is to avoid creating a dependency of the client on the consultant — where the client cannot capably participate in the organization without the ongoing services of the consultant. However, it is not uncommon that the client strongly believes that the quality of the relationship with the consultant is as important as the consultant's expertise. The client might choose to use that consultant wherever and whenever they can in the future.

13.7   Tracking the Value

The last aspect of the project is to measure the actual improvement to various operational and performance metrics and compare it against the planned improvement to see if the project was a success or not. The comparisons are made based on the value of these metrics at a point in time. Trend charts show if further improvement is expected.

For example, for a client, we calculated the annual benefits of better monthly demand and supply planning at $2 million per year. This was computed based on the expectations that the finished goods (FG) days of supply would improve within 12 months after the go-live to 60 days from its current value, and raw material (RM) days of supply would improve to 55 days from its current value, owing to forecast accuracy improvement from 40% to 60% at a service level of 95%. In such a scenario, the success of the project would be based on meeting or exceeding these metrics.

In addition, we forecast ongoing savings opportunities in year 2: increasing forecast accuracy to 70%, resulting in FG days of supply of 37 and RM days of supply of 34, leading to additional savings of $0.44 million per year. The ongoing success of the project is not only based on sustaining year 1 metrics, but improving upon them to achieve year 2 targets.

13.8   Summary

Although it is obvious in hindsight, the best-designed processes, organization, and technology are no better than their implementation. People need to understand the change and the motivations behind it. They need to be trained in the new processes, which in turn, must be aligned with the capabilities of the enabling technology. A change process run by a committed, qualified team including knowledgeable consultants when necessary and guided by strong executive governance focused on achieving success has the best chance of turning a vision into positive change in the balance sheet and income statement.

14 Conclusion

In this last chapter, we'll come full circle and return to a high-level examination of demand management, but this time with greater understanding of the details gleaned from the preceding chapters to add perspective and depth. To retain their independence, organizations must deliver at least as much value as their competitors to customers and investors alike. A well-run demand management process can support this, and a well-integrated technology platform can enable that process.

14.1 Financial and Strategic Implications of Managing Demand

Let's review the financial implication of demand and supply chain management or mismanagement by looking at a real-world example. In April 2001, Cisco reported that it would write-off an astonishing $2.5 billion worth of parts. This was the largest write-off in history at that time. The stock price was beaten down some 84%, and the media was calling it "Cisco's $2.25 billion mea culpa." Some alleged that investors had lost as much as $400 billion in wealth. Whereas all of it could not be attributed to failure to manage demand (though some would argue otherwise), that was definitely a factor in the $400 billion of share holder value erosion. A number of heads must have rolled as a result of this incident.

Analysts and investors expect management teams to achieve certain revenue and profit targets while keeping costs within a given tolerance. These financial metrics along with the remaining balance sheet and income statement items serve as a general assessment of the financial health of the company and can be compared to other potential investment opportunities. Of course, results show that Cisco did learn from is mistake and is a much better run organization today. It also made it to the list of the most efficient 25 supply chains by AMR Research.

Senior management and analysts and officials within the financial community continually interact, whether through the filing of mandatory documents or in freeform interviews and announcements. Together they arrive at projections for future performance based on existing internal sales projections and competitive benchmarks from capital markets and competitors.

Whereas demand management is a continuous process, the announcement of any guidance to the investment community is the beginning of a cycle. Existing sales forecasts and investment plans must be reconciled with the corporate performance targets. Where gaps exist, decisions must be made and resources committed to close them.

Beginning or deferring projects, launching and discontinuing products, entering markets, and dissolving or engaging in partnerships are all examples of strategic decisions that organizations might make based on projections of demand. Specifically, the forecast for sales volumes, sales revenue, and expense inherent in these options are lined up against gaps between current expectations and financial targets. Resources in the form of organizational talent, capital and other assets will be committed to realizing these gains.

14.2   Project, Impact, Realize, Correct

Companies that more efficiently leverage talent and knowledge across the entire enterprise and beyond can beat not only competitors selling similar products, but also all of the other organizations vying for investors' capital. Visibility to historical trends, leading indicators, downstream demand, and actions being taken internally and by competitors to impact demand each provide incremental clarity and accuracy, enabling resources to be committed to greater effect.

Figure 14.1, which we first saw at the beginning of Chapter 2, illustrates the collection and assimilation of multiple demand signals into a coherent probabilistic projection of demand. Whereas some information reinforces other sources, certain insights expand or refine the projections of demand at various levels.

Changes in product, price, place, and promotions and focusing on the most productive products and customers can have a significant impact on demand. These decisions are driven in part by the gaps between financial guidance and implications of existing demand projections, but they themselves recursively impact demand projections, ideally closing the gaps.

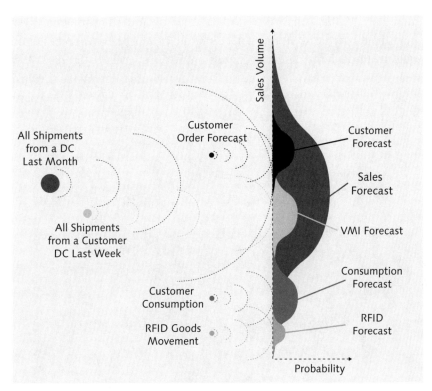

Figure 14.1 Seeing Insight from Multiple Demand Signals

Sales and marketing activities can only be successful when the product can be effectively supplied to meet the incremental demand that they create. Therefore, decisions must be made in consensus with operations and logistics functions within the company and with key customers and suppliers.

Similarly, operations and logistics teams must manage resources to meet asset utilization and expense budget targets. Product launches, sales drives, marketing promotions, and so on that drive incremental revenue at the expense of disproportionately higher costs are not profitable over short time horizons.

Because nearly every stakeholder in the demand management process thinks of demand in different time horizons and categories, the single consensus demand plan must be translatable to provide information relevant to the context of each individual stakeholder's role. Not only must the demand projection be available to individual stakeholders in relevant contexts, but they must also be available at the level and time horizon that supports that individual in committing resources. For instance, over the longer term, strategic decisions are made to help address manufacturing capacity through the capital budgeting process. However, in the very short term, the focus is on tactical and execution-related decisions to deploy the finished goods inventory to achieve customer demand. Figure 14.2 reviews the decisions and the relevant levels and time horizons that we discussed in Chapter 11.

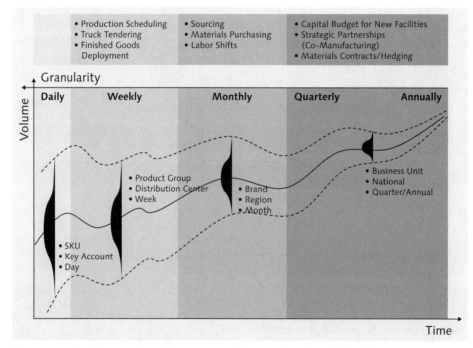

Figure 14.2   Decisions to Commit Resources and Relevant Levels and Time Horizons

Demand management itself constantly receives input and generates projections and associated decisions without beginning or end. There are cycles within demand management, however, when the time horizon for a projection rolls into the present, and projected demand can be compared to actual demand. This provides the opportunity for continuous improvement if performance measurement is aligned with the time and level at which the demand projection impacts the commitment of resources and accountability is assigned to the stakeholders involved in developing the demand projection. Without alignment and accountability, it matters little if bias is identified or relative accuracies of component demand projections are discovered.

Any organization can improve the contribution of its demand management process to its balance sheet and income statement, but no one individual or even an isolated team within the organization can succeed alone. Knowledge about future demand and its implications exists in too many pockets inside and outside of an enterprise for an isolated individual or group to be successful. In addition, whereas the scale and sophistication of calculations require technology to facilitate the capture and analysis of the data, acting upon the data necessitates fluency in the business, and achieving consensus is impossible without an efficient process to communicate updates across the organization. As Figure 14.3 suggests, people, process, and technology are all crucial enablers to a demand management function.

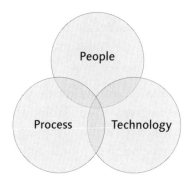

Figure 14.3 Three Pillars of Successful Demand Management

14.3 SAP Solutions

To communicate and plan effectively within the four walls of an organization and beyond, harmonized master data is critical. Advanced statistical algorithms and collaborative forecasts from key customers are completely irrelevant if different stakeholders know the products or customers by different names or numbers.

Once master data is mastered, a rich repository of demand-related transactions such as shipments and orders can be employed as the foundation for demand projections. Extrapolating demand statistically would be nearly impossible without accurate visibility into past demand that can be realigned as customers, regions, and channels shift and merge.

SAP ERP provides these capabilities and serves as the platform for executing many of the decisions supported by demand management. Production schedules, pricing changes, inventory deployment, and customer orders and shipments all flow through SAP ERP.

Business Planning and Consolidation is an application and a process in which current demand projections can be brought together with the expectations of the financial community to identify gaps and begin to propose action plans.

Both SAP ERP and SAP APO can serve as platforms to store and manipulate demand history and project future demand through statistical techniques. Unlike SAP ERP, however, SAP APO offers more advanced capabilities and algorithms that enable it to bring leading indicators and downstream demand data into the demand projection. With a more flexible data structure that enables stakeholders to view and manipulate data within their individual business contexts and programmable macros that facilitate routine calculations and deliver threshold-sensitive alerts, SAP APO is the backbone of a company's demand management technological infrastructure.

Supplier Network Collaboration (SNC) permits manufacturers and retailers to exchange demand information such as sales, shipments, inventory, and forecasts at a more detailed, granular level. The fact that SNC runs on a web-based frontend makes it a tool that a company and its customers can both use to form a better overall picture of demand.

Because sales executives are so frequently out talking to customers, they are one of the best sources of demand information. Conversely, however, because they are so often away talking to customers, they are also among the most difficult to engage in the demand management process. Duet demand planning offers the sales executive or any other demand management stakeholder the familiar interface of Microsoft Excel as a portal into demand planning information. Stakeholders can work on- or offline to view and manipulate their contribution to the demand plan.

Visibility into demand data from further downstream in your supply chain can be invaluable in anticipating unforeseen changes in demand. Because this data is by its nature extremely granular and voluminous, it makes sense to store it in a separate repository to be aggregated to the levels necessary to supplement a forecast or support a decision-making process. Vision Chain offers a demand signal repository that integrates into SAP ERP and SAP APO.

When storing and tracking the accuracy of consensus demand plans and all of the component demand projections that go into them at multiple time lags, it quickly becomes possible to overwhelm an application like SAP APO, which is tuned for performance in calculation rather than high-volume reporting. Fortunately, information in SAP APO is easily offloaded into SAP NetWeaver BW, which can provide static and dynamic ad hoc reporting capable even of reaching into SAP APO itself to report on live data.

SAP BusinessObjects applications such as SAP BusinessObjects Explorer can make the analysis of a very high volume of data in SAP NetWeaver BW faster and easier through either preconfigured dashboards or web-based analytical tools.

14.4 Case Study

Demand planning software packages can help manufacturers establish baseline sales forecasts incorporating multiple inputs, perform sophisticated analysis to calculate the impact of promotions and new product introduction on customer demand, and enable marketers to better understand their markets and customers. Yet merely implementing a solution does not give benefits. It's important to approach this problem strategically and first focus on those products and customers that produce the biggest benefit and then phase in the remaining ones. In this section, we'll illustrate this through a case study.

A large high-tech company was seeking to overhaul its demand planning processes and systems because they were saddled with inventory and believed the problem lay in the demand management area. The first meeting revealed that the forecast accuracy was 90%. Just looking at the forecast accuracy metric, one would think that the problem lay in some other areas — but always remember the old adage: If something sounds too good to be true, it probably is. The company had 90% forecast accuracy, but their environment was riddled with large inventory and low levels of delivery performance — at under 65%! When we peeled back a few layers of the onion, we discovered the issues were with the metric definition itself. They reported forecast accuracy using the revenue for the business unit, not by

SKU quantity at a location level (such as a distribution center). The problem was further masked by the period over which the accuracy was being measured: quarterly rather than monthly. This was a moment of enlightenment. The metric can be used to stop and starve progress. After further discussions and diagnostics, it was determined that the actual forecast accuracy number was very low.

The next step was to determine the starting point. This company had thousands of products and thousands of customers. It was important to determine what and who to focus on. Business analysis was essential to determining the focus areas. The results were worse than we expected:

▸ 5% of products contributed over 80% of revenue.

▸ 75% of products contributed 5% of revenue.

▸ Less than 5% of customers contributed 80% of revenue.

▸ 85% of customers contributed 5% of revenue.

This analysis identified the products and customers that required the focus, that is, the products and customers that had the biggest impact on business.

The company decided to focus on streamlining and automating the demand planning process for the 5% of the products that contributed over 80% of the revenue. This analysis also raised a number of questions: Why were there so many products? Was the new product introduction process effective? Why did they have so many customers? What would be the strategic implications if they did not serve the rest and focused on the most profitable and strategic? Would they grow faster? The demand planning engagement leveraged best business practices, and we focused on:

▸ Improving the demand planning processes

▸ Better organizational alignment

▸ Performance management

The key take-aways of this engagement were:

▸ Process

  ▸ One consensus demand plan: a single demand forecast was computed with inputs from multiple roles in the organization.

▶ Tight integration with the order management process: This was required to ensure that there was no latency in data.

▶ Ability to segment the demand forecasts based on key product-customer characteristics.

▶ Ensure that the forecast is at the SKU level.

▶ Organization

    ▶ Define a clear owner for the consensus forecast.

    ▶ Deploy internal collaboration: Whereas statistical forecasts generated from the demand planning solutions provide a solid foundation to work with, the real value comes from augmenting systems with organizational knowledge.

▶ Performance management

    ▶ Ability to measure KPIs such as delivery performance and forecast accuracy.

Three months after the completion of the project, we revisited the metrics to identify the improvements. The metrics had improved substantially.

▶ Forecast accuracy improved by more than 20%.

▶ Forecast cycle time reduced by 50–75%.

▶ Inventory turns went from 5 to 36.

▶ Cash-to-cash cycle time was reduced by 13 days.

▶ Planner productivity significantly increased.

The estimated annual benefit came close to $2.6 million; put another way, it increased the company's operating profit by 25%.

14.5   Benefits of Demand Planning Systems

Clearly, the demand planning implementation brings in financial gains as a result of optimizing the supply chain. However, to get the quickest return on investment, you have to focus on what is important. Some of the benefits from demand planning systems are discussed as follows.

1. **Increased revenue**

    The accurate forecast from Demand Planning helps give a clear picture of the product demand at different locations. Therefore, it reduces the potential for loss of revenue opportunity due to the right product not being at the right location at the right time. In addition, the sales volume increases owing to higher customer service levels.

2. **Reduce inventory-related costs**
Demand Planning is one of few tools that leverages a multivariate forecasting technique to develop a system-generated forecast on the basis of causal and historical data. The forecast can be validated by internal or external partners through an easily accessible, Internet-based, portal-supported collaboration. With an accurate forecast, a business can correctly calculate requirements for its products at different supply chain nodes. This capability facilitates developing an accurate distribution and production plan to make optimum inventory available at the supply chain nodes. A company can then maintain a higher service level for the customer and avoid a stock-out situation while spending the minimum amounts on inventory storage, transportation, ordering cost, carrying cost, and resources.

3. **Aids decisions on capital investment**
Demand Planning gives an unconstrained demand plan indicating the market potential and, as a result, helps a company identify growth the opportunity of its products in the market. A company can use this information to decide if they want to allocate capital resources to close the gap between unconstrained demand and what they can meet with acceptable service levels.

4. **Streamlined new product launches**
New products keep the cycle of innovation going. The demand planning solution provides lifecycle management techniques to help identify the demand of a new product at its launch stage, thereby helping a company identify the right amount of resources needed for a proper launch.

5. **Focus on the right things**
Because Demand Planning enables collaborative forecasting across hierarchical levels and partners, it's possible to manage a shared plan rather than creating multiple versions of same information. The planners can therefore focus on other business imperatives rather than spend time on accurately aggregating demand from various sources.

6. **Reduce production and operating costs**
Characteristics-based forecasting (CBF) enables the user to streamline forecasting of many different variants of the same product. By being able to forecast variants, manufacturers can easily react to changes in market demand and address

wastage. By easily creating a forecast of variants, manufacturers can confidently place orders with their suppliers.

7. **Reduce costs of data handling**
   Demand Planning manages all available information about historical sales, budgets, strategic company plans, and sales targets. This data can come from different sources and can be transferred from any source to InfoCubes in SAP NetWeaver BW. From there, the data can be read directly or transferred first to the live cache to improve performance. This way, a company can maintain all of its sales-related data in SAP APO Demand Planning, thus reducing the cost of maintaining such information in multiple places.

8. **Reduce costs by managing exceptions**
   SAP APO Demand Planning can communicate any exception through alerts when a forecast bias crosses the threshold. Managers can then concentrate their effort and focus on such exceptions.

Other benefits that would result in savings include:

▸ Reduction in warehousing costs

▸ Reduction in obsolescence-related write-offs

▸ Reduction in expediting costs (transportation costs)

▸ Better plant throughput

▸ Potential increase in revenue growth

▸ Visibility of RM demand to suppliers

▸ Reduced RM delivery variability

▸ Ability to negotiate better terms with suppliers

Companies with best-in-class demand planning have already reaped benefits by deploying a demand management process to drive dynamic marketplace prioritization and choice.

Best-in-class companies recognize that demand management programs need to be continuously reassessed to generate improvements in key customer-facing performance. Therefore, even after the demand planning implementation is stabilized, companies search for newer ways to get more value form their processes.

Some of the actions that companies take are listed as follows.

1. **Rework the business rules.**

   The business rules in the system need to be altered on an ongoing basis, because the environment changes, and the rules no longer reflect the reality. For example, an after-sales service firm stored fast-moving components at all of its regional depots. Company leaders decided to shift all of the slow-moving spare parts to a central warehouse. They decided the parts would be flown to the different regions on an as-needed basis. Instead of forecasting all of the components at each location, a few components now are stored and forecast only at the central location, significantly increasing accuracy.

2. **Use postponement.**

   More and more organizations are embracing postponement, which enables you to do final assembly much closer to the customer and without any major increase in cost. In such a scenario, forecasting should also be moved downstream.

3. **Recognize the goal.**

   Firms are not in business to make accurate forecasts; they're in business to make more money. Forecasting is merely a tool that helps along the way. Forecasting is bound to be inaccurate, but it is nonetheless necessary for a firm's survival — especially when an organization has increasing product variants due to a dynamic global marketplace. Software solutions provide some assistance, but these current tools will never be 100% accurate. Thus, operations management professionals must refocus their efforts to create processes that can deliver standard output with acceptable accuracy.

4. **Educate before training.**

   Because the demand planning process is cross-functional, people may provide input to the forecast without realizing the importance of their contributions. As a result, the quality of their contributions may suffer. A good educational program helps everyone understand their contribution and impact on the performance of the demand plan.

5. **Cleanse the data.**

   Cleanse the data so you don't spend all of your time questioning it and losing confidence in the process, which can cause others to second-guess the demand plan and produce their own version. Demand planning deals with huge quantities of data, and robust processes are required to keep the data cleansed.

6. **Trust the numbers.**

   Trust the numbers and manage by exception. Eighty percent of your return can be achieved by reviewing 20% of the items.

7. **Use the error in your forecast to positive effect.**
   A good statistical forecast has an appropriate error that drives an appropriate safety stock target. This leads to good inventory management and delivers higher service with lower total inventory.

8. **Analyze results frequently.**
   It's important to know what influences the true demand signal. A leading consumer goods manufacturing company developed its consensus forecast and focused on what they sold to retailers. At the end of every quarter, they would get products back or they would have to provide rebates owing to existing price protection agreements. This was primarily because they didn't know the level of inventory a particular retailer was carrying. Eventually, they improved the process by getting the sell thru information from the retailer, and considered that in the short-term demand planning process. This ensured that they were not starving some customers and over stocking others.

Recognizing that effectively monitoring demand management requires additional resource and knowledge skills, companies are turning to solution vendors for managed service offerings, also called business process enablement (BPEs). Acting like an extension of the company's demand planning team, the vendor's BPE team members monitor and assess the demand management functions for the company. Planners in BPEs take on additional functions such as preparing the data, cleaning it, and more.

Demand planners rarely get credit when the forecast is right, but when things go wrong, people notice them. Nevertheless, they perform one of the key functions to keep the supply chain engine humming. The Demand Planning solution in SAP APO provides demand planners with all of the required tools to aid them in this key task.

14.6 Summary

This book is about managing demand. More specifically, it's about projecting, managing, and impacting the sales of a business to its customers. Readers have learned about the different methods that businesses use to project demand, such as statistical analysis of past customer orders and sales. They've also gained an appreciation for the efforts of sales and marketing professionals to better adapt customer demand to a company's goals and capacity. Similarly, the book included the role of operations personnel in meeting demand.

The beginning is the foundation for the future, limiting possible outcomes by strengthening those that resonate with what has come before. To best profit in the future, it's necessary to build a projection of the future firmly rooted in a broad knowledge of the present, choose how and where to act, and then use the insight and experience from the process to go forward.

Technology is a lever that enables an organization to better project, impact, and realize demand by automating the rote work, giving analysts and executives the time and attention to focus on decision making. The time, talent, and money invested in improving an organization's demand management capabilities can yield significant returns if the focus is sustainable change targeted at meaningful goals.

A Business Planning

In the first part of the book, we introduced demand management concepts and their relevance to organizations. This appendix explores individual components of the demand management process in more detail.

We'll begin with the business planning process because it's the main driver of the demand management process in most companies, especially those that are publicly traded because their business cycles inevitably begin and end with shareholder expectations.

We'll touch on the SAP BusinessObjects Planning and Consolidation (BPC) solution and its relation to the other SAP solutions enabling the demand management process.

A.1 Expectations and Guidance by Public Companies

Shareholders in public companies have invested money because they expect a return. They may hope to one day use it to buy a house, send their children to college, retire from work, or accomplish any of a number of financial goals. To safeguard their investments, they want to know the business plans of the companies in which they have invested. Companies with better prospects for making more money in the near future pay better dividends, and their stock price may rise as well.

In buying a company's stock, shareholders own a small share of the company, which gives them the right to vote for board members who have the authority to hire and fire senior executives. So in a very real way, the CEO of a multibillion dollar company reports to the teachers and dentists, parents and retirees who own equity in that company and is responsible for meeting their expectations.

These expectations are often guided by financial analysts who are paid by individual investors to understand the markets and business plans of a number of organizations within some logical grouping, such as automotive manufacturers, retailers, or even software companies. With their deep knowledge of individual business segments and access to executives across multiple companies, analysts tend to influence the decisions of many of investors with respect to whether to buy, hold, or sell a company's stock.

We hope this background will enable us to approach a question that historically has baffled employees for generations. Where did the leadership team get these revenue and margin targets? The answer is, more often than not, that the analysts who advise the shareholders have looked at the price of the company's stock and compared it to a number of factors such as the previous year's earnings, the customer base for the company and its competitors, any risks involved in strategic projects the company is undertaking (for instance, changing the way that it does demand management), and more. Having gone through this exercise and built many sophisticated models to support their initial theses, the analysts are then able to tell their customers the revenue and profit margins the company must deliver over the ensuing quarters and year to continue to be worth its stock price.

The management team, however, is not without the ability to influence the expectations set by the analysts. On a quarterly basis they report business results back to the shareholders and analysts. Most senior executives also take the chance to offer guidance on how plans for the coming quarters and maybe years will go. If the financial market's expectations for revenue and profit margin are inputs to the business planning process, then one of the most important outputs would be the guidance delivered back to the market.

Why does the stock price matter so much to senior executives anyway? The stock price is the cost to purchase a portion or share of the company. The price of an individual share multiplied by the number of shares available for purchase dictates the value of the company as a whole.

If by failing to meet revenue or profit expectations or another measure, a management team allows the price of the stock (and therefore the value of the company) to drop, the company can become a target for purchase by another company or group of investors. This is likely to lead to some or most of the original management team and board members losing their jobs.

The revenue and profit margin guidance delivered by management teams must be broken down into actionable plans that can be executed by the individual departments. Stated simplistically, the profit margin is whatever is left over of the revenue after expenses are subtracted. So with this expense target, an organization can begin the budgeting process from which the capital expenditure plan, headcount and staffing plan, and cash flow plan can be derived.

Whereas budgeting and allocation of capital is critical to both the strategic and day-to-day management of the business, it is not per se a demand management activity, so we won't go into much more detail on the topic. Sales planning, however, is very much a demand management process, which we covered in detail in Chapter 9.

For now, we can understand that sales planning is the process of spreading the revenue targets across business units, regions, accounts, and any other way that an organization might divide its sales force. This might include brand, sales channel (i.e., direct sales, resellers, Internet sales, sales to original equipment manufacturers, etc.).

Another way to look at the sales target is to spread it across those products that the customers will buy, which is what we'll discuss in the next section.

A.2 Establishing the Product Mix

Whereas allocating sales targets across products or product groupings can be important to organizations that have product or product-area-specific sales teams, it is important to all organizations that are bringing new products to the market. Also, unlike sales expenses, which are normally fairly consistent across accounts of similar size and continental regions, the expense and resources required to produce and distribute a product can vary greatly from product to product, as can the profit margin. So the product mix that a company has planned impacts not only the sales plan, but the capital expenditure, headcount, and cash flow plans as well.

In this balancing of sales targets and budgeting, we begin to see the interplay among the various processes. Sales executives know their "patch" (i.e., region, accounts, channel, etc.) and understand which products their customers will be willing to buy. With this knowledge they can provide an important input back to the business planning process: namely, the gap between what they believe they can sell and what their sales targets are.

This gap becomes a major input for the marketing planning process, which we discussed in Chapter 8. It's relevant to business planning, though, in that one method of closing this gap is the introduction, or *launch*, of new products. Although many new products can cannibalize sales, eating into the amount of existing products that the organization plans to sell to customers, they are designed to expand the current market for the product and to take market share from competitors' products.

The design, development, and launch of new products, often referred to as *new product design and introduction* (NPDI), is traditionally a marketing function for most companies. However, senior management closely monitors this process and in some cases directly controls it. The reasoning behind this is that whereas new products can help a company grow market size and market share, for many companies the research and development portion of NPDI is a large share of their total expenditure. This is certainly true in the pharmaceutical industry, where new drugs can take over a decade and numerous expensive clinical trials to bring to market.

Discussions regarding methods for developing statistical forecasts for new products, the impact of leading indicators such as pricing, deriving intelligence from downstream data for product launches, and other aspects of demand management for new products are covered in more detail in Chapters 5 through 9. The important take-away from this section is that product mix and the NPDI process impact equally the sales planning and budgeting processes, and because of their potential to impact revenue and profit growth, they are highly visible to shareholders and analysts.

Resource and Project Management (RPM) is the SAP solution that can be leveraged to support the "pipeline" of new products and the activities necessary to bring them to market. It includes the cProjects collaborative project management tool to plan and monitor product development and launch activities and a dashboard enabling executives to assess their portfolio of new product projects for risk, readiness, and resources.

A.3   Setting Sales Targets

With the product portfolio adjusted to fill a portion of the gap between demand projections and the guidance to the financial community, the next step is to adjust sales targets. Most companies employ a hierarchy of sales executives reporting to managers who report to vice-presidents who report to senior vice-presidents, and so on. Figure A.1 shows an example of a sales hierarchy.

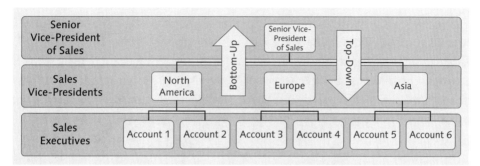

Figure A.1   Sales Hierarchy Example

Changes to the demand plan made at any level of this hierarchy must be communicated upward and downward to keep the sales plan synchronized. If a sales executive in Asia believes an account will buy more than is currently projected, then the demand projection for that account needs to go up, as does the sales vice-president's demand projection for the region and the senior vice-president's global projection. Having begun at the detailed level, this would be considered a bottom-up change.

Similarly, when the sales projection falls short of the guidance to the financial community, then the global sales projection needs to change, and that change needs to be reconciled down to all of the individual regions and their respective accounts. This is a top-down change. In demand management, professionals speak of top-down and bottom-up or often of aggregation (the process of adding up all of the component data into the next-higher-level categories) and disaggregation (the process of breaking data down into component categories).

Figure A.1 includes arrows that suggest how the top-down and bottom-up information flows. In the case of an increase in the global demand projection, the new demand target would move top-down and be spread (disaggregated) down to the lowest level of detail. Sales executives and vice-presidents could then change their own demand projections, which are aggregated (bottom-up) to reflect the new demand projection.

Aggregation is a fairly simple and straightforward exercise, with detailed data simply being added together to arrive at the next-higher level of data. Disaggregation, however, can be extremely contentious, especially when sales targets are being adjusted up.

Figure A.2 begins with a simple bottom-up aggregation across accounts in the Annual Forecast column. The percentage contribution of each account to the total is calculated in the Percent Breakout column. However, the current demand projection must be increased by 25% from 200,000 to 250,000 to meet guidance. These percentages can then be used to disaggregate the newly increased Annual Target proportionally across the accounts top-down.

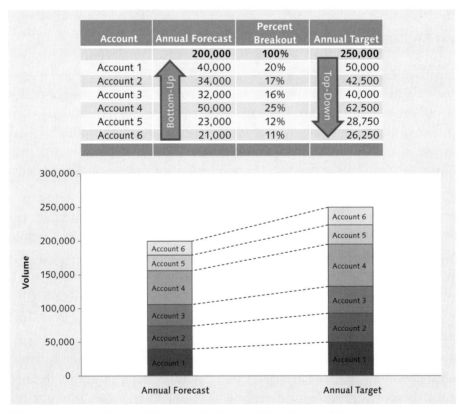

Account	Annual Forecast	Percent Breakout	Annual Target
	200,000	100%	250,000
Account 1	40,000	20%	50,000
Account 2	34,000	17%	42,500
Account 3	32,000	16%	40,000
Account 4	50,000	25%	62,500
Account 5	23,000	12%	28,750
Account 6	21,000	11%	26,250

Figure A.2 Aggregating and Disaggregating Demand Projections and Targets

Disaggregation is made more complex by the need to spread top-down changes across multiple hierarchies. Figure A.2 focuses on the sales hierarchy, but there are other hierarchies as well (products, regions, sales channels, etc.). Figure A.3 illustrates three simple two-tier hierarchies, each aggregating up to the single 200,000 annual demand projection.

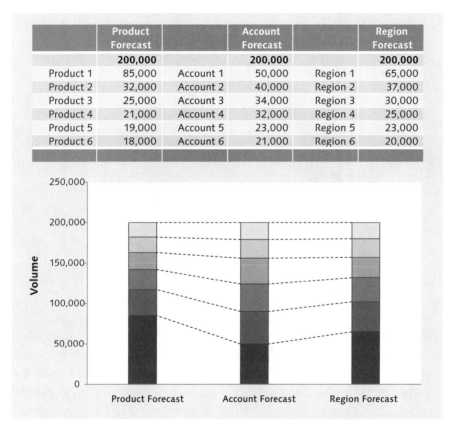

	Product Forecast		Account Forecast		Region Forecast
	200,000		**200,000**		**200,000**
Product 1	85,000	Account 1	50,000	Region 1	65,000
Product 2	32,000	Account 2	40,000	Region 2	37,000
Product 3	25,000	Account 3	34,000	Region 3	30,000
Product 4	21,000	Account 4	32,000	Region 4	25,000
Product 5	19,000	Account 5	23,000	Region 5	23,000
Product 6	18,000	Account 6	21,000	Region 6	20,000

Figure A.3   Multiple Hierarchies to Aggregate and Disaggregate Demand

It's important to remember that there are many ways to break down a global demand projection. Responsibility for closing the gap between guidance and the demand projection is not limited to the sales organization. Marketing activities, such as the adding of new products discussed in the previous section, can be planned and executed with the intention of positively impacting demand. Figure A.4 shows a bottom-up and top-down product-focused demand planning process in which a marketing team might engage.

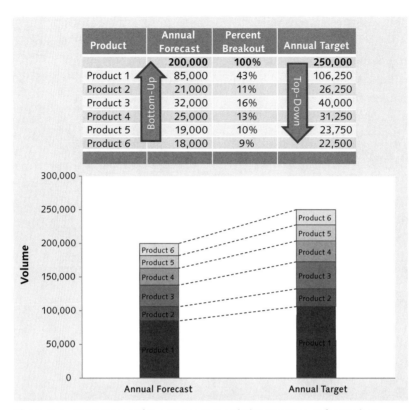

Product	Annual Forecast	Percent Breakout	Annual Target
	200,000	100%	250,000
Product 1	85,000	43%	106,250
Product 2	21,000	11%	26,250
Product 3	32,000	16%	40,000
Product 4	25,000	13%	31,250
Product 5	19,000	10%	23,750
Product 6	18,000	9%	22,500

Figure A.4 Bottom-Up and Top-Down Demand Planning Process for Products

The setting and changing of sales targets and the aggregation and disaggregation of data that accompanies it can be a computationally intensive task. Without supporting technology, it's probable that executives, managers, and analysts would spend more time collecting, formatting, and synchronizing spreadsheets and less time applying their professional judgment to the numbers.

Whereas SAP APO is capable of aggregation and disaggregation of multiple demand projections across an exceptionally flexible hierarchy, the breadth and depth of its capabilities configured for planners can be intimidating to more casual users. SAP BusinessObjects BPC is an application that is at once more friendly to the more casual user and capable of supporting a business planning process in which sales targets are adjusted.

A.4 Business Planning and Consolidation

The business planning process, at its heart, concerns reconciling the discrepancies between planned actions and expected results. SAP BusinessObjects BPC captures plans and budgets from across the enterprise and presents them through the familiar interface of Microsoft Excel. The underlying SAP NetWeaver architecture stores the information, including textual comments made by individuals, and makes all of it available to the relevant stakeholders.

The process is driven by a configurable workflow that can be adapted to the unique aspects of an organization's business planning process. Data can be brought in from across the enterprise and subjected to predictive analysis, automated variance analysis, and root-cause analysis.

A.5 Summary

Business planning offers direction to a demand management process of projecting, impacting, and realizing demand. It links the financial objectives of the organization with its plans to commit resources in the most economical manner.

However, the business plan must be anchored in reality. Senior executives can influence the expectations of the financial community provided they have a well-thought-out basis for argument.

B   The Authors

Chris Foti has fifteen years of experience working directly with Fortune 500 companies mainly in the consumer products industry and supply chain functional areas. He has been with SAP since the turn of the century where he has done solutions architecting, business consulting, marketing, customer networking, and management. Chris keeps an undergraduate and graduate diploma from Rensselaer Polytechnic Institute and the Massachusetts Institute of Technology respectively on the wall of his home office in New Hampshire.

Jessie Chimni is the Vice President of Consulting Services at Bristlecone, an SAP centric supply chain consulting company. He has over 19 years of supply chain management experience, spanning a number of industries, including CPG, High Tech, Semiconductor, and Automotive industries. Jessie has extensive experience in SAP Supply Chain consulting and is regarded by many as a thought leader in this field. Jessie has played a key role in Bristlecone's growth over the last 9 years, and has led Bristlecone's journey to transition to an Intellectual Property centric company. Jessie has a Master of Management Studies, degree from Carleton University and a Bachelor of Economic, Punjab University, Chandigarh, India.

Index

Within timelines, 360
Work area, 111

X

XML, 167

Y

Y2K, 80

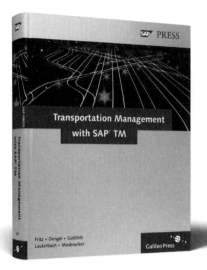

Teaches readers how to implement and integrate SAP TM 6.0

Covers all business processes from planning to shipment cost settlement

Contains comprehensive information on SAP Event Management

Up-to-date for SAP SCM TM 6.0

Rüdiger Fritz, Till Dengel, Jens Gottlieb,
Bernd Lauterbach, Bernd Mosbrucker

Transportation Management with SAP TM

This is a practical reference that teaches consultants and project teams how to implement the new Transportation Management components of SAP SCM. It teaches users what SAP SCM TM is, what it can do, and how to implement and configure it into their systems. With clear and straightforward examples, this is a must-have reference for anyone interested in mastering the new SAP tool for transportation management.

654 pp., 2009, 79,95 Euro / US$ 79.95
ISBN 978-1-59229-237-0

>> www.sap-press.com

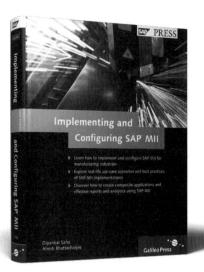

Learn how to implement and customize SAP MII for manufacturing

Explore real-life implementation scenarios of SAP MII in different industries

Discover how to create composite applications and effective reports using SAP MII

Abesh Bhattachargee, Dipankar Saha

Implementing and Configuring SAP MII

Implementing and Customizing SAP MII is your guide to the product features of SAP MII, how to implement it, and how to configure and customize it for different manufacturing tasks and issues. The book will help manufacturing teams get processes and systems working together by showing how to create composite applications that connects them. Once the systems are linked and generating comprehensive and accurate data, the book details how to use MII tools to generate accurate reports for analysis and planning.

468 pp., 2009, 79,95 Euro / US$ 79.95
ISBN 978-1-59229-256-1

>> www.sap-press.com

Interested in reading more?

Please visit our Web site for all
new book releases from SAP PRESS.

www.sap-press.com